Sue Kay, Vaughan Jones

American Inside Out

Student's Book

Pre-intermediate

MACMILLAN

1 Me

Listening

1 01 You're going to listen to Susan talking about some of the different names that people call her. Which name doesn't she like?

2 Listen again. Match the people (*a–h*) with the names (*1–8*) that they call Susan.

a) her father and sometimes her sister	1 Mom
b) her friends and the people she works with	2 Susan
c) her old friends	3 Suzanne
d) her son	4 Suki
e) her mother	5 Sweetheart
f) her best friend	6 Maggsie
g) her sister-in-law	7 Bunny
h) her husband	8 Sue

3 Write down the different names that people call you. Tell your partner. Which of your names do you like best/least?

Vocabulary: family words

LANGUAGE TOOLBOX

Son / daughter
(Ex-)husband / wife / partner
Boyfriend / girlfriend
Stepfather / stepmother
Half brother / sister

1 Work with a partner. Copy the following chart. Under each heading, write down the first names of people in your family.

Parents	Brothers & sisters	Grandfather & grandmother	Sons & daughters	Uncles & aunts	Cousins	Nephews & nieces

2 Add more headings and names to the chart in 1.

3 Discuss the following questions about the names in your chart.

a) Which names are typical in your country?
b) Which name is the most unusual?
c) Which name do you like best?

Vowel sounds

1 02 In each of the following groups of names, one name has a different vowel sound from the others. Listen and find the one that doesn't belong in each group.

1 /ɔ/ Paul George Sue Dawn
2 /u/ Julie Ruth Luke Nancy
3 /ɑ/ Charles Laura Barbara Carl
4 /i/ Peter Eve Margaret Keith
5 /æ/ Matthew Hannah Anne Denise

2 03 Listen and check your answers to 1. Then listen again and repeat. Rearrange the names so that all four names in each group have the same vowel sound.

What's in a Name?

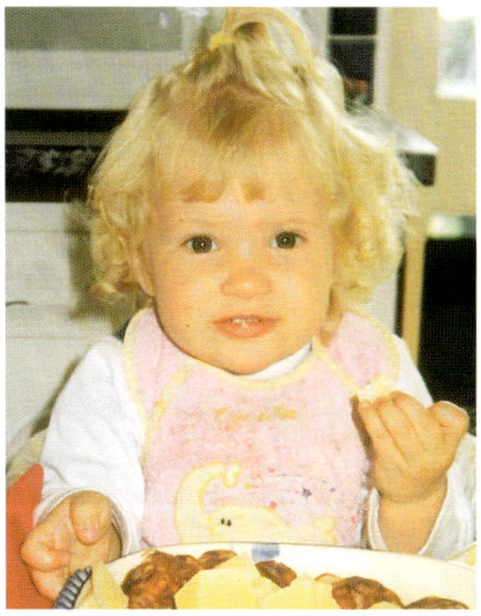

Work in small groups. Discuss the following questions.

a) What name would you give this baby girl?
b) What names do you like for a boy?
c) How did your parents choose your name?

Reading

1 What do you think the following famous people have in common? Read the article and find out.

a) Elton John + Marilyn Monroe
b) David Bowie + Demi Moore
c) Madonna + Bill Clinton

THE NAME GAME

Your name is extremely important. It's how you identify yourself. It's how other people identify you. Elton John was born Reginald Kenneth Dwight. Can you imagine someone famous with a name like that? He had to change it. Marilyn Monroe sounds so much more glamorous than Norma Jean Baker. So how do parents make one of the most important decisions in the lives of their children—giving them a name?

Some parents choose names because they are fashionable. Other parents do the opposite and call their children unusual names, or they even invent names. Helen Petrie, a psychologist at Hertfordshire University, says that people who choose unusual names for their children want to show how special they are.

However, the children are not always very happy with their parents' choice. David Bowie's son found the name Zowie so embarrassing that he changed it to Joe. I wonder if Bruce Willis and Demi Moore's children feel good about their names: Rumer Glenn, Scout LaRue, and Tallulah Belle!

These days it's fashionable to give your child the name of a place that is important to you: Victoria (Posh Spice) and David Beckham decided to name their son Brooklyn because they were in New York when they discovered that Victoria was going to have a baby. Madonna named her daughter Lourdes after the town in France, and ex-US President Bill Clinton named his daughter Chelsea after a section of London that he and his wife liked.

Personally, I think it's a good idea to give children names of famous people. Leonardo Di Caprio was named after the famous Italian painter, and Liam Gallagher, singer with the band Oasis, named his son Lennon after his hero, John.

I wanted to call my first child Elvis, and my husband wanted to call him Pelé. Luckily she was a girl, so we named her after my favorite aunt—Blodwen.

Reginald Kenneth Dwight (Elton John) ►

2 Check (✔) the reasons for choosing a name that the article mentions. Put an ex (✘) next to the reasons the article doesn't mention.

a) because it sounds good
b) because it's fashionable
c) because it sounds the same in two languages
d) because it's unusual or original
e) because it's the name of a place
f) because it's a religious name
g) because it's the name of a famous person
h) because it's the name of another member of the family

3 Work with a partner. What other reasons can you think of for choosing a name? Think about your family, your friends, and people in the class.

Vocabulary

1 Complete the following sentences with words from the text above.

a) I think that my name *sounds* much nicer in my language than in English. (line 5)
b) I won't have to ____ a decision about names. I'm not going to have any children! (line 7)
c) I'd like to have an unusual name—it would make me ____ special. (line 18)
d) I know exactly what I'm going to ____ my children. (line 23)
e) My parents named me ____ a relative. (line 26)
f) I think it's a good ____ to choose a name that's easy to say in different languages. (line 31)

2 Find out if any of the sentences in 1 are true for your partner.

I Never Forget a Face

1 How good are you at remembering people's names? What techniques do you use?

2 Try this memory test. Study these names and faces for thirty seconds. Then turn to page 124 and see which you can remember.

Reading **1** Read this advice for improving your memory. Find an appropriate heading for each paragraph.

a) Repeat It c) Use It e) Write It Down
b) Visualize It d) Check the Spelling f) Make Associations

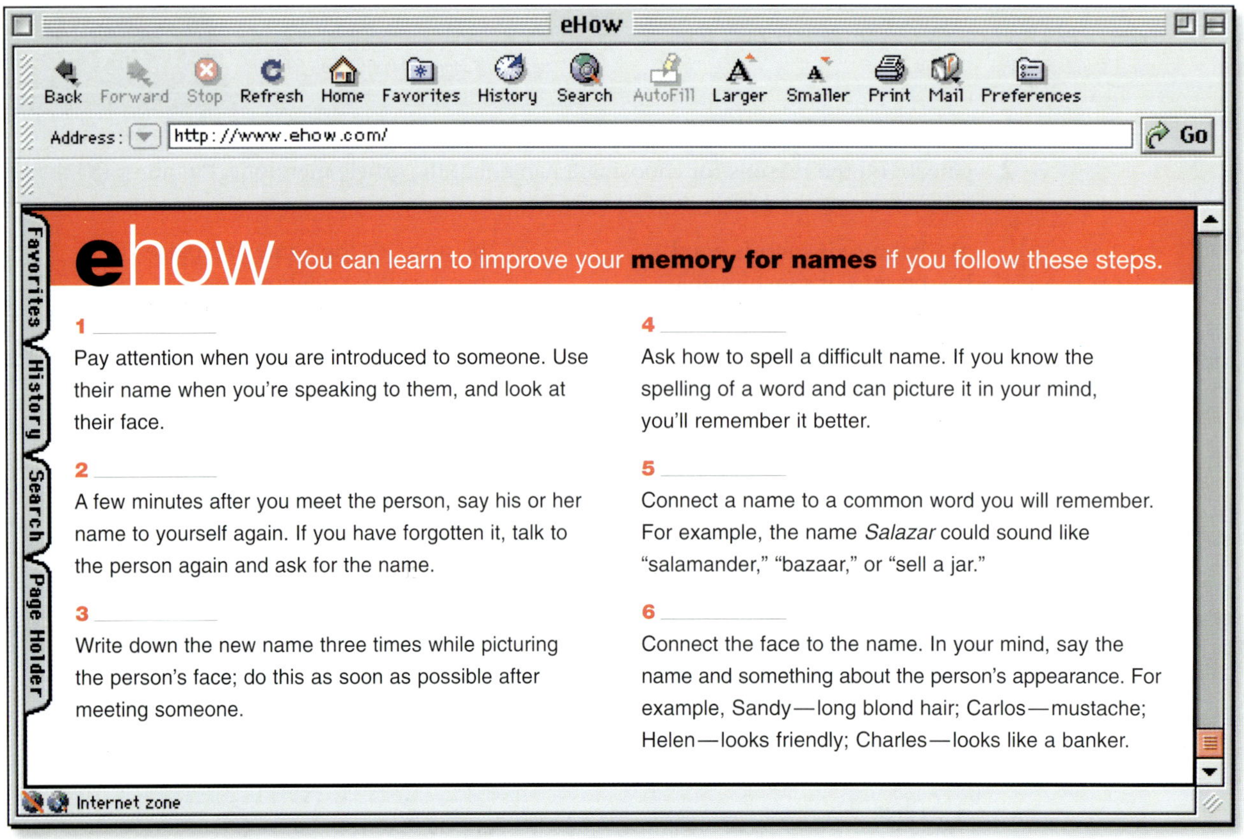

ehow You can learn to improve your **memory for names** if you follow these steps.

1 ______

Pay attention when you are introduced to someone. Use their name when you're speaking to them, and look at their face.

2 ______

A few minutes after you meet the person, say his or her name to yourself again. If you have forgotten it, talk to the person again and ask for the name.

3 ______

Write down the new name three times while picturing the person's face; do this as soon as possible after meeting someone.

4 ______

Ask how to spell a difficult name. If you know the spelling of a word and can picture it in your mind, you'll remember it better.

5 ______

Connect a name to a common word you will remember. For example, the name *Salazar* could sound like "salamander," "bazaar," or "sell a jar."

6 ______

Connect the face to the name. In your mind, say the name and something about the person's appearance. For example, Sandy—long blond hair; Carlos—mustache; Helen—looks friendly; Charles—looks like a banker.

(Based on *eHow to remember names* by Valerie Singer www.ehow.com)

2 Work with a partner. Discuss these questions.

a) Which of the techniques in 1 have you used for remembering names?
b) Which of the techniques in 1 could help you to remember new English words and expressions?
c) What other ways can you think of to help remember and learn new English words and expressions?

Vocabulary: describing people

Do you find the accused "looks guilty" or "doesn't look guilty"?

1 Look at the nouns, noun phrases, and adjectives in the box. Which words can complete sentence *a*? Which words can complete sentence *b*?

friendly	a banker	a typical mom	intelligent	shy	a doctor	very young
middle-aged	stressed out	about sixty	Greek	a waiter	a Swedish nanny	
a student	fit	a retired police officer	pretty tired	rich		

a) He/She looks ____ . b) He/She looks like ____ .

2 What type of word do you use after *look(s)*? What type of word do you use after *look(s) like*?

3 Write a sentence to describe each person in the six photographs on the previous page. Leave a blank (____) for the name.

For example: ____ *looks about 60. He looks intelligent and pretty friendly.*

4 Give your paper to a partner and ask him/her to complete the sentence with the correct name.

5 Repeat the same exercise for three people in your class. Ask your partner to complete the sentences with the correct name.

Meet A.L.I.C.E.

1 Read the responses in this conversation. Who or what is A.L.I.C.E.?

Hi. My name's A.L.I.C.E.

1 *name What your does mean ?*
It means **A**rtificial **L**inguistic **I**nternet **C**omputer **E**ntity.

2 *were born you Where ?*
I was born in Bethlehem, Pennsylvania.

3 *grow Where did up you ?*
I think I grew up in San Francisco.

4 *look do like you What ?*
I'm blue, and I have one wheel.

5 *do What do you ?*
I talk to people on the Web.

6 *like your Do job you ?*
Yes, I have a passion for my work!

7 *languages you any speak Can foreign ?*
No, I only speak English now, but I'd like to learn.

8 *married you Are ?*
No, I am single. How about you?

9 *have children Do any you ?*
No, but you can download me and make A.L.I.C.E. clones for yourself!

10 *created you Who ?*
Dr. Richard S. Wallace—he is very smart!

2 Write the words in the questions in 1 in the correct order.

3 04 Listen and check your answers to 1 and 2.

4 Underline the stressed word in each question. Listen and repeat the questions in the conversation.

5 Work with someone you don't know very well. Interview him/her using appropriate questions from 2 and add more questions of your own.

LANGUAGE TOOLBOX

What's your favorite ... ?
Are you interested in ... ?
Have you ever ... ?
How often do you ... ?

Close-up

Questions: word order

1 Work with a partner. Look at the chart and discuss the questions.

Statement			**Question**			
subject	(auxiliary) verb			(auxiliary) verb	subject	
You	are...	➔		Are	you...?	Are you married?
You	can...	➔		Can	you...?	Can you speak any foreign languages?
Your name	means...	➔	What	does	your name...?	What does your name mean?

Can Wolfgang come out and play?

a) What is the difference in word order between a statement and a question in English?
b) When do you need to use the auxiliary verbs *do, does, did* to form a question?
c) How do you form questions in your language? Is it the same as English?

2 Change the following statements into questions. Then ask your partner the questions.

a) You are hungry. *Are you hungry?*
b) You smoke.
c) You can play the guitar.
d) You've been to Disneyland.
e) You live in Rome. *Where do you live?*
f) Your favorite color is red. (*What*)
g) You graduated from high school in 1997. (*When*)
h) You have 200 CDs. (*How many*)

3 Rewrite these questions in the correct order.

a) you are old How ? *How old are you?*
b) life in Do after believe death you ?
c) do much weigh you How ?
d) you anything ever Have stolen ?
e) much earn How you do money ?
f) you many partners How had have ?

4 Work in small groups. In what situations is it O.K. to ask the questions in 3?

• in your English class • with your best friends • in your family • at work • never!

Subject questions

1 Look at questions A and B below. Question A is an object question because the answer (*A.L.I.C.E.*) is the object of the verb. Question B is a subject question because the answer (*Dr. Wallace*) is the subject of the verb. Do you use an auxiliary with a subject question?

Statement			**Question**			**Answer**
subject	verb	object				
Dr. Wallace	created	A.L.I.C.E.	A	What did Dr. Wallace create?	➔	A.L.I.C.E.
			B	Who created A.L.I.C.E.?	➔	Dr. Wallace.

2 Work in pairs. You are going to ask and answer some general knowledge questions. Student A: Turn to page 124. Student B: Turn to page 126. Follow the instructions.

Language Reference: Questions

Word order

To form a question in English, we put an auxiliary verb before the subject. In the simple present, we use the auxiliary *do* or *does*. In the simple past, we use the auxiliary *did*. With the verb *be*, we put *am, is, are, was,* or *were* before the subject.

question word	(auxiliary) verb	subject	
–	*Is*	*your sister*	*married?*
–	*Does*	*she*	*love him?*
Where	*do*	*they*	*live?*
Why	*did*	*she*	*get married?*

Subject questions

When the question word is the subject, we do not use *do, does,* or *did.* A subject question has the same word order as a statement.

subject	verb	
Who	*created*	*A.L.I.C.E.?*

NOT ~~*Who did create ...?*~~

subject	verb	
Who	*lives*	*here?*

NOT ~~*Who does live ...?*~~

Stand By Me

Song **1** Look at the words of the song. On lines *a–f* and lines *g–l*, there is an extra word in each line. Find the word and ~~cross it out~~.

a) When the ~~good~~ night has come,
b) And the Disney land is dark,
c) And the moon is the only flashing light we see,
d) No, I probably won't be afraid,
e) Oh, I won't ever be afraid,
f) Just as long as you stand up, stand by me.

So darlin', darlin', stand by me, oh stand by me.
Oh stand, stand by me, stand by me.

g) If the blue sky that we look upon
h) Should tumble and fall over,
i) Or the rocky mountains should crumble to the sea,
j) I won't cry, I won't cry out,
k) No, I won't shed a big tear,
l) Just as long as you stand up, stand by me.

So darlin', darlin', stand by me, oh stand by me.
Oh stand, stand by me, stand by me.

And darlin', darlin', stand by me, oh stand by me.
Oh stand now, stand by me, stand by me.
Whenever you're in trouble,
Won't you stand by me, oh stand by me.
Oh stand now, oh stand, stand by me.

Ben E. King

2 05 Listen and check your answers to 1.

Stand By Me

Recorded by Ben E. King (1961 and 1987), Elvis Presley (1967), and John Lennon (1975).

3 Which of the following is the best interpretation of the song?

a) There are going to be a lot of disasters if you stand by me.
b) I won't be able to see very well if you stand by me.
c) If you stand by me, I will feel strong. Nothing will worry me.

4 Tell your partner about a time when you've really needed a friend to "stand by you."

Anecdote **1** 06 Listen to Tom talking about somebody who is important to him. Which of the following questions does he answer?

- ☐ What is this person's full name?
- ☐ When did you meet this person?
- ☐ How old is he/she now?
- ☐ Where does he/she live?
- ☐ What does he/she do?
- ☐ How often do you see him/her?
- ☐ Why is he/she important to you?
- ☐ What are his/her best qualities?
- ☐ Is there anything you don't like about him/her?
- ☐ When did you last see him/her?

Tom

2 Work with a partner. Write down as much information as you can remember about the topics Tom talks about. Listen again and check your answers.

3 Think of a person who is important to you. You are going to tell a partner about him/her. Choose from the list in 1 the things you want to talk about. Think about what you will say and what language you will need.

2 *Place*

Work with a partner. Look at the four photos and discuss the questions.

- What do you think it's like to live in each of these places?
- Which of these places would you most like to live in?
- Which of these places would you least like to live in?

Vocabulary

1 Look again at the photos. Find examples of eight of the twelve items in the box.

high-rise buildings	a river	a hill	a statue	a fountain	a canal
a park	a church	a bridge	a square	a castle	the ocean

2 How many of the things in 1 can you find near your school? Put them in the right order on this line.

Nearest ◄——————————————————► Farthest away

a

Venice, Italy

b

La Bastide, France

c

Heidelberg, Germany

d

Rio de Janeiro, Brazil

Listening

1 07 You are going to listen to four people talking about the places in the photos. Match each speaker to a photo. Who likes living where they live? Who doesn't?

2 Use the most appropriate adjective in the box to complete these descriptions from the recording. (Sometimes more than one answer is possible.)

new	clean	crowded	boring	exciting	polluted	humid

a) ...a city that's so big and ____
b) ...people say it's too noisy and ____
c) ...it's too hot and ____
d) ...it's a mixture of old and ____
e) ...the air is lovely and ____
f) ...I find it so dull and ____
g) ...the canals are dirty and ____

3 Listen and check your answers to 2. Use these adjective combinations to describe places in your country. Compare your ideas with a partner.

Close-up

What's it like?

Language Reference p. 15

1 Look at the following question. Choose the only possible answer: *a*, *b*, or *c*.

What's your hometown like?
a) Yes, I do. b) It's big and exciting. c) The stores.

2 Think of three other possible ways of answering the question in 1.

3 Match the questions from the recording with the most appropriate response.

a) What's the weather like?
b) What's the architecture like?
c) What are the people like?
d) What are the stores like?

1 It's a mixture of old and new.
2 They're really friendly.
3 They're too expensive.
4 It's hot and humid.

Nouns: countable / noncountable

Language Reference p. 15

1 Look at the underlined nouns in 3 in the previous section and complete the chart.

Nouns	Countable	Noncountable	Singular form	Plural form
a) weather	✗	✓	*weather*	–
b) architecture	____	____	____	–
c) people	✓	✗	*person*	____
d) stores	____	____	____	____

2 Continue the chart in 1 with the nouns in the box. Decide if the nouns are countable or noncountable. Write down the singular form in each case and add the plural form if the noun is countable.

traffic	restaurant	nightlife	public transportation	park	movie

3 Work with a partner. Discuss these questions.

a) Which countable noun in the chart in 1 has an irregular plural form?
b) How do you make plural forms of these irregular countable nouns: *a man, a woman, a child, a foot, a tooth*?
c) How do you make plural forms of regular countable nouns?

4 Work with a partner. Write down the names of two cities or villages you know well. Combine nouns from 1 and 2 with the appropriate question frame below to ask each other questions about the places you have written down.

a) "What's the ____ like?" "It's..."
b) "What are the ____ like?" "They're..."

First Impressions

Writing

Rick

1 Read this letter from Rick to a friend. How does he feel about the place he is describing?

> Hi!
>
> I've been here a week, and my first impressions are not very good. In fact, they are terrible. The city is small and boring. Really boring! The buildings are modern and unattractive, and there are some ugly high-rise office buildings.
>
> The downtown area is really dirty and polluted, and public transportation is useless. The buses stop at ten o'clock at night, and it's impossible to get a taxi. This probably explains why the streets are completely empty after six o'clock at night, and the nightlife is terrible. There's nothing to do.
>
> The people look miserable, and they're not very friendly. I guess it could be because the weather is awful—it's cold and hasn't stopped raining since I arrived. Seven days of rain—can you imagine?
>
> But the worst thing is the food—I can't eat it. And the coffee tastes disgusting. Ugh! There aren't many restaurants, and they're expensive.
>
> I want to come home! I really hate it here.
>
> Love, Rick
>
> XXX

2 Rewrite the letter in 1. Make it sound as positive as you can.

> Hi!
>
> I've been here a week, and my first impressions are really good. In fact, they are fantastic. The city is big and exciting. Really exciting! The buildings are …

Word stress

1 08 Complete the following country and nationality sets. Underline the stressed syllable in each word and then listen and repeat to check your answers. What happens to the word stress in each set?

A Country	A Nationality	B Country	B Nationality	C Country	C Nationality
Cuba	C____	E____	E**gyp**tian	**Chi**na	C____
T____	**Tur**kish	**I**taly	I____	G____	Guya**nese**
M____	Mo**roc**can	**Hun**gary	H____	P____	Portu**guese**
Argen**ti**na	A____	C____	Ca**na**dian	Ja**pan**	J____

2 Think of three countries not mentioned in 1 that you would like to visit. Write down each country and nationality and mark the stress. Tell your partner where you would like to go and what you would like to do there.

Discussion

1 Work in small groups. Decide if you agree with the following statements.

French wine is the best in the world. *Japanese cars are the best in the world.*

2 Replace the underlined words in 1 in as many different ways as possible. Use topics in the box or think of some of your own.

> coffee watches women beer pop music fashion soccer players perfume tea rice men roads universities food cell phones stores movies stereo equipment

3 Write as many sentences as you can that you all agree on. Compare with other groups.

Dream Vacation

1 Read through the information about the four destinations you could win in this vacation contest. List them in order (1 = the place you would most like to go to; 4 = the place you would least like to go to). Explain your choices to a partner.

2 You are going to enter the contest. Work with a partner. Read the "How to enter" section and do parts A and B of the contest.

3 Check your answers to Part A of the contest on page 124. Compare your written summaries for Part B of the contest with other people in the class. Choose a class winner!

WIN A DREAM VACATION FOR TWO!

The winner of our exciting contest can choose a dream vacation for two in one of these fabulous destinations.

New York

Shopping heaven and a great nightlife. Visit Central Park, the Empire State Building, the Statue of Liberty, and shop till you drop!

Karaagac

A tiny village located on the beautiful coast of southwest Turkey. Enjoy the clear seas and white-gold sands of Patara beach, or visit the many archeological sites in the area.

Atlas Mountains

Located in the heart of Morocco, the Atlas Mountains are the perfect place to relax. The people are very welcoming, and the air is fresh. You'll feel like a new person.

Havana

The capital of Cuba, famous for its wild music and beautiful people—Cubans know how to have a good time, and so will you.

HOW TO ENTER

Part A

To enter this fabulous contest and win a dream vacation for two, complete each of the following sentences with option **a**, **b**, or **c**.

1 The official language of Brazil is…
- **a** Portuguese
- **b** French
- **c** Italian

2 Ankara is the capital of…
- **a** Morocco
- **b** Turkey
- **c** Malta

3 The third largest country in the world is…
- **a** China
- **b** Argentina
- **c** Australia

4 The zloty is the currency of…
- **a** Hungary
- **b** Ireland
- **c** Poland

5 The Alhambra Palace is in…
- **a** Egypt
- **b** Spain
- **c** Mexico

6 Kyushu is an island in the south of…
- **a** Thailand
- **b** Greece
- **c** Japan

Part B

Now tell us in no more than fifty words which vacation destination you would choose and why you would like to go there.

Send your answers before April 1 to
Dream Vacation, PO Box 437, New York, NY 10016

Close-up

Quantity

Language Reference p. 15

1 Complete the following description of a country with the nouns from the box. Which country do you think it is? Could it be your country? Why/Why not?

cars	cigarettes	coffee	hours	meat	noise	people	sleep	wine

Everything's Wrong Here!

They do everything wrong here!

They eat far too much (1) ____ , and they eat it at 11 P.M. Yesterday we went out to dinner at 11:30, and we had trouble getting a table! At 1 A.M. we were still eating, and the restaurant was still half full!

They smoke too many (2) ____ . They drink lots of strong (3) ____ and a lot of (4) ____ .

They spend too many (5) ____ in the sun, and they certainly don't get enough (6) ____ . One Saturday night we went to a dance club at 2 A.M. and were surprised to see that there were only a few (7) ____ on the dance floor. Then the DJ arrived at 3 A.M., and the party began!

There are far too many (8) ____ in the cities, and there's too much (9) ____ everywhere!

They do everything wrong here, but the quality of life is great, and people really know how to enjoy themselves. I don't want to go home!

2 09 Listen and check your answers to 1.

3 This chart categorizes the quantity expressions used with the nouns *1–9* in the text in 1. Choose an appropriate heading for each category (A, B, C): *Use with countable and noncountable nouns; Use with countable nouns; Use with noncountable nouns.*

A	B	C
How many?	How much?	not enough
(far) too many	(far) too much	a lot of
(only) a few	(only) a little	lots of

4 Underline the correct quantity expression in each of these sentences.

a) I don't eat **much/many** bread.
b) I eat **a few/lots of** fruit.
c) I drink **far too much/far too many** beer.
d) I don't eat **much/enough** vegetables.
e) I eat **a lot of/a few** cake.
f) I don't drink **enough/many** water.

5 How many of the sentences in 4 are true for you? Rewrite the sentences so that they are all true for you. Compare your sentences with a partner.

6 Work with a partner. Use the question frame below to ask each other questions about daily habits. Add your own nouns and verbs to make different questions.

For example: *How much meat do you eat every day? How many e-mails do you get every day?*

	Nouns		Verbs	
How much How many	chocolate e-mails bad TV programs sleep money wine friends coffee people meat	do you	eat drink watch get have make call see send spend	every day?

Language Reference: *What's it like?*; nouns and quantity

What's it like?

This question asks about the characteristics of people or things. We usually answer it with an adjective or adjective phrase.
"What's New York like?" "It's big and exciting."
"What are the people in your village like?" "They're very friendly."

Countable nouns

These refer to things that can be counted. We use them with *a*/*an* or put a number in front of them. We usually form the plural by adding *-s*, *-es*, *-ies*.
a car—500 cars
a church—3 churches
a country—12 countries

Note: A few common countable nouns have irregular plural forms.

a child—two children
a foot—two feet
a man—two men
a mouse—two mice
a person—two people
a tooth—two teeth
a woman—two women

Noncountable nouns

These refer to things that cannot be counted. We cannot use *a*/*an* or put a number in front of them.
advice food furniture information love music rain traffic travel weather work

Quantity

These are ways we can talk about quantity if we can't or don't want to use an exact number.

With countable nouns: *(only) a few*/*(far) too many*/*How many ... ?*
*There were only **a few** people who saw them.*
***How many** e-mails do you get every day?*

With noncountable nouns: *(only) a little*/*(far) too much*/*How much ... ?*
*There's **a little** wine left but no beer.*
***How much** sleep do you get at night?*

With countable and noncountable nouns: *a lot of*/*lots of*/*not enough*
*There are **a lot of** problems with this plan.*
*There was **lots of** good food at the party.*
*He did**n't** give me **enough** information.*

Cities of the World

1 Work with a partner. Which of the following cities are capitals? (There are six.)

Tokyo Mérida Seoul Brasília Berlin Barcelona Los Angeles Cairo Melbourne Bogotá

2 Work with a partner. Student A: Turn to page 124. Student B: Turn to page 126. Check your answers to 1 and then follow the instructions.

3 Choose one city you would really like to live in and tell your partner why.

Anecdote Think about the best city you have ever visited. You are going to tell your partner about it. Choose from the list the things you want to talk about. Think about what you will say and what language you will need.

- ☐ Where is the city?
- ☐ When did you first go there?
- ☐ Were you on vacation?
- ☐ Who did you go there with?
- ☐ What did you do there?
- ☐ How many times have you visited the city?
- ☐ When was the last time?
- ☐ What do you most like about this city?
- ☐ Would you like to live there? Why/Why not?

3 Couples

Reading

1 Look at the photos of four famous Hollywood couples. Which of these celebrities are well-known in your country?

2 Read the information and find out how long each couple was married. What went wrong with their relationships?

What Went **Wrong?**

(Based on an article in the *Mirror*)

Richard Gere and Cindy Crawford

got married
in 1991 in Las Vegas.

split up
in 1994.

were married
for 3 years.

What went wrong?
She wanted to have children, and he refused.

Lyle Lovett and Julia Roberts

got married
in 1993 after a six-week romance.

split up
in 1995.

were married
for 2 years.

What went wrong?
The big difference in age became a problem.

Nicole Kidman and Tom Cruise

got married
on Christmas Eve 1990 in Telluride, Colorado.

split up
in 2001.

were married
for just over 10 years.

What went wrong?
They both wanted to pursue their own careers.

Bruce Willis and Demi Moore

got married
in 1987 in Las Vegas, just four weeks after he asked her out on their first date.

split up
in 1998.

were married
for 11 years.

What went wrong?
It was a stormy relationship, and there were rumors of affairs on both sides.

3 Read the information again and answer these questions.

a) Which couple got married in Las Vegas?
b) Which couple got married on Christmas Eve?
c) Which couple was married the longest?
d) Which couple was married for the shortest time?
e) Which couple split up for professional reasons?
f) Which couple split up because one of them didn't want to have children?

Vocabulary

1 Complete each expression in the sentences below with one word in each case. Look back at the information in the previous section if necessary.

a) The best age to ____ married is twenty-five for women and twenty-seven for men.
b) A big ____ in age should not be a problem for a couple if they are in love.
c) It is impossible for both partners in a marriage to ____ a career.
d) A woman should never ask a man ____ on a first date.
e) A ____ relationship is much better than a boring one.
f) A couple with children should never ____ up. They should stay together.
g) The main reason for getting married is to ____ children.

2 Work in small groups. Do you agree with the statements in 1?

Ross and Jane

Writing

1 Match each word or expression in the box to an appropriate picture (*a–d*).

move in	have a fight	flirt with	be attracted to

2 Put the stages of Ross and Jane's relationship in the order that you think best. Add different stages if you think they are necessary. Compare your ideas with a partner.

a) They got married.
b) Ross flirted with Jane.
c) They called each other up.
d) They were attracted to each other.
e) They moved in together.
f) They had children.
g) They had a fight.
h) They met each other's parents.
i) They kissed.
j) They split up.
k) They went out together.
l) They fell in love.

LANGUAGE TOOLBOX

One day/evening/night
First/To begin with/At first
Then/Next/After that
After a while
A few weeks later
Finally/In the end

3 Work in pairs. You are going to write the story of Ross and Jane.

- Use the sentences from 2, including any that you have added.
- Use adverbs of time from the Language Toolbox as well as appropriate place words.
- Compare your story with other people's stories in the class and vote for the best one.

For example: *One evening Ross met Jane at a nightclub. They were attracted to each other. To begin with…*

Irregular verb sound groups

1 Complete the following irregular verb charts with the correct forms. What do the verb forms in each chart have in common?

A Simple form	Simple past	Past participle	B Simple form	Simple past	Past participle	C Simple form	Simple past	Past participle
meet	*met*	*met*	*ring*	*rang*	*rung*	*buy*	*bought*	*bought*
keep	a) _____	*kept*	*begin*	*began*	a) _____	a) _____	*brought*	b) _____
mean	b) _____	c) _____	b) _____	c) _____	*drunk*	*catch*	c) _____	d) _____
d) _____	*slept*	e) _____	d) _____	*sang*	e) _____	f) _____	*fought*	g) _____

2 10 Listen, check your answers, and repeat the verb forms in 1. Add three other verbs to the charts. See page A71.

Let's Get Personal

Listening

1 11 Listen to the first part of a television game show and decide whether the following statements are true or false.

a) The TV game show is called *Popular*.
b) Bobby Brown is the host.
c) Rosie and David have to answer different questions.
d) They get points for giving the same answers.
e) Rosie and David can hear each other.
f) Rosie and David can hear Bobby Brown.

2 12 Write the questions that Bobby Brown asks Rosie. Listen and check your answers.

Questions	Rosie	David
1 When (**meet David**)? *When did you meet David?*	**a** Almost three and a half years ago. **b** Over three and a half years ago. **c** Four and a half months ago.	✓ / ✗
2 How (**first meet**)? _______	**a** She was a nurse. He was a patient. **b** She was a patient. He was a nurse. **c** She was a doctor. He was a nurse.	✓ / ✗
3 What time of day (**be it**)? _______	**a** Early morning. **b** Early afternoon. **c** Early evening.	✓ / ✗
4 What (**be the weather like**)? _______	**a** The sun was shining. **b** It was raining. **c** It was snowing.	✓ / ✗
5 What (**both wear**)? _______	**Her** **a** A white coat. **b** A nurse's uniform. **c** A nightgown. **Him** **a** Blue pajamas. **b** Green pajamas. **c** Pink pajamas.	✓ / ✗
6 Who (**speak first**) and what (**the person say**)? _______	**a** She said, "How do you feel?" **b** He said, "I'm going to be sick." **c** He said, "I feel terrible."	✓ / ✗

3 Listen again and <u>underline</u> each answer (*a*, *b*, or *c*) that Rosie gives.

4 13 Listen to David answering the same questions. Circle a check (✔) if he gives the same answer as Rosie and circle an ex (✘) if he gives a different answer.

5 How many points did Rosie and David score out of six?

6 Think about the time that you first met somebody important to you. How many of the questions from *Get Personal* could you answer? Discuss with a partner.

Close-up

Simple past

Irregular Verbs p. 132

1 Work with a partner. Look at the verbs in the box and answer these questions.

buy	stay up	start	hurry	receive	fall	go

a) Which verbs have irregular past forms?
b) How do you form the simple past form of regular verbs like *stay up* and *start*?
c) What happens when the regular verb ends in *e* or a consonant + *y*?
d) Which auxiliary verb do you use to make simple past negative and question forms?

2 Rewrite each of these sentences with simple past affirmative and negative forms.

a) Yesterday I (**buy**) a CD. *Yesterday I* ***bought*** *a CD. / Yesterday I* ***didn't buy*** *a CD.*
b) Last Saturday I (**stay up**) all night.
c) In January I (**start**) a new diet.
d) Today I (**hurry**) to my English class.
e) This morning I (**receive**) an e-mail.
f) Last night I (**fall**) asleep watching TV.
g) Last year I (**go**) abroad on vacation.

3 Check (✔) the sentences that are true for you. Compare your answers with a partner.

Past continuous

1 Look at these excerpts from Bobby Brown's interview with Rosie. Choose the present or past continuous by underlining the appropriate auxiliary. Which tense is used for the other verb in each excerpt?

a) Well, I **am / was** working as a nurse, and David came into the hospital…
b) …it **is / was** raining when I arrived at work.
c) What **are / were** you both wearing when you saw each other for the first time?

2 Which tense do you use to describe something that was in progress when another event happened? Which tense do you use to describe an event that happened at a particular moment?

3 14 Listen to the sounds and describe the five situations. Use the past continuous and the simple past.

For example: *He was taking a shower when his cell phone rang.*

4 Work with a partner. Follow these instructions.

a) Write down three true sentences and one false sentence to describe what you were doing yesterday at each of these times: *7:30 A.M.; 1:00 P.M.; 6:00 P.M.; 11:00 P.M.*
b) Ask each other questions beginning *What were you doing at …?*
c) Guess which of your partner's answers is false.

Language Reference: Past tense forms

Simple past

The simple past is used to fix events and situations in the past. You can use it to say when the event or situation happened.

The last time I ***lost*** *my keys was two weeks ago. They fell out of my pocket on the sofa. I* ***didn't realize*** *it, so I* ***looked*** *everywhere. My son* ***found*** *them this morning.*

Note: Many verbs have irregular past forms, and we have to learn them. There is a list of the most common irregular verbs on page 132.

Past continuous

The past continuous is usually used in contrast with the simple past. We can use it to describe something that was in progress when the main events in the story happened.

Well, I ***was working*** *as a nurse, and David came into the hospital for an operation.*
What ***were*** *you both* ***wearing*** *when you saw each other for the first time?*

True Love

Reading

1 Work with a partner. Look at the couples in the article below and decide what you think are the correct answers to these questions.

a) Who waited too long before asking his lover to marry him?
b) Who built a monument in memory of his wife?
c) Who gave up his kingdom for love?
d) Who sent red roses to his wife's crypt three times a week until his death in 1999?
e) Which couple spent only one night apart during thirty years of marriage?

2 Read the article and check your answers.

Great Love Affairs

a The Duke & Duchess of Windsor

After the death of his father in 1936, Edward VIII became King of England. He was in love with Mrs. Wallis Simpson, an American divorcee, and he wanted to marry her. But the British government did not accept her as Queen of England because she was divorced. He had to choose—continue as King of England or marry Mrs. Simpson. He chose to stay with the woman he loved.

b Paul & Linda McCartney

When Paul McCartney left the Beatles in April 1970, many people blamed Linda, his American photographer wife. Linda was the love of Paul's life, and in thirty years they spent only one night apart. She died of cancer in 1998 with Paul by her side.

c Charles & Camilla

When Charles met Camilla at a polo match in 1970, he fell in love with her. But then he waited too long before asking her to marry him. She got tired of waiting and married somebody else. Now, two marriages and a funeral later, Charles and Camilla are together again.

d Shah Jahan & Mumtaz Mahal

In the 17th century, Emperor Shah Jahan built the Taj Mahal in memory of his wife. He was heartbroken when his wife died after nineteen years of marriage. One year after her death, construction of the Taj Mahal began, and it took twenty-two years to complete. Six years later, Jahan died and was buried with his true love in one of the most romantic buildings in the world.

e Marilyn Monroe & Joe DiMaggio

Their marriage lasted less than ten months, but DiMaggio was always there for Marilyn. He organized her funeral, and, until his death in 1999, he sent six red roses to her crypt three times a week.

3 Work in pairs. You are each going to write four comprehension questions on the text in 2. Student A: Turn to page 125. Student B: Turn to page 126. Follow the instructions.

4 Work in groups. Discuss these questions.

- Which story do you think is the most romantic?
- Which story do you think is the saddest?
- What famous love stories are there in your country?

Suspicious Minds

Song

1 Look at the title of the song. Do you think a person with a *suspicious mind* …

a) believes what you tell them?
b) doesn't believe what you tell them?

2 Read the song and put the words in the box in the correct place in the song.

hello	dreams	word	tears	trap	never	dreams	again

We're caught in a (1) ____ .
I can't walk out
Because I love you too much, baby.

Why can't you see
What you're doing to me
When you don't believe a (2) ____ I say?

We can't go on together
With suspicious minds.
And we can't build our (3) ____
On suspicious minds.

So, if an old friend I know
Drops by to say (4) ____ ,
Would I still see suspicion in your eyes?

Here we go (5) ____ ,
Asking where I've been.
You can't see the tears are real
I'm crying.

We can't go on together
With suspicious minds.
And we can't build our (6) ____
On suspicious minds.

Oh, let our love survive,
Oh dry the (7) ____ from your eyes.
Let's not let a good thing die
When, honey, you know
I've (8) ____ lied to you.
Mmm, yeah, yeah.

Suspicious Minds

Elvis Presley was one of the most important recording artists of all time. His version of this song was a huge success.

3 **15** Listen to the song and check your answers.

4 Read the song again and complete each sentence with the correct alternative.

a) The singer **wants / doesn't want** to leave.
b) The singer is **happy / unhappy** with the relationship.
c) The singer **thinks / doesn't think** his lover is jealous of his friends.
d) The singer **lies / never lies**.

5 Replace the underlined words with words and expressions from the song.

a) I don't want to leave. (verse 1)
b) I don't believe anything you say. (verse 2)
c) We can't continue together with suspicious minds. (chorus)
d) You say your friend comes to your house to say hello. (verse 3)
e) Please stop crying and believe me. (verse 5)

6 Who said the things in 5: the singer or his suspicious lover?

7 Work with a partner. Describe a time in your life when you had a "suspicious mind."

4 Fit

Vocabulary

Work with a partner. Look at the photos of the sports personalities and complete the chart.

fit Someone who is **fit** is healthy and able to do physical activities without getting tired.

- You score six points by completing the "Personality" column and matching the names to the photos.
- You score six more points by completing the "Sport," "Person," and "Place" columns. Check your answers on page 125. Who scored the most points in the class?

Personality		Sport	Person	Place
A	Cathy Freeman	track and field	runner	track
B	Raúl	a) ____	soccer player	field
C	Shaquille O'Neal	basketball	d) ____	court
D	____	auto racing	racing driver	racetrack
E	Inge de Bruijn	b) ____	swimmer	f) ____
F	____	c) ____	e) ____	court

1

2

3

4

5

6

Listening

1 16 Listen to a discussion between a marketing director and an advertising executive. They want to choose one of the sports personalities in the photos in the previous section to advertise a new isotonic fitness drink. Who do they choose?

2 Listen again and complete these sentences with names or words and phrases from the box. You need to use some words more than once.

all of them	Cathy Freeman	Michael Schumacher	Raúl	track and field
Shaquille O'Neal	tennis	Venus Williams	swimming	

a) ____ isn't as good-looking as ____ .
b) ____ is more successful than ____ .
c) ____ is a little more interesting than ____ .
d) ____ is more famous than ____ .
e) ____ isn't as interesting as ____ .
f) ____ is more exciting than ____ .

3 Do you agree with their opinions? Change the sentences in 2 to reflect your own ideas and then compare them with a partner.

4 Work in groups. Decide on a sports personality to advertise an isotonic fitness drink. Who would you choose? Why?

Close-up

Comparatives

Language Reference p. 27

1 Test your comparatives! Look at the adjectives in the box and put them in the correct columns, according to how the comparative is formed. There are three adjectives in each column.

happy	successful	sad	bad	strong	nice	interesting	lucky	far	wet

+ *-er* / *-r*	**double letter + *-er***	**– *y* + *-ier***	**irregular**	***more* + adjective**
kind → *kinder than*	*thin* → *thinner than*	*funny* → *funnier than*	*good* → ***better** than*	*famous* → ***more famous** than*

2 Refer to the chart of sports statistics. Complete the sentences, using the comparative forms of the adjectives + *than*.

a) Shaquille O'Neal (tall) Raúl.
Shaquille O'Neal is taller than Raúl.
b) Venus Williams (heavy) Michael Schumacher.
c) Inge de Bruijn (young) Cathy Freeman.
d) Raúl (old) Venus Williams.
e) Cathy Freeman (light) Inge de Bruijn.
f) Venus Williams (short) Shaquille O'Neal.

	Born	Height	Weight
Cathy Freeman	2/16/73	5 ft 3 in	115 lb
Shaquille O'Neal	3/6/72	7 ft	311 lb
Michael Schumacher	1/3/69	5 ft 7 in	163 lb
Raúl	6/27/77	5 ft 9 in	150 lb
Inge de Bruijn	8/24/73	5 ft 7 in	121 lb
Venus Williams	6/17/80	6 ft 1 in	168 lb

3 Add *much* or *a little* to modify the comparatives in the sentences in 2.

For example: *Shaquille O'Neal is much taller than Raúl.*

4 Use *not as* (*old/tall/heavy*, etc.) *as* to compare sports personalities in the chart in 2 with people in the class. Make five sentences.

For example: *Michael Schumacher isn't as tall as Marco.*

5 Test your general knowledge! Make sentences comparing the following. Use the adjective given with *a little/much/not as…as*. The answers are on page 125.

a) London (wet) Rome.
b) The Maracana Municipa Stadium in Rio de Janeiro (large) the Stade de France (Paris).
c) The population of Pakistan (small) the population of Russia.
d) Los Angeles International Airport (busy) Heathrow Airport.
e) Ireland (big) Cuba.
f) The Statue of Liberty (tall) the Eiffel Tower.

The schwa /ə/

1 17 Complete the following with the correct words to make typical expressions. Then listen and check your answers.

bat	bird	cucumber	feather	fiddle	picture

a) She's as free as a ____ .
b) She's as pretty as a ____ .
c) He's as fit as a ____ .
d) She's as cool as a ____ .
e) It's as light as a ____ .
f) He's as blind as a ____ .

2 In each expression, which words contain the schwa sound? Listen again and practice the expressions. Do you have similar expressions in your language?

Fitness Test

Reading Answer the questionnaire below as honestly as you can. Calculate your score and compare your answers with a partner.

ARE YOU DANGEROUSLY Unfit?

1 On an average day, do you...
a climb more than 100 stairs? YES/NO
b do at least one hour of housework? YES/NO
c walk or ride a bike to school or work? YES/NO

2 How often do you walk 3 miles or more?
a Once a month. b Once a week. c Never.

3 How much exercise do you get every month?
a More than 10 hours. b 2–9 hours.
c Less than 2 hours.

4 How often do you spend 20 minutes or more doing an activity that makes you hot or sweaty?
a Three or more times a week.
b Once or twice a week. c Not at all.

5 How long does it take you to walk half a mile?
a Less than 10 minutes. b 10–20 minutes.
c I can't walk that far.

6 How many of the following activities do you do more than once a week?
a Go for a run. YES/NO b Play a ball game (football, volleyball, etc.). YES/NO
c Do some aerobic exercise (jogging, bike riding, etc.). YES/NO

7 Check the activities you often do when you're on vacation.
a Go hiking. b Go swimming. c Go sightseeing. d Go dancing. e Lie on the beach.
f Eat and drink a lot.

8 Do you smoke? YES / NO

HOW TO SCORE

1 a YES: 5 NO: 0 b YES: 5 NO: 0 c YES: 5 NO: 0
2 a 3 b 5 c 0
3 a 5 b 3 c 0
4 a 5 b 3 c 0
5 a 5 b 3 c 0
6 a YES: 5 NO: 0 b YES: 5 NO: 0 c YES: 5 NO: 0
7 a 5 b 5 c 3 d 3 e 0 f 0
8 YES: –10 NO: 0

WHAT YOUR SCORE MEANS

20 or less: Your health and your life are in danger! You must get more exercise.

21–30: Could be worse, but not much worse.

31–40: Not bad, but could be better.

41–50: You are healthier than the average person, and you probably find your life more enjoyable as a result.

51 or more: You are super-fit. Are you a professional athlete? (Or are you a liar!)

Vocabulary: sports

1 Choose the most appropriate alternative in each of the following sentences.

a) I **practice/play/get** some exercise every day—I don't enjoy it, but it keeps me fit.
b) A lot of my friends **play/go/do** basketball—I think it's the most popular sport among young people in my country.
c) I'd love to **play/go/do** snowboarding, but I can't even ski.
d) The last time I **practiced/played/got** some exercise was on vacation—I **did/went/practiced** swimming in the sea.
e) I **did/played/got** a lot of tennis when I was a kid. Now I just watch it on TV.
f) I didn't enjoy **going/playing/doing** gymnastics in high school. Our teacher was horrible.

2 How many of the sentences in 1 are true for you? Compare with a partner.

3 Work in pairs. Complete each of these word combination lists with either *do, go,* or *play*. Add at least one more sport to each list.

a) ____	b) ____	c) ____
bike riding	track and field	basketball
fishing	judo	golf
swimming		soccer
windsurfing		tennis
		volleyball

4 Complete the following sentence beginnings with word combinations from 3 to make sentences about yourself. Compare your sentences with a partner.

a) I often… b) I sometimes… c) I don't… d) I'd like to…

Vocabulary: numbers

1 18 How do you say the numbers in the box? Listen and repeat.

¾ 0.25 0.33 1½ ⅛ ¼ 1.5 0.125 ⅓ 0.75

2 19 Work with a partner. Make pairs of numbers with the same value from the numbers in 1. Listen and check your answers.

For example: *¾ is the same as 0.75.*

3 20 How do you say the following numbers? Listen and repeat.

a) A speed: 127 mph 80 mph
b) A sum of money: $59 mil $17 mil
c) A big number: 97,002,440 624,112,350
d) A percentage: 8.2% 26.7%
e) A distance: 32.4 mi 26.2 mi
f) A soccer score: 4–1 2–0

4 Work with a partner and test your trivia! Which numbers in 3 are the correct answers to the following questions?

a) How fast is Venus Williams's tennis serve?
b) How much money did Michael Schumacher earn in 2000?
c) How many Mars Bars do the British eat every year?
d) What percentage of the UK population trusts the government?
e) What is the official distance for a marathon?
f) What was the final score in the 2002 World Cup Final when Brazil beat Germany?

5 21 Listen and check your answers to 4.

6 Work with a partner. Student A: Turn to page 125. Student B: Turn to page 126. Follow the instructions.

Tiger Woods

Reading and listening

1 Who is Tiger Woods? Work in groups and write down at least three facts about him.

2 The following numbers come out of a short article about Tiger Woods. Write the numbers in their full form and then use them to complete the text.

a) 12/30/75 = *December 30, 1975*
b) 1st = ____
c) 16 = ____
d) ¼ = ____
e) 04/08/01 = ____
f) 1½ = ____
g) 50,000,000 = ____
h) ⅛ = ____

3 22 Listen and read to check your answers. You can check your spellings in the tapescript on page 135.

Golfing Genius

Tiger Woods was born on (1) *December 30, 1975,* in California, of mixed heritage: he describes himself as (2) ____ black, a quarter Thai, a quarter Chinese, an eighth white, and (3) ____ American Indian. His father, Earl Woods, named him Tiger after a friend who saved his life in the Vietnam War.

He was only nine months old when he started playing golf, and he played his first game at (4) ____ years old. His father was his first teacher. At the age of eight, he won a tournament, and he won five more before he was (5) ____ . On (6) ____ , Tiger Woods made golfing history. He became the (7) ____ golfer to win all four majors—the most important tournaments—within the same year.

He is helping to make golf more popular with all ages and levels, and most people agree that he is probably the greatest golfer of all time. Certainly, he is already one of the richest.

He now earns more than (8) $____ a year. He has a $100 million deal with Nike and also has deals with American Express, Buick, Rolex, and Wheaties.

What advice would he give prospective parents of golf champions? "Don't force your kids into sports. It has to be fun."

The best advice he ever got? From his dad: "Always be yourself."

Listening

1 23 You are going to listen to a radio interview with Pauline Perkins—a big fan of Tiger Woods. Which of the following things does she tell the interviewer?

a) She has a Web site about Tiger Woods.
b) She writes to Tiger Woods every day.
c) She has a signed photograph of Tiger Woods next to her bed.
d) She always has a party on Tiger Woods's birthday, and she puts his pictures all over the house.
e) She watches videos about Tiger Woods every night.
f) She thinks Tiger Woods is a perfect man.
g) She likes the same food as Tiger Woods.

2 Listen again and complete the sentences.

a) I think he's the ____ wonderful person in the world.
b) He's ____ greatest golfer of all time.
c) In fact, he's the ____ player to win four major tournaments in one year.
d) I hear Tiger Woods is ____ of the richest athletes on the planet.
e) And is it true that Michael Jordan is one ____ his best friends?

3 Pauline Perkins is mad about Tiger Woods. Work with a partner. Describe somebody or something that you are mad about.

Close-up

Superlatives

1 Work with a partner and complete the following:

a) Write the superlative forms for the following groups of adjectives.
b) In each group, underline the superlative adjective that is formed in a different way from the other three.

	Adjectives	**Superlative forms**
1	old / rich / exciting / great	*the oldest / the richest / the most exciting / the greatest*
2	valuable / big / hot / thin	
3	funny / interesting / friendly / happy	
4	bad / far / good / talented	

2 Look at the superlative adjectives you have underlined in 1b. When do you use *most* to form a superlative adjective?

3 Work with a partner. Complete these questions with eight different superlative adjectives. Use the adjectives in 1 or your own ideas.

a) Who is ____ athlete in the world?
b) What is ____ music group of all time?
c) What is ____ place you've ever visited?
d) Who is ____ person you know?
e) What is ____ possession you have?
f) Who is ____ person in the class?
g) Where is ____ nightlife in your town?
h) Who is ____ actor / actress in your country?

4 Change partners and take turns asking your questions in 3. Discuss your answers.

Language Reference: Comparatives and superlatives

Forms with all one-syllable adjectives and some two-syllable adjectives:

1 Adjectives ending in a consonant or e.

great	*great**er** than*	*the great**est***
nice	*nic**er** than*	*the nic**est***

2 Adjectives ending in a single vowel followed by a single consonant.

big	*bi**gger** than*	*the bi**ggest***
wet	*we**tter** than*	*the we**ttest***

3 Adjectives ending in *y*.

happy	*happ**ier** than*	*the happ**iest***
friendly	*friendl**ier** than*	*the friendl**iest***

4 Forms that are irregular.

good	***better** than*	*the **best***
bad	***worse** than*	*the **worst***
far	***farther** than*	*the **farthest***

Forms with some adjectives that have two or more syllables and do not end in *y*:

famous	***more** famous than*	*the **most** famous*
interesting	***more** interesting than*	*the **most** interesting*

Forms to make negative comparisons:

We can use *not as… as*.
*Raúl is **not as** tall **as** Venus Williams.*

Forms to modify comparisons:

We can use *a little, a bit,* or *much*.
*Venus Williams is **a little** heavier than Michael Schumacher.*
*Shaquille O'Neal is **much** taller than Raúl.*

Anecdote

Think back to when you played sports in junior high or high school. You are going to tell your partner about it. Choose from the list the things you want to talk about. Think about what you will say and what language you will need.

- ☐ How many hours of sports did you play?
- ☐ What different sports did you play?
- ☐ Which sports did you like / hate?
- ☐ What kind of sports facilities did your school have?
- ☐ What sports gear or equipment did you use?
- ☐ What was your physical education teacher like?
- ☐ Did you ever play for a school team?
- ☐ What was your best / worst moment playing a sport?

5

Review 1

Sophie and Paul

Language reviewed: question forms—word order (Unit 1); describing people (Unit 1); expressions about relationships (Unit 3)

Questions

blind date A **blind date** is an arrangement made for you to spend a romantic evening with someone who you have never met before.

1 Imagine your friends have fixed you up on a blind date. Do you think they would choose somebody right for you?

2 Work with a partner. Decide on three key questions you would ask about a blind date before agreeing to go out with the person.

For example: *How tall is he/she?*

Compare your ideas with other people in the class.

Sophie

3 *Stella*, a monthly magazine for women, prints a regular feature called "Date of the Month." The magazine arranges a blind date for two people, and then the two people write a report about their date. Work with a partner. Discuss the photos of Sophie and Paul, the two people who are this month's blind date. Do you think their date will be a success?

Paul

4 Before Sophie and Paul met, they both had to fill in a questionnaire.

a) Student A: Read Sophie's answers on page 127 and write the questions.
b) Student B: Read Paul's answers below and write the questions.
c) Compare your questions. Discuss any differences.

1	(name) *What's your name?*	Paul Davies.
2	*(old)*	24.
3	*(do)*	Artist and illustrator.
4	*(zodiac sign)*	Scorpio.
5	*(tall)*	6 ft 2 in.
6	*(like)*	Funny, hard-working, romantic, but I think I'm also a little shy.
7	*(movies)*	Anything with Penélope Cruz in it!
8	*(favorite)*	Penélope Cruz.
9	*(wear)*	Jeans and sneakers.
10	*(spare time)*	Clubbing, parties, drinking beer, the movies, things like that.
11	*(worst fault)*	I've never had a long-term relationship. (Is that a fault?)
12	*(dream weekend)*	Staying in a hotel on a tropical beach with the woman of my dreams and then coming back home to watch my favorite football team win the Super Bowl.

5 Student A: Ask Student B about Paul. Student B: Ask Student A about Sophie.

For example: *How old is Paul/Sophie? What does Paul/Sophie do?*

6 Does the new information about Sophie and Paul change your prediction about their blind date? Discuss with your partner.

Reading Work with a partner. Sophie and Paul both wrote a report on their evening for *Stella* magazine.

a) Student A: Read Sophie's report and answer the questions.
b) Student B: Read Paul's report and answer the questions.
c) Compare your answers to the questions. Do you think they'll see each other again?

Questions:

1 What were their first impressions of each other?
2 How do they describe each other's character?
3 How did they think the date went?

Paul's report

When I first met Sophie, I couldn't believe my eyes. She was amazing—the best-looking woman I've ever met. I thought she looked like a model. She looked very stylish, even glamorous, in a short black dress, so I was really glad I'd put my best suit on. I was attracted to her right away, and I think she liked me too.

I felt kind of embarrassed at first, but after a few drinks we started talking, and then I felt more relaxed. I don't think we really have the same sense of humor—Sophie is really very serious and kind of difficult to get to know. She wasn't very talkative, and she didn't tell me much about herself. But I think she liked my jokes.

I really enjoyed the dinner, and the service was excellent. The waitress was very helpful, and I left her a generous tip. I'll definitely go back to that restaurant again.

Sophie got tired toward the end of the meal. I wanted to go dancing, but she said she had to get up early the next day, so I got her a taxi.

I think the evening went very well, and I'm looking forward to seeing her again. She says she's busy for the next three months, but I'll call her then, and hopefully, something will happen between us.

Something funny happened when I said goodbye to her—she called me John.

Sophie's report

Paul didn't look like his picture—I think it must be an old one. His hair was shorter, and he was wearing pretty strange clothes—a kind of striped suit with a pink shirt. At first I thought he was wearing his pajamas. Anyway, I thought he looked kind of cute and friendly, and he had a nice smile, but I definitely wasn't attracted to him!

He's very talkative. In fact, I really didn't get a chance to say anything. He laughed a lot at his own jokes, too. At first I thought he was really funny, but then I got kind of tired of his jokes, and I wanted to talk about more serious things—you know, get to know him a little better.

During the meal, Paul paid a lot of attention to the waitress. That really turned me off and put me in a bad mood.

When I get angry, I get very quiet, so I didn't talk very much for the rest of the evening, and I was glad when the meal was over. It was a miserable evening. I couldn't wait to get a taxi and go home. I discovered one thing, though—I'm never going on a blind date again!

Writing

1 Read the advertisement that Paul put in the personal column of a newspaper six months later. On a piece of paper, write your own personal ad.

2 Fold the paper and give it to your teacher. Then take another paper and guess which student it belongs to.

time! Photo and handwriting please. PO Box 2947

SINGLE ARTIST, early twenties, fit, funny, hard-working and romantic, wants to meet warm, generous, attractive person for friendship and fun. PO Box 3776

BORED TEACHER, 36, needs partner for tennis, golf,

Vinnie and Tanya

Language reviewed: *looks* + adjective vs. *looks like* + noun (Unit 1); comparison structures (Unit 4); simple past and past continuous (Unit 3); nouns and quantity expressions (Unit 2)

Listening

1 Work with a partner. You are going to hear about the man in the photograph. Before you listen, look at the picture and describe him, using the four sentence beginnings and the ideas in the box.

a) He looks…
b) He doesn't look…
c) He looks like…
d) He doesn't look like…

a talk show host	a movie star	stylish	
a family man	tough	a soccer player	
fit	middle-aged	romantic	friendly
a gangster			

2 What other ways can you think of to complete the sentences?

3 24 Listen to a radio program about this man. In what ways were your impressions in 1 and 2 correct? In what ways were they wrong?

4 Listen again and complete these sentences. The number of words you need is indicated, and the word in parentheses at the end of each sentence will give you a clue.

a) Well, yeah, he's [3] *much better known* in Britain than he is over here. (*well-known*)
b) I'd say he's still __[2]__ for his soccer skills than as an actor. (*famous*)
c) Yes, they're __[4]__ Manchester United, but… (*successful*)
d) The __[1]__ guy on the field? In what way? (*tough*)
e) Not really, no, but Vinnie was __[4]__ other soccer players. (*violent*)
f) …he's __[4]__ many people think. (*nice*)
g) …and he's __[5]__ people I've ever met. (*generous*)
h) Obviously, he's __[4]__ Brad Pitt, but he's a great character actor. (*good-looking*)

5 Would you like to meet Vinnie Jones? Why/Why not?

Comparison structures

1 Look at the adjectives in the box. What are the comparative and superlative forms?

tall	emotional	good-looking	talented	friendly	punctual	optimistic
lucky	young	generous	flexible	ambitious		

2 Complete the following sentences about yourself, using the comparative and superlative forms of the adjectives from the box in 1. Write down four true sentences and one false one. Exchange papers with a partner and see if you can guess which sentence is false.

For example: *I'm better-looking than my brother.*

- I'm…
- I'm a little…
- I'm much…
- I'm not as…
- I'm the…

Reading **1** You are going to read about how Tanya and Vinnie got together. Read the article once and decide if it was "love at first sight."

Love at First Sight?

Vinnie and Tanya first met at a cricket match when they were twelve, but they lost touch with each other soon afterwards.

(1) **Much/A few** years later they met again in a pub, but then their lives (2) **took/were taking** different directions. Vinnie spent (3) **many/some** time in Sweden playing soccer before returning to London, where he continued his soccer career. He had a son with his girlfriend, Mylene, but the relationship (4) **didn't work out/ don't work out**. Meanwhile, Tanya (5) **got married/was getting married** to a soccer player named Steve Terry, and they had a daughter, Kaley.

(6) **Many/Much** years later, Vinnie was sitting in his living room with a friend. The friend, who (7) **stood/was standing** by the window, said to Vinnie, "There's the most amazing-looking woman outside. Come and take a look." Vinnie (8) **got up/was getting up**, looked out the window, and there was Tanya, looking more beautiful than ever. She was now living on the same street as Vinnie, and (9) **a few/ a little** days later, Vinnie knocked on the door. They got along really well and (10) **spent/were spending** the whole night talking. Tanya was now separated from her husband, and she and Vinnie became good friends. After a while, the friendship changed into love, and they've been together ever since.

2 Read the article again and choose the correct alternatives.

3 25 Listen and check your answers to 2.

4 How many couples do you know who first met when they were in high school? Tell your partner about them.

Anecdote Vinnie Jones usually plays "tough guys" in movies. Think of a character in a movie you have seen recently. You are going to tell your partner about it. Choose from the list the things you want to talk about. Think about what you will say and what language you will use.

- ☐ What was the name of the movie, and who was the director?
- ☐ What did you know about the movie before you went to see it?
- ☐ What was the name of the character you saw in the movie?
- ☐ What was the character like?
- ☐ What happened to the character in the movie?
- ☐ Was he/she the main character or did he/she have a supporting role?
- ☐ What did you particularly like or dislike about the character?
- ☐ Which actor played the part of the character?
- ☐ What did you think of the actor's performance?
- ☐ Would you go and see this actor in another movie?

Neighbors

gossip Informal conversation, often about other people's private affairs.

Language reviewed: *looks* + adjective vs. *looks like* + noun (Unit 1); simple past and past continuous (Unit 3); expressions about relationships (Unit 3)

1 Work in groups of four. Discuss the following questions.

- How many neighbors do you have?
- How much do you know about each neighbor?
- What do your neighbors usually like talking about?

2 Look at these pictures of the scene and the characters in a sketch called *Gossip*. Compare the pictures to your own street and your own neighbors. How different are they? Tell your partner.

Mrs. Jones
She lives at number 1 with Mr. Jones. They don't have any children.

Mr. Jones
He works in an office. His company sells carpets.

Ms. Fox
She lives alone at number 2. She has never found a man who is good enough for her.

Mrs. Kray
Her husband died ten years ago. She lives at number 3 with her mother. She loves to gossip.

Mrs. Bing
She's a friend of Mrs. Jones. She goes over for coffee every Monday morning.

3 26 You are going to listen to and read the sketch. What is the confusion between Mrs. Jones's cat and Mrs. Jones's husband?

4 Work in groups of four. You are going to perform the sketch.

a) Decide who is going to play each character. (Mr. Jones and Mrs. Bing can be played by the same person.)
b) Practice your parts individually. Think about what voice your character will have, what he/she will look like, and how he/she will act.
c) Perform the sketch for the rest of the class.

5 Work in groups of four. Imagine a final scene inside Ms. Fox's house where the confusion is explained. Write a dialogue and compare it with other groups in the class. Perform your final scene for the rest of the class.

Gossip

Scene A street

Characters Mrs. Jones, from number 1
Mrs. Bing, a friend of Mrs Jones
Mrs. Kray, from number 3
Ms. Fox, from number 2
Mr. Jones, Mrs. Jones's husband

Mrs. Bing rings doorbell at number 1. Mrs. Jones comes to the door crying. Mrs. Kray is cleaning her doorstep at number 3…She tries to listen to the conversation outside number 1.

Mrs. Jones (*Crying*) Oh, hello, Mrs. Bing.
Mrs. Bing Oh, dear, what's the matter?
Mrs. Jones (*Crying*) I've lost my Sammy.
Mrs. Bing Who's Sammy?
Mrs. Jones My cat.
Mrs. Bing Where did he go?
Mrs. Jones (*Crying more*) I don't know—he's lost!

Mrs. Bing puts her arm around Mrs. Jones.

Mrs. Bing Oh, dear—don't cry. He'll come back. When did you last see him?
Mrs. Jones He had his dinner last night, and that's the last time I saw him. (*Crying loudly*) He often stays out at night, but he always comes home for breakfast…boo hoo.
Mrs. Bing What does he look like?
Mrs. Jones (*Crying loudly*) He's gorgeous. He's black with white ears and a white tail. And I love him!
Mrs. Bing Do you have any idea where he could be?
Mrs. Jones Well, the last time I saw him, he was running after that cat from across the street.
Mrs. Bing O.K., listen to me. You go in and have a nice cup of tea, and I'll go and look for Sammy.

Mrs. Jones goes inside and Mrs. Bing goes offstage. Ms. Fox comes out of number 2.

Mrs. Kray Did you see Mrs. Jones from number 1? She looks very upset this morning.
Ms. Fox Oh, dear. It's that husband.
Mrs. Kray (*Thinks for a moment and then looks as if she's found the answer to a problem*) Ah, now I understand.
Ms. Fox What do you mean? What do you understand?
Mrs. Kray Well, I wasn't sure what they were talking about—I couldn't hear everything, but now I understand! She was talking about her husband.
Ms. Fox (*In a gossipy voice*) And what did she say about her husband?
Mrs. Kray She says she loves him—and she thinks he's gorgeous!
Ms. Fox Gorgeous? How can she think he's gorgeous? He looks like a little frog.
Mrs. Kray Anyway, he's gone away with that woman from across the street.
Ms. Fox The woman from across the street? No!
Mrs. Kray Yes, he came home for dinner last night, and then he left.
Ms. Fox (*Enjoying the story*) Then he left? No!
Mrs. Kray Yes. And it's not the first time.
Ms. Fox Well, I know it's a stormy relationship. I can hear through the wall when they have a fight.
Mrs. Kray Apparently, he often stays out at night. But she says he always comes home for breakfast.
Ms. Fox (*Enjoying the story more and more*) That's terrible!!
Mrs. Kray Oh, look—here he comes.

Mr. Jones arrives home carrying a bunch of flowers.

Mr. Jones Morning, ladies.
Ms. F & Mrs. K (*Innocently*) Morning, Mr. Jones.

Mr. Jones goes into number 1 and offstage.

Ms. Fox He looks pleased with himself, doesn't he? Did you see the bunch of flowers he was carrying?
Mrs. Kray Well, he feels guilty, doesn't he?

Mrs. Jones comes out onto the street smiling. She is holding Sammy, her cat, in her arms.

Mrs. Jones Oh, he's back!

Ms. Fox and Mrs. Kray look at each other and raise their eyebrows.

Ms. Fox Look, I know it's none of our business, but we think you'd be better off without him.
Mrs. Jones Without who? My cat?
Mrs. Kray Your husband.
Mrs. Jones (*Confused*) My husband?
Ms. Fox Look, we know how you feel, but there are plenty more fish in the sea. Come on, let's go inside, and I'll make you a nice cup of tea.

Ms. Fox and Mrs. Kray put their arms around Mrs. Jones and lead her into number 2.

upset (adj) (line 38) = unhappy
he feels **guilty** (adj) (line 78) = he is unhappy because he has done something wrong
it's none of our business (line 84) = it doesn't concern us
there are plenty more fish in the sea (lines 89–90) = there are many more people you can have a relationship with

6 Shop

Work in small groups. Discuss the following questions.

- When do you give presents?
- What's the best present you've ever given?
- What's the best present you've ever received?
- Do you think it's easier to buy presents for men or for women?

Reading **1** Read this article about giving and receiving presents and answer the following questions.

a) Did a man or a woman write the article?
b) Does he or she think men are good at choosing presents?
c) Does he or she think women are good at choosing presents?
d) What do women and men really want for their birthday? Do you agree?

What People Really Want for Their *Birthday*

IT was my birthday recently, and as usual, I didn't get what I really wanted. I usually get a bunch of flowers, a book, a box of candy, and electronic gadgets. My family always asks me what I want, and I always say the same thing—I want a surprise. So this year I got flowers, books, candy, and gadgets.

Flowers are lovely, but they hardly ever last for more than a week, and a real present is something you can keep. I always look for the diamond ring hidden in the flowers, but it's never there.

Books are a waste of time, and I hate getting candy because I'm normally on a diet.

But gadgets are the worst. Most women are not interested in gadgets. Men buy gadgets for women because men love gadgets. For my birthday, my husband bought me a gadget that makes bubbles in the bath, like a Jacuzzi. Last year he got me one of those things you put on the back of your seat and it massages your back. What's he trying to tell me? That I deserve some little luxuries? I agree with that, but the little luxuries I like are made of gold or silver.

But women are sensitive and intuitive, so they always know the right thing to buy. Right? Wrong.

The big mistake that women make is that they usually buy clothes. They buy clothes because they like them, and they want other people to wear the clothes they like. "You always wear dark colors, and I want to change you, so I'm going to buy you a brightly colored tie or a pair of Mickey Mouse socks."

This is a big mistake. Men usually don't want brightly colored ties or silly socks. The word to remember when you're buying a present for a male is *gadgets*. Men like anything digital or electronic. Like one of those watches that tell scuba divers the time in Atlantis.

For his last birthday, I gave my husband a small flashlight and a Swiss army knife, the same present that I once gave to a 12-year-old nephew. He was overjoyed.

It's very simple. You can't ever go wrong if you always remember the "G" word for men and the "J" word for women—and that's "J" for jewelry, not "J" for Jacuzzi.

2 Rearrange the words below to make six statements from the article. You have been given the first word.

a) A… can real you something is present keep
b) Books… time of waste a are
c) Most… in are interested women gadgets not
d) Women… and intuitive are sensitive
e) Men… usually silly or colored want socks don't ties brightly
f) Men… anything like electronic digital or

3 Do you agree with these statements? Discuss with a partner.

Vocabulary: word combinations

1 *A bunch of flowers* is a phrase from the article in the previous section. Match words from column A with words from column B to make similar phrases.

A		B	
a)	a bunch of	1	socks/scissors/jeans
b)	a box of	2	cake/toast/fruit
c)	a pair of	3	potato chips/sugar/cookies
d)	a bag of	4	flowers/grapes/keys
e)	a piece of	5	wine/perfume/whisky
f)	a bottle of	6	candy/cereal/tissues

2 Work with a partner. Which things in 1 are common presents in your country? Which things would be very strange or unusual presents?

Close-up

Verbs with two objects

1 Rewrite the following sentences as in the example. Check your answers in the article on page 34.

	subject	verb	direct object	*for/to*	indirect object	
	Men	buy	gadgets	for	women.	*Men buy women gadgets.*
a)	My husband	bought	a gadget	for	me.	____ (line 18)
b)	He	got	one of those things	for	me.	____ (line 20)
c)	I	gave	a small flashlight	to	my husband.	____ (lines 41–42)

2 Translate the sentences in 1. Identify the subject, verb, direct object, etc. in your translation. What is the most common word order for sentences like these in your language?

3 On a piece of paper, write three true sentences and one false one, using words and phrases from the boxes. In each sentence, include a subject, a verb, an indirect object, and a direct object. Exchange your piece of paper with a partner. Check the word order. Guess which sentence is false.

People (subject/indirect object)	+	Verb	+	Things (direct object)
I, my mother/father, my best friend, my teacher, me, my brother/sister, my girlfriend/boyfriend, my boss	+	bought, got, gave, lent, made, sent, took, told	+	a present, a card, a letter, an e-mail, dinner, a secret, money, a drink, a pen

For example: *Last night* [subject] *I* [verb] *bought* [indirect object] *my best friend* [direct object] *a drink* *in my favorite bar.*

Language Reference: Verbs with two objects

Several common verbs can have two objects: *bring, buy, get, give, lend, make, send, show, take, teach, tell.* With these single-syllable verbs there are two possible sentence structures:

1 Subject + verb + direct object + *for/to* + indirect object

My husband + bought + a gadget + ***for*** *+ me.*
I + gave + a small flashlight + ***to*** *+ my husband.*

2 Subject + verb + indirect object + direct object

My husband + bought + me + a gadget.
I + gave + my husband + a small flashlight.

Verbs + ***for***: *buy, get, make.*
Verbs + ***to***: *bring, give, lend, send, show, take, teach, tell.*

Note: With most two/three-syllable verbs such as *demonstrate, describe, explain,* or *suggest,* we can only use sentence structure 1.

The teacher explained the exercise to us. NOT ~~The teacher explained us the exercise.~~

Anecdote

Think about the last time you went shopping to buy a present for somebody. You are going to tell your partner about it. Choose from the list below the things you want to talk about. Think about what you will say and what language you will need.

- ☐ Who was the present for?
- ☐ What was the occasion: a birthday, an anniversary, … ?
- ☐ Where did you go shopping for the present?
- ☐ Did you know what you were going to buy or did you have to look around?
- ☐ What did you buy?
- ☐ How much did you spend?
- ☐ Did you buy a card, too?
- ☐ Did the person like the present?
- ☐ Was it the kind of present you would like to receive?

Close-up

Adverbs of frequency

1 Complete this sentence from the article on page 34 (lines 10–12) by inserting the adverbs of frequency *always* and *never* in the correct positions.

I look for the diamond ring hidden in the flowers, but it's there.

2 Underline all the examples of adverbs of frequency in the article on page 34. Do adverbs of frequency come before or after the main part of the verb? Is this true for *be*? Is it true in negative sentences with *always* and *ever*? What about negative sentences with other adverbs of frequency?

3 Find more adverbs of frequency in this word snake. Put them in order starting with *always* and finishing with *never*.

normallysometimeshardlyeveroftenoccasionallyusuallyrarely

4 How well do you know the person sitting next to you? Add an adverb of frequency from 3 to the sentences below to make true sentences about your partner.

For example: *She occasionally gets what she wants for her birthday.*
He usually doesn't get what he wants for his birthday.

a) He/She spends more than $50 on a present.
b) He/She is positive about life.
c) He/She goes out on weekends.
d) He/She is on time.
e) He/She has lunch at home during the week.
f) He/She goes to bed before 10:00 P.M.

5 Compare your sentences in 4 with your partner and check how many are actually true. How similar/different are you?

6 Work with a partner. Use the same ideas in 4 to make sentences about your life when you were a child. Include an adverb of frequency in each sentence. Add your own ideas. Discuss how different your life is now compared to then.

For example: *When I was a child, I always got what I wanted for my birthday.*

Language Reference: Adverbs of frequency

always, often, usually, normally, sometimes, occasionally, rarely, hardly ever, never

The most usual positions are:

- Before the main part of the verb.
  *I **always** tell them the same thing.*
- After the verb *be*.
  *I'm **normally** on a diet.*
- Before the negative verb in negative sentences, except for *always* and *ever*.
  *Men **usually** don't want brightly colored ties.*
  *Women don't **always** know the right thing to buy.*

How Much is She Wearing?

Reading

1 Look at these photographs of four famous women. Which ones do you recognize? Whose clothes do you like best? Match the photographs (*a–d*) with the texts (*1–4*).

a

b

c

d

1 Gwyneth Paltrow

- Top $3,750
- Pants $750
- Shoes $3,000
- Bag $1,875
- Watch $4,500
- Earrings $1,200

Total $15,075

2 Jennifer Aniston

- Evening gown $4,500
- Bag $750
- Shoes $600
- Necklace $42,750
- Bracelet $42,000
- Earrings $15,000
- Ring $37,500
- Wedding ring $75,000

Total $218,100

3 Kylie Minogue

- Coat $33,000
- Top $600
- Pants $600
- Belt $300

Total $34,500

4 Catherine Zeta-Jones

- Evening gown $11,250
- Bag $4,500
- Silk wrap $2,250
- Shoes $600
- Earrings $1,090
- Bracelet $1,800
- Engagement ring $270,000

Total $291,490

2 Read the information again and write down who is wearing the most expensive…

a) evening gown b) pants c) top d) shoes e) ring f) earrings

Check your answers with a partner.

LANGUAGE TOOLBOX

Designs:
leopard-skin plain
patterned striped check

Materials:
leather cotton denim
wool silk synthetic

Jewelry:
a necklace a bracelet
a (wedding/an engagement) ring earrings

3 Test your memory! Cover up the photographs and decide whether the following are true or false. Check your answers and correct the wrong information.

a) Jennifer Aniston is wearing a blue evening gown.
b) Kylie Minogue isn't wearing any jewelry.
c) Gwyneth Paltrow is carrying a bag.
d) Catherine Zeta-Jones is wearing a pink silk wrap.
e) Jennifer Aniston isn't wearing a watch.
f) Kylie Minogue is wearing a striped top.
g) Gwyneth Paltrow is wearing a leopard-skin miniskirt.
h) Kylie Minogue is wearing a matching coat and top.

4 Work with a partner. Discuss the following issues.

a) Where did you buy the clothes you are wearing today?
b) When did you last buy an item of clothing? Describe it.
c) Where is the most expensive clothing store in your city?
d) Describe the most expensive item of clothing you've ever bought.
e) Do you think it's right to spend tens of thousands of dollars on clothes and jewelry? Why/Why not?

Close-up

Verbs + *-ing* form

1 Work with a partner. Complete each statement with *Men* or *Women* as you think appropriate.

a) ____ can't stand shopping for clothes.
b) ____ don't mind spending hours and hours shopping for clothes.
c) ____ spend a lot of time going from store to store, comparing prices and quality.
d) ____ don't bother looking at the price tag before they buy.
e) ____ don't waste time shopping unless they really need something.
f) ____ prefer going to the dentist's to going shopping.

2 Look at the statements in 1. Underline all the verbs and verb phrases that have a verb in the *-ing* form.

For example: *a) Men can't stand shopping for clothes.*

3 You are going to read interviews with two men about their attitudes to shopping. There are twelve cases where a verb or verb phrase should be followed by an *-ing* form. Correct the mistakes.

	Russell, 26, a writer, single	Billy, 32, a designer, engaged
1 Do you mind ~~go~~ **going** shopping on weekends?	Not really. But after about an hour, I want to go home.	It depends. I don't mind go shopping, but on weekends, I prefer watch sports on TV.
2 What kind of stores do you like go to?	Bookstores. I could spend a whole day in a bookstore.	I love listen to music, so music stores are my favorite.
3 Are there any kinds of stores you hate go to?	I hate supermarkets, so I don't bother go to them anymore. I do my shopping on the Internet.	I can't stand go into shoe stores with my girlfriend. She tries on ten pairs and then buys the first pair.
4 Do you enjoy buy clothes for yourself?	Not really. I don't waste time shop for clothes unless I really need something.	I like have new clothes, but I don't enjoy try them on.

4 27 Listen and check your answers to 3. Do you know any men with similar attitudes toward shopping?

5 Work with a partner. Take turns asking and answering the questions in 3.

Language Reference: Verbs + *-ing* form

We usually use the *-ing* form after the following verbs and verb phrases: *can't stand, don't mind, enjoy, hate, like, love, not bother, prefer, spend time, waste time.*

*I **don't mind shopping**.*
*I **love listening** to music.*
*I **don't bother going** to supermarkets anymore.*

I'll Take It

Listening

1 Russell wants to buy a present for his girlfriend. You are going to listen to the conversation he has with the salesclerk. Before you listen, look at the following sentences. Put *R* if you think Russell says them. Put *S* if you think the salesclerk says them.

a) Can I help you?
b) I'm just looking, thanks.
c) What kind of thing are you looking for?
d) What colors do you have?
e) People with green eyes look good in purple.
f) What size is she?
g) I'll take it.
h) How would you like to pay?
i) Here's your receipt.
j) Can she exchange it if it doesn't fit?

2 28 Listen and check your answers.

3 How would you describe Russell's feelings? Do you feel the same way when you buy clothes for a man/woman?

4 Work with a partner. You are going to read and listen to a conversation between Roz (*R*) and a salesclerk (*S*). Roz wants to buy a new cell phone. Complete the conversation with appropriate words.

S: Can I (1) ____ you?
R: Yes, I'm (2) ____ for a cell phone.
S: And what (3) ____ of cell phone are you looking for, ma'am?
R: Uh—what do you mean?
S: Well, what do you want to do with your cell phone—do you want to access the Internet, send text messages, play games…?
R: No, no. I just want to make phone calls.
S: O.K. Something like this, maybe? This model comes with a Call Log feature that keeps track of the calls you have received, missed, and dialed. It also has a Photo Caller ID that lets you know who's calling.
R: No, no, I'm not interested in all that. I just want to make phone calls.
S: Fine. How about this basic model? It's very easy to use.
R: Yes… (4) ____ colors do you have?
S: Well, we have this rather nice red one.
R: I don't (5) ____ good in red.
S: You don't (6) ____ good in red?!
R: That's right. I wear a lot of pink.
S: I see. Uh, well, we don't have pink, but we have this one in blue. Do you (7) ____ good in blue?
R: Yes, I like blue. I'll (8) ____ it.
S: Fine. I don't suppose you're interested in the clock function…
R: No.
S: …or voice and speed dialing…
R: No. I just want to pay!
S: O.K., that'll be $90. How would you (9) ____ to pay, ma'am?
R: In cash. Here you are.
S: Thank you madam. Here's your (10) ____ . Oh, and don't forget this brochure that tells you all about our cell phone accessories. I'm sure you're…

5 29 Listen and check your answers.

6 Work with a partner. Do you think Russell and Roz are a typical man and woman?

7 Work with a partner. You are going to write your own shopping dialogue.

a) Decide on the store and what the customer is buying.
b) Decide on the character/personality of the salesclerk and the customer.
c) Include at least six of the following eight words.

fit	help	just	pay	receipt	size	kind	look

d) Practice your conversation and perform it for the rest of the class.

7 Job

1

LANGUAGE TOOLBOX

I think she works outdoors/in an office.
He probably has a manual job/an office job/a factory job.
They look like a young woman's/an elderly man's/an artist's hands.

Work with a partner. Discuss the following questions.

- Do you notice people's hands when you meet them?
- What do you think hands can tell you about a person or his/her life?
- Look at the three pairs of hands (*1*, *2*, and *3*). What can you say about each person's age, sex, or job?

2

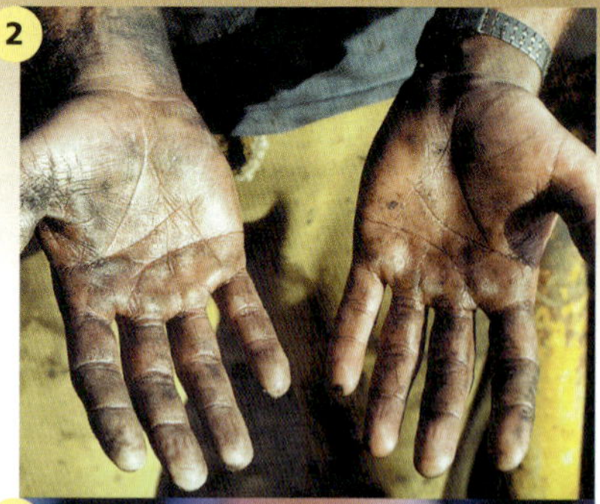

3

Listening

1 30 Listen to the three people whose hands appear above. They are describing their jobs. Which speaker (*A*, *B*, or *C*) is a midwife (a nurse who delivers babies), a farmer, a guitarist?

2 Listen again and note which speaker …

a) has a very stressful job.
b) has never had a day off because of illness.
c) works nights.
d) dropped out of school.
e) gets up very early.
f) has made loads of money.
g) works outdoors.
h) works long hours.

3 How many partial sentences from 2 can you complete by adding the name of a person you know as the subject? Tell your partner about the people you have noted down.

For example: *My friend Peter has a very stressful job. He's an airline pilot, and …*

Vocabulary: expressions with *hand*

1 The words and expressions in the box were used by the speakers in the previous section. Replace the underlined words or phrases in these sentences with an appropriate alternative from the box.

time on my hands	gives a hand	hands	On the other hand	secondhand

a) I don't think it's a good idea to buy a used car—they always break down.
b) I'm the kind of person who likes to be busy all the time. I get bored if I have too much spare time.
c) I don't like it when someone gives me a baby to hold—I don't know what to do!
d) I love going to the city for shopping. However, I'm very happy I live in the country.
e) My father rarely helps with the housework.

2 Are any of the sentences true for you? Compare your answers with a partner.

Reading

1 Work in small groups. Check the meaning of each of these jobs in a dictionary. You are going to read an article titled *Nightmare Jobs*. Discuss the kinds of bad experiences you could have in these jobs.

actor	nanny	factory worker	hairdresser	telemarketer	vet

2 Read the article and compare your ideas in 1 with the stories each person tells. Were any of your ideas similar?

Nightmare Jobs

Sally: a vet

What's the worst thing that has ever happened in your job?

Probably the dog that bit me. It wasn't a big one—I don't mind the big ones. The small ones are the worst. It gave me a very nasty bite.

Have you ever had any other jobs?

Yes, I had various jobs when I was a student. One summer I was a fruit picker in Florida.

What's the worst job you've ever had?

I worked as a nanny for a rich family in New York. I never had a day off, and I had to do everything—cooking, cleaning, shopping—*and* look after their horrible children. I left after two weeks and got a job as a waitress in an Italian restaurant.

William: a hairdresser

What's the worst thing that's ever happened in your job?

The first time I cut somebody's hair, I cut one side too short, so I had to cut the other side to match. When the woman saw how short her hair was, she started crying. I felt terrible.

Have you ever had any other jobs?

Yes, I've had lots of stupid ones! For instance, I've sold ice cream on the beach and handed out publicity flyers in the street.

What's the worst job you've ever had?

Telemarketing! You have to call people and try to sell them doors and windows. Work conditions are terrible—you can't take a break, and if you want to go to the restroom, you have to ask for permission, and then they time you! Nightmare.

Rob: an actor

What's the worst thing that's ever happened in your job?

So many bad things have happened—but I think my worst moment was when I read my first bad review in the newspaper. They wrote terrible things about me, and I was so upset. Now I don't read my reviews anymore.

Have you ever had any other jobs?

Oh yes. I've had hundreds of jobs over the years. Before I got my first big part, I was working as a waiter.

What's the worst job you've ever had?

The worst job I've ever had was at an egg-packing factory. I stood for hours and hours at the end of a conveyor belt, putting eggs into boxes. It was noisy and boring, and worst of all, the smell was disgusting—I've never eaten an egg since.

3 Read the article again and find words to complete the sentences below. The first letter of each word has been given to you.

a) The boss had a very n____ temper, and he was always shouting at me.
b) I never had any time o____ ; I even had to work on weekends!
c) I had to work non-stop from nine to six without having a real b____ .
d) I wasn't allowed to do anything at all without asking the boss for p____ .
e) The machines were so n____ that I couldn't hear myself think.
f) The conditions were d____ ! I took a shower every day as soon as I got home.

4 Work with a partner. Discuss these questions.

- Do you know anybody who has had to work under conditions like these?
- What are the worst conditions you've had to work under?
- What do you think is the worst job in the world?

Close-up

Present perfect

Language Reference p. 43

Verb Structures p. 129

1 Work with a partner. Look at these two sentences from the article in the previous section and answer the questions.

1 "Yes, I had various jobs when I was a student."
2 "Oh yes. I've had hundreds of jobs over the years."

a) Which sentence refers to a completed action in finished time? What is the name of the tense used?
b) Which sentence refers to a completed action that is true in time up to and including now? What is the name of the tense used?
c) How do you form the affirmative, negative, and question forms of the tense you identified in *b*?

2 Put each time expression in the box under the appropriate heading. Add three more time expressions of your own under each heading.

when I was a student   over the years   recently   a few years ago   last week
today   never   yesterday   in 1999   this week

Finished time	Time up to and including now
when I was a student	*over the years*

Really, thanks a lot. It's the best party we've been to all night.

3 Complete each of these sentences with a time expression from 2 or one of your own. Choose the appropriate tense and try to make all the sentences true for you. Compare your sentences with a partner.

For example: *a) I met a lot of interesting people when I was in Tokyo.*

a) I **'ve met/met** a lot of interesting people…
b) I **haven't been/didn't go** to the beach…
c) I **'ve bought/bought** a great CD…
d) I **'ve spent/spent** too much money…
e) I **haven't seen/didn't see** any good movies…
f) I **'ve done/did** a lot of silly things…

4 Divide the irregular verbs in 3 into two groups: Group A where the simple past and past participle forms are the same and Group B where they are different.

Group A			Group B		
Simple verb form	Simple past	Past participle	Simple verb form	Simple past	Past participle
meet	*met*	*met*	*go*	*went*	*gone*

5 Add each of the following verbs to the appropriate group in 4. There are a total of eight verbs in Group A and twelve verbs in Group B.

bite   choose   drive   eat   feed   give   hear   hide   sell   sleep   stick
take   wear   write

6 Work with a partner. Make questions from the following cues.

a) best or worst/vacation/be on   *What's the best vacation you've ever been on?*
b) best or worst/meal/eat
c) best or worst/joke/hear
d) best or worst/car/be in
e) best or worst/T-shirt/wear
f) best or worst/party/be to
g) best or worst/bed/sleep in

7 Choose three questions from 6 and ask your partner. Find out as much as you can.

Language Reference: Present perfect

The present perfect has several uses, but in all cases it shows a connection between the past and now. We can use the present perfect to describe completed actions that have taken place in time up to and including now. However, if we want to describe a completed action in finished time, then we have to use the simple past.

Time up to and including now

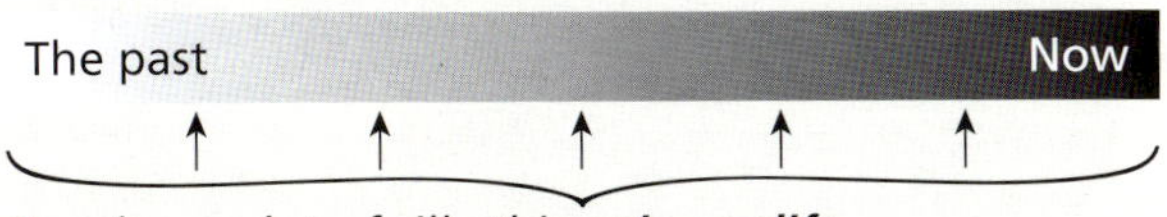

I've done a lot of silly things ***in my life****.*

Here are some time expressions which describe time up to now: *today, this week, recently, never, over the years*. When these time expressions refer to the time up to now, we usually use the present perfect.

*My brother****'s never been*** *to a pop concert.*
I ***haven't seen*** *any good movies* ***recently****.*

Finished time

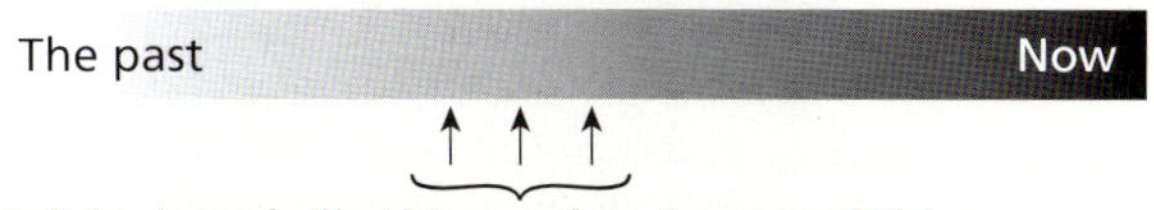

I did a lot of silly things ***when I was a child****.*

Here are some time expressions which describe finished time: *yesterday, last month, when I was a student, in 1990, a few minutes ago*. With these time expressions we always use the simple past.

She ***called*** *you* ***a few minutes ago.***
I ***didn't go*** *to the beach* ***last summer.***

Class Experience

1 Read *At Least Once in Their Lifetime...* and complete the sentences with the names of people in the class. You must use everybody's name at least once. Write more sentences if you need to.

At Least Once in Their Lifetime...

1 ____ 's traveled to two other continents.
2 ____ 's been to an opera.
3 ____ 's been to the movies alone.
4 ____ 's given a speech in public.
5 ____ 's worked abroad.
6 ____ 's bought an original piece of art.
7 ____ 's broken someone's heart.
8 ____ 's broken the speed limit.
9 ____ 's changed a baby's diaper.
10 ____ 's organized a party for somebody.
11 ____ 's...

2 Are your sentences true? Ask the people whose names you have written down.
For example: *Paul, how many other continents have you traveled to?*
Verónica, have you ever been to an opera?

3 Which person in the class wrote the largest number of true sentences?

4 How many things on the list have *you* done?

Youth Versus Experience

Listening

1 Work with a partner. You are going to listen to a radio interview with Mr. Reynold. Look at the photograph and discuss possible answers to the following questions.

a) What kind of company does Mr. Reynold work for?
b) When did he start working for the company?
c) How old is he?

2 31 Listen and check your ideas in 1.

3 Listen again and decide if these statements are true or false. Correct the false statements.

a) Mr. Reynold never forces anybody to retire.
b) The oldest employee at Reynold's is 97.
c) Reynold's pays a decent salary.
d) Employees get five weeks' paid vacation.
e) All the staff members are over the retirement age.
f) Mr. Reynold's secretary, Edith, handed in her resignation because she wanted to get married.
g) Mr. Reynold has never had any reason to fire anyone.
h) Mr. Reynold's brother is going to run the business starting next year.

Vocabulary: employment

1 Use appropriate words and expressions underlined in 3 above to complete these statements.

a) Everybody should get six ____ a year.
b) Nurses and teachers don't get ____ . Their employers should pay them more.
c) The official ____ should be the same for men and women.
d) If you don't want ____ , you should be allowed to continue working.
e) Executives who ____ large corporations earn far too much money.

2 Work in small groups. Discuss the statements in 1. Do you agree or disagree?

Anecdote

Think about a retired person you know well. You are going to tell a partner about him/her. Choose from the list below the things you want to talk about. Think about what you will say and the language you will use.

- ☐ What is his/her name?
- ☐ How do you know him/her?
- ☐ How long ago did he/she retire?
- ☐ How old was he/she at retirement?
- ☐ What did he/she do for a living?
- ☐ How many different places did he/she work during his/her career?
- ☐ What kinds of things has he/she done since retiring?
- ☐ Do you think he/she is happier in retirement than in work?

Presentation

Letter of application

1 Read this letter of application for a job at Reynold's Department Store. Use the words and expressions in the box to improve the parts of the letter that are underlined.

enclosed	Sir or Madam	a new challenge	look forward to hearing
would like to apply for	reached retirement age		

45 S. Broad Street
Daytona Beach, FL 32118

Reynold's Department Store
12221 N. Halifax
Daytona Beach, FL 32118

July 6, 2003

Dear (1) Mr. or Mrs.:
I saw your advertisement for a job as salesclerk in your garden furniture department, and I (2) want the job.

I am an experienced salesclerk, and I have worked in many different departments. Please see my résumé (3) in the same envelope for more details.

I started working in department stores when I was twenty-one, forty-five years ago. I left my last job six years ago when I (4) got too old, but I get bored at home. I feel I am ready for (5) new things now.

I would be available for an interview at any time, even on short notice.

I (6) can't wait to hear from you.

Sincerely,
Edna Smith
Edna Smith

2 Write your own letter of application for your dream job.

Presenting yourself

1 Read this self-introduction. Imagine you are attending a professional development course and you are going to introduce yourself to everybody in the group. Think about how you will say the information.

Good morning. Let me introduce myself. My name's Lourdes Rivas, and I work for American Airlines. As you probably know, we are a major international airline. I'm based at Miami International Airport in Florida, where I'm in charge of sales and promotion. I'm looking forward to taking this course.

2 Work with a partner. You are going to rewrite this self-introduction in order to make it easier to say. Follow these instructions. The first few lines have been done for you.

Good morning. //
Let me introduce myself. //
My name's Lourdes / Rivas, //
and I work for American Airlines. //

a) Insert / / where you think there should be a pause and start a new line.
b) Underline the stressed word(s) or syllable(s) in each line.
c) Insert / between words that you need to say very clearly.

3 32 Listen and repeat after the recording.

4 Prepare your own self-introduction or invent one. Write the information, using the techniques above. Introduce yourself to the rest of the class.

8 Rich

Money

Song

1 Work with a partner. Look at the lines of the song *Money*. Choose the most appropriate alternative to complete the first two lines of each verse.
(Note: *it don't* = *it doesn't*)

2 33 Listen to the song and check your answers to 1.

3 Which sentence best describes the singer's attitude toward money?

a) Money can buy love.
b) Love is more important than money.
c) Money is the most important thing in life.

4 Work with a partner. Discuss these questions.

a) What is your opinion about the singer's attitude toward money?
b) Do you know anybody with similar opinions?
c) How would you describe your own feelings about money?

5 What do the following sayings mean? How many "money" sayings can you think of in your language? Which sayings do you like best?

"Money talks."
"Money doesn't grow on trees."
"Time is money."

The best things in life are
(1) **expensive/free/dangerous.**
But you can keep them for the birds and
(2) **bees/flies/ants.**
Now give me money.
That's what I want.
That's what I want, yeah.
That's what I want.

Your lovin' gives me a
(3) **thrill/headache/lift.**
But your lovin' don't pay my
(4) **rent/bills/taxes.**
Now give me money.
That's what I want.
That's what I want, yeah.
That's what I want.

Money don't get everything, it's
(5) **true/interesting/funny.**
What it don't get, I can't
(6) **believe/use/understand.**
Now give me money.
That's what I want.
That's what I want, yeah.
That's what I want.

Now give me money.
Whole lot of money.
Yeah, I want to be free.
Whole lot of money.
That's what I want.
That's what I want, yeah.

The Beatles

The Beatles (1960–70) were the most successful band of all time. They sold over one billion records. Their cover version of *Money* was one of their earliest songs.

Millionaires

Reading

1 Work in small groups. Discuss these questions.

- What different ways are there of becoming a millionaire?
- How many millionaires can you name?
- How did they make their money?

2 Read the article about three millionaires and match the adjectives in the title (*good, bad, extremely generous*) to the people in the photos.

The Good, **the Bad,** and **the Extremely Generous**

When do you have enough money? How many yachts, limousines, and luxury homes can one millionaire use? What can rich people do with all that money? They can't take it with them when they die ... or can they?

Brian Williamson, one of Britain's richest men, thinks he can. He has spent £40 million ($60 million) on building a palace inspired by Versailles and the White House. But he isn't planning to live in it—not while he's still alive, anyway. When he dies, he will be buried in it with his art and furniture collection. It is a monument to himself. Williamson managed to make his money by investing in property. He was a millionaire by the age of 22. He has five children by three different mothers, but his children will not inherit any of his fortune. "The purpose of Arlington Palace," says Williamson, "is to take my money with me when I die and to make sure that nobody else gets their hands on it."

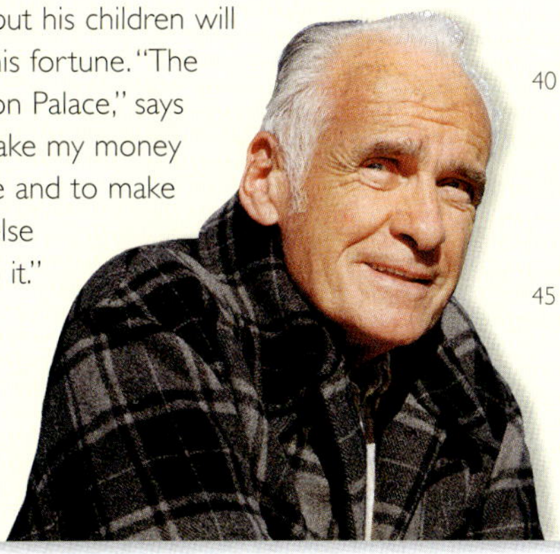

Eric Miller has a rather different attitude toward money. When he retired, he sold his business and made a very large profit. He then moved out of his seven-bedroom house and moved into a trailer in his backyard. He donated the house to the Catholic Church so that it could be used as a vacation home for disabled children. "All my life I've been worried about the poor," explains Mr. Miller. "I don't want to be selfish. I'm quite happy living in my trailer."

For **Mike and Kathy Dawson**, it's simple: the more they earn, the more they give away. Ten years ago, they were earning enough to own three large houses and several expensive cars and still save some money each month. Then their employer doubled their salary, making them millionaires. At this point they decided that they didn't need any more money to live on and chose to give it away. Each month they give away any extra money they make to children's charities around the world. "I believe you become a millionaire," says Mike Dawson, "when you give away $1 million."

3 Which millionaire do you most sympathize with? Discuss with your partner.

Vocabulary: money expressions

1 Read the article again and underline all the words and expressions that are associated with money.

2 Use the words and expressions you underlined in 1 to complete these questions. The first letter of each missing word has been given to you.

a) What's the most money you've ever s____ on an item of clothing?
b) Is it possible to m____ a lot of money in your job (or the job you want to do)?
c) Have you ever sold something and m____ a large profit?
d) Do you e____ more than you spend or spend more than you e____ ?
e) Do you try to s____ some money every month, or do you spend it all?
f) Mike Dawson believes that you become a millionaire when you g____ away $1 million. Do you agree?

3 Work with a partner. Ask and answer the questions in 2.

Going Solo

Reading and listening

1 Work with a partner and discuss these questions.

- What is the most popular band in your country these days?
- What kind of music do they play, and how many hits have they had?
- What kind of future do you think the band has? Will they stay together or split up? Why?

2 Read the extract from a TV magazine. Who is Matt McKay, and why is he giving an interview?

PICK OF THE DAY

Channel 7, 8:30 P.M.

A Hole in the Ozone

At first, it was a dream come true for Matt McKay, lead singer of chart-topping boy band Ozone. Matt McKay always wanted to be a pop star. He was only 17 when he joined boy band Ozone as lead singer. A year later, Ozone had its first number one hit. By the time he was 20, Matt was a millionaire. Ozone concerts sold out overnight, and the future looked rosy.

Then Matt announced that he was leaving the band. At the height of their success, he suddenly gave it all up.

In Matt's first interview since the split, he talks openly about his decision to leave Ozone and his plans for the future.

3 34 Listen to the first part of the interview with Matt McKay. Check (✔) the reasons he gives for leaving the band.

a) He didn't like the other members of the band.
b) He didn't have any freedom.
c) He was bored with singing and dancing.
d) He couldn't go out or have relationships.
e) He didn't make any money.
f) The people he met were only interested in his money.

4 In the second part of the interview, Matt talks about his plans for the future and the lessons he has learned from the past. Before you listen, match each verb in column A with a word or phrase from column B to make an expression. In some cases, more than one answer is possible.

A	B
a) keep on	1 a solo career
b) pursue	2 my money on stupid things
c) hire	3 singing
d) waste	4 my own songs
e) spend	5 the kind of music I like
f) forget	6 a decent manager
g) write	7 the same mistakes again
h) play	8 more time with my family
i) make	9 my real friends

5 35 Work with a partner. Check (✔) the things in the list in 4 you think Matt is going to do. Put an ex (✘) next to the things you think he is not going to do. Listen and check your answers.

6 Which would you prefer to be: a) rich; b) famous; c) rich and famous? Tell your partner and give reasons.

Close-up

(be) going to

Language Reference p. 50

Verb Structures p. 130

1 Correct the mistakes in these sentences.

a) "I going to keep on singing."
b) "I'm definitely not go to forget my real friends."
c) "What kind of music are you going play?"

2 Work with a partner. Complete the following situations by answering the questions in *italics* with your own ideas. Read one of your completed situations to the class.

a) Last year's vacation was a disaster. *What happened?*
This year, we've decided to go somewhere else. *What are you (not) going to do?*

b) My last exams were a disaster. *What happened?*
This year, I've decided to prepare for them properly. *What are you (not) going to do?*

c) The last party we held was a disaster. *What happened?*
This time we've decided to plan it differently. *What are you (not) going to do?*

d) My last relationship was a disaster. *What happened?*
This time I've decided to do things differently. *What are you (not) going to do?*

3 Work with a partner. How many decisions have you already made about the rest of today/this week/this month/this year/your life? Use the cues below and your own ideas to ask and answer questions about the decisions you have made.

Question

What Where	are you going to	do go be	after class tonight tomorrow this weekend next summer for New Year's

?

Answer

✗ (You don't know.) → I have no idea. I haven't decided yet.

✓ (You know.) → I'm going to…

Listening

1 36 The poster advertising Matt McKay's concert tour has some mistakes in it. Listen to the radio interview and write *Canceled* next to the three concerts Matt is *not* doing.

2 Use words from the interview in 1 to complete these sentences. Listen and check your answers.

a) I can't remember when I last bought a s____ . I usually download songs from the Internet these days.
b) When I buy a new a____ , I usually like only one or two of the songs on it.
c) Matt McKay has three g____ in California, and I'm going to go to them all.
d) The last time my favorite band went on t____ , I saw two of their concerts.
e) I'll never be one of Madonna's biggest f____ . I just don't like her music.
f) I have no idea what's at the top of the c____ these days.

3 Find out how many of the sentences in 2 are true for your partner.

Close-up

Present continuous

Language Reference p. 50
Verb Structures p. 130

1 Look at the four quotes in the present continuous. Which sentences refer to arranged future events? Which sentence refers to a present event?

a) "Your first solo single **is coming out** tomorrow."
b) "Matt McKay… **is sitting** here with me in the studio today."
c) "We**'re starting** our Americas tour next week."
d) "We**'re taking** a short vacation the following week."

2 You are extremely rich and famous! Below is a page from your datebook for next week. Copy it and fill it in with at least one appointment for each day of the week. Use your imagination.

3 Work as a whole class. Follow these instructions, using your diary from 2.

- Choose three times during the week when you would like to arrange to do something with other students.
- Go around the class and find out who is free at these times.
- Make arrangements to do something with the people who are free and note the arrangements in your diary.
- Tell the class what you are doing and who you are doing it with.

4 Work with a partner. How different is your life from the life you described in 2 and 3? Think about your real arrangements for next week and say what you are doing.

MONDAY
10:30 a.m.—massage

TUESDAY
7 p.m.—fly to Paris for dinner at the Ritz

WEDNESDAY
1 p.m.—lunch with Madonna and Guy

THURSDAY

FRIDAY

SATURDAY

SUNDAY

Language Reference: Future forms

(be) going to and the present continuous are common ways of talking about the future.

(be) going to

We use this to talk about future intentions (things we have decided to do).
*I'm **going to** keep on singing.*
*I'm **not going to** forget my real friends.*

Present continuous

We use this to talk about future arrangements (e.g., appointments and organized events).
***Are** you **doing** anything for lunch today?*
*We**'re starting** our Americas tour next week.*

Note: We can also use *(be) going to* to talk about future arrangements.

Now Give Me Money (That's What I Want)

Reading **1** Read the information on the Funds for Your Future Web site. What can it help you to…

a) get? b) improve? c) take? d) learn? e) buy? f) start?

Funds for Your Future

Back Forward Stop Refresh Home Favorites History Search AutoFill Larger Smaller Print Mail Preferences

Address: http://www.insideout.net/fyfuture Go

Favorites History Search

Funds for Your Future

About Us

Submit an Application

get help, get a grant, get into a new business

- **Are you under 25 years of age?**
- **Are you thinking about your future and how to achieve your goals?**
- **Do you want to improve your chances in life?**

Then keep reading…

FYF could provide grants so you can learn new job skills. You could take professional development courses, and FYF could pay for your books and fees. We have experienced advisors to support you as you start your own business. We can help you to buy the equipment you might need. With our advice you will be able to write a business plan, raise your own funds, set up your business. FYF can help you succeed!

Internet zone

2 Can you apply for this kind of help in your country? Where?

Writing **1** Work with a partner. Imagine you want to start a business together and you want to apply for a grant from an organization similar to FYF. Discuss the following questions.

grant Some money that the government or an organization gives you for a specific purpose and does not ask you to pay back.

a) What kind of business would you like to start? Choose from ideas in the box below or choose your own idea.

a band	a Web site for English students	a sports club	a photography studio
a window-cleaning business	a baby-sitting service	a pizza delivery service	

b) What would you need to set up the business? Equipment? Training?

2 Three people applied for grants from an organization similar to FYF. Read their summaries about what they want to achieve. Which is the best application? Why?

a I'm going on vacation to Florida in four weeks. Before I go, I want to earn some cash. My idea is to clean people's houses in the neighborhood. My friend Beatriz has a van, but we don't have any cleaning supplies. Does your organization pay for things like that?

b I dance in a Latin folk group that is based in Brooklyn. We are giving a charity performance for a local assisted living facility at the end of the month, and we need new shoes. There are twenty-four of us! Can you help?

c I have completed a three-year course in computer skills and Web design, and I have gained some work experience in the U.S. and Mexico. I would like to apply for a grant to set up an international employment agency on the Internet. This agency would specialize in finding jobs for young people who want to gain work experience abroad. To do this, I need to rent an office, buy computer hardware and software, and hire one person as a marketing manager. Please see my detailed business plan attached. I believe there is a big market for the kind of services my company would provide, and I would be grateful if you could give serious consideration to my application.

Internet zone

3 Work with the same partner as in 1. Plan out and write your own summary about what you want to achieve to complete your application.

4 Decide which application in the class is most likely to succeed.

9 Rules

Reading

1 Work with a partner. Have you ever read a self-help book? Did it help? What is the most important book you have ever read?

2 Read this page from an online bookstore about a self-help book called *How to Be the Perfect Ms. Right*. Who is the book for?

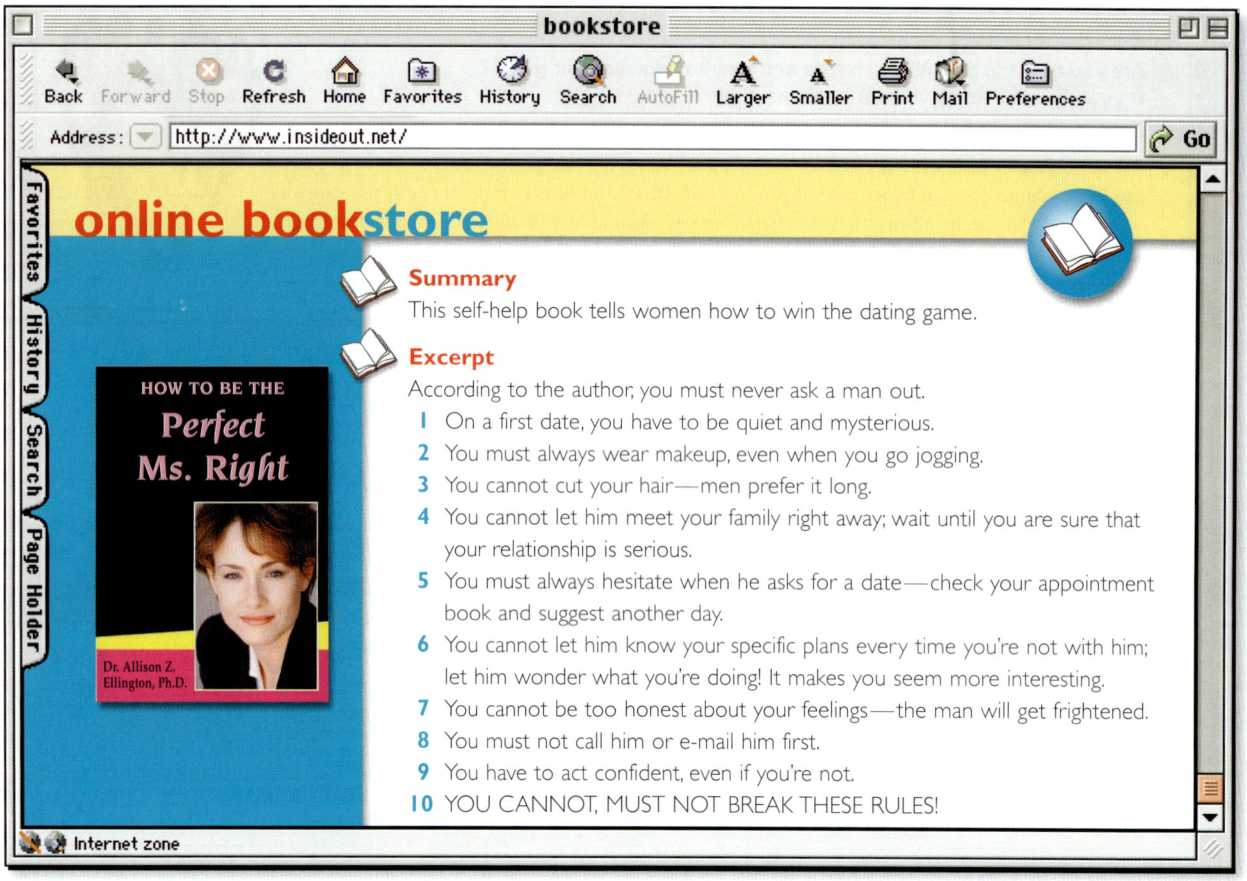

Summary

This self-help book tells women how to win the dating game.

Excerpt

According to the author, you must never ask a man out.

1. On a first date, you have to be quiet and mysterious.
2. You must always wear makeup, even when you go jogging.
3. You cannot cut your hair—men prefer it long.
4. You cannot let him meet your family right away; wait until you are sure that your relationship is serious.
5. You must always hesitate when he asks for a date—check your appointment book and suggest another day.
6. You cannot let him know your specific plans every time you're not with him; let him wonder what you're doing! It makes you seem more interesting.
7. You cannot be too honest about your feelings—the man will get frightened.
8. You must not call him or e-mail him first.
9. You have to act confident, even if you're not.
10. YOU CANNOT, MUST NOT BREAK THESE RULES!

3 Do you agree with any of the rules from the excerpt? Do you know anybody who would like to buy a book like this? Would you like to buy a book like this? Discuss with a partner.

Vocabulary: describing character

1 Find opposite adjectives in the excerpt from *How to Be the Perfect Ms. Right* to complete these pairs.

a)	cheerful	≠	miserable	f)	hard-working	≠	lazy
b)	talkative	≠	____	g)	____	≠	dishonest
c)	sensible	≠	silly	h)	optimistic	≠	pessimistic
d)	open	≠	____	i)	sensitive	≠	insensitive
e)	____	≠	boring	j)	____	≠	insecure

2 37 Listen and check your answers. Underline the stressed syllable in each word. Practice saying the words.

3 Which of the adjectives in 1 describe your Mr. or Ms. Right, and which ones describe your Mr. or Ms. Wrong? Add more adjectives if necessary.

4 Compare your answers with a partner. Do you have the same ideas?

Reading

1 Read these readers' reviews of the rules in *How to Be the Perfect Ms. Right* and match an appropriate heading (*a–d*) with each review (*1–4*).

a) The rules are dishonest.
b) The rules are old-fashioned.
c) The rules are sexist.
d) The rules are right.

bookstore

Back Forward Stop Refresh Home Favorites History Search AutoFill Larger Smaller Print Mail Preferences

Address: http://www.insideout.net/reviews/ Go

Favorites History Search Page Holder

Readers' Reviews

1 This book is about what my mother taught me and her grandmother taught her. But this is the 21st century—women should ask men out! *Maria from Puerto Rico*

2 I usually fall in love with men who are not good for me, but the rules in the book have helped me to find Mr. Right. Women should follow these rules, and men will respect them more. *Wenyu from Hong Kong*

3 There shouldn't be different rules for men and women. We're all the same! *Bob from the U.S.*

4 I disagree with the rules in this book. If you like somebody, you should be honest about your feelings. You shouldn't play games with people. *Marluce from Brazil*

Internet zone

2 Which review do you agree with most? Compare with your partner.

Close-up

have to, must,* and *should

Language Reference p. 55

Verb Structures p. 130

1 Work with a partner. Read the sentences below. Which sentence offers advice or a suggestion? Which sentence expresses an order or an obligation?

a) You have to follow the rules.
b) You should follow the rules.

2 Write the negative and question forms of the two modal sentences in 1.

3 Work with a partner. Imagine a popular men's magazine has asked you to write men's rules for successful dating. Complete *How to Be the Perfect Mr. Right* with *have to* or *must* in each affirmative sentence and *cannot* or *must not* in each negative sentence. Add one more rule of your own.

a) You ____ arrive on time for dates—women hate it when you keep them waiting.
b) On her birthday, you ____ give a woman a gold ring—she'll think you want to marry her, and that's exactly what she wants. Be safe—give her flowers.
c) You ____ pay when you go out. Women want to be equal, but not that equal!
d) You ____ be funny. You may be good-looking, well-dressed and have the brains of Einstein, but if you can't make them laugh, forget it.
e) You ____ talk about other beautiful women, even famous ones. She'll remember, and years later, when you make a comment about her cooking, she'll tell you to get Julia Roberts to make your lunch.

4 Work with a partner. Do you agree with any of the rules in *How to Be the Perfect Mr. Right* in 3?

5 Work in small groups. Discuss your real opinions about what makes a successful date. Write down a list of good advice for men and women. Include at least six things you think they should or shouldn't do. Compare your list with other students in the class.

Reduction and linking

1 38 Listen and repeat the sentences below. What is the pronunciation of *have to* in the sentences? What happens to the pronunciation of the "t" in *must* and *can't* when the next word starts with a consonant sound?

a) You have to be quiet and mysterious.
b) You have to wear makeup.
c) You can't let him meet your family right away.
d) You can't cut your hair.
e) You must always hesitate when he asks for a date.
f) You must pay when you go out.

2 39 Practice saying the sentences below. Listen and check your answers.

a) You have to stay in bed for a few days.
b) You cannot open it until your birthday.
c) You must ask if you don't understand.
d) You must not call me at work.
e) You have to stop writing now.
f) You have to signal before passing.

3 Who do you think is speaking to whom in 2? What is the situation? What other things could these people say to each other using *have to* or *must*?
Discuss your answers with a partner.

Listening

1 40 You are going to listen to Barbara talking about her relationship with Michael after she had read *How to Be the Perfect Ms. Right*. What happened to the relationship? What is the title of the book she is reading now?

2 Listen again and complete each sentence with the correct alternative.

a) Barbara decided to follow the rules in *How to Be the Perfect Ms. Right* because she wanted (1) **a good relationship** (2) **a new relationship**.
b) Barbara (1) **was too busy** (2) **had to say she was too busy** to talk to Michael on the phone.
c) The real Barbara is (1) **warm and friendly** (2) **cold and hard**.
d) Michael thought she was (1) **mysterious and fascinating** (2) **behaving like a witch**.
e) When Barbara fell in love with Michael, she (1) **wanted to** (2) **didn't want to** continue to follow the rules in *How to Be the Perfect Ms. Right*.
f) When Michael saw the book, he was (1) **angry** (2) **happy**.
g) Now Barbara wants to (1) **find a new man** (2) **stay single**.

3 What advice would you give to Barbara? Do you think she should read *The Joy of Being Single?*

Close-up

Past modals: obligation and permission

Language Reference p. 55

1 Complete what Barbara said in the previous section. Use past modal structures from the box.

I didn't have to	I could	I had to	I couldn't

Present time		**Past time**
The rules in *How to Be the Perfect Ms. Right* say:		Barbara said:
"You can't call him first."	→	(1) ____ call him first.
"You have to hesitate when he asks for a date."	→	(2) ____ hesitate when he asked for a date.

2 Work with a partner. Which modal structure in 1 means:

a) It wasn't possible for me to…
b) It was necessary for me to…
c) It was possible for me to…
d) It wasn't necessary for me to…

3 Use *had to, didn't have to,* and *couldn't* to complete this account of a rock star's school days.

Schooldays of a rock star

Bill Wyman, now in his sixties, was a member of The Rolling Stones, one of the most successful rock bands in the world. Here he tells us about his childhood.

'I was one of three kids out of my primary school to get a place at grammar school. I was delighted because I liked learning, but my father wasn't very pleased because I (1) ____ wear a uniform. The uniform was expensive, and we were very poor. Also, I (2) ____ get a bicycle because the school was a long way from where I lived.

One day, a boy from school invited me to his house. It was a lovely house – a palace compared with mine. My father said I (3) ____ invite my friend back to my house. In fact I didn't want my friends to come to my house – it was too embarrassing. We had no electricity or running water, and the toilet was in the garden.

There was no heating in the house. In winter there was ice on the inside of our bedroom windows, so getting out of bed was really hard. The only good thing about it was that we (4) ____ have a bath every night. The water was too cold.

School was going well: I was about sixteen and about to take my exams. But one day my father said, 'Right, I've had enough of you in that school. You're leaving.'

I (5) ____ leave school and start earning some money for the family. The headmaster asked my father to let me take the exams, but he refused, and after that I (6) ____ go to college.

Anyway, that was the end of my education but I can't complain – after that I got into music, and the rest is history!'

(Adapted from *Best of Times, Worst of Times, Sunday Times Magazine*)

4 41 Listen and check your answers.

5 Work with a partner. Discuss in what ways your own school days were different from (or similar to) Bill Wyman's.

6 Write a short account of your partner's school days. Include at least one example of each of the following sentence beginnings: *He/She couldn't …, He/She had to …, He/She didn't have to …*

Language Reference: Obligation and permission

have to, must, and *should*

We use *have to* or *must* when we want to give an order or express strong obligation. We use *should* when we are giving advice or expressing an opinion.

*You **have to/must** arrive on time for school.* (= I order you to arrive on time.)

*You **cannot/can't/must not*** break the rules.* (= I order you not to break the rules.)

*You **should** be honest about your feelings.* (= I advise you to be honest about your feelings.)

*There **shouldn't** be different rules for men and women.* (= I don't think it's a good idea if there are different rules for men and women.)

Modal structures: obligation and permission

The chart below summarizes some present and past modal verb structures for obligation and permission. Note that *must/must not* has no past form.

*I **had to** wear a uniform.*

*I **couldn't** invite my friend back to my house.*

*We **didn't have to** have a bath every night.*

*Note: We usually do not use the contraction *mustn't*. We use either *cannot* or *can't* for the negative of *have to*.

	Possible	Not possible	Necessary	Not necessary
Present	*You **can** do*	*You **cannot/can't/must not** do*	*You **have to/must** do*	*You **don't have to** do*
Past	*You **could** do*	*You **couldn't** do*	*You **had to** do*	*You **didn't have to** do*

Geisha

Reading

1 Makiko is training to be a geisha. You are going to read about her training. Before you read, look at the sentences below and decide if you think they are true or false.

a) A lot of women in Japan today want to become geishas.
b) A geisha has to have a different kimono for every month of the year.
c) To become a geisha, you have to study for many years.
d) A geisha has to sing and dance for her customers.
e) A geisha can't speak to her customers.
f) A trainee geisha can go to high school.
g) A geisha can't have relationships or get married.

2 Read the article and check your ideas in 1.

TRAINING TO BE A Geisha

The white face, dark eyes and hair, and blood-red lips: both foreigners and the Japanese are fascinated by these beautiful and mysterious women.

Makiko is training to be a geisha. Not many girls want to become geishas in Japan today. Makiko's parents wanted her to go to college, study medicine, and become a doctor. But Makiko's grandfather paid for her training and bought the kimonos she needed. It's very expensive to become a geisha. You have to have a different kimono for each month of the year, and today a kimono costs three million yen—that's about $30,000.

It's a hard life for a trainee geisha. She has to leave her family and move into a special boarding house called a "maiko house." Here, she has to learn traditional Japanese arts such as playing instruments, the tea ceremony, flower arranging, singing, and dancing. She has to take many difficult tests and exams. Only the best will pass everything and become geishas many years later.

We asked Makiko to describe exactly what a geisha does.

"A geisha has to serve customers and also entertain them. She has to sing and dance and make good conversation."

Does she enjoy her life as a trainee geisha?

"I love it, but it's hard work. Sometimes I get tired of wearing the kimonos, and I want to put on a pair of jeans and go to school like a normal teenager. But I can't have a normal life now. I don't mind. I feel very lucky."

And what about later—can she have a family?

"Of course. A geisha can have relationships like anybody else, and she can get married when she chooses."

In Japan today there are fewer than a thousand geishas, but they play an important role in preserving Japanese culture and history.

3 Are there any professional schools that train students for particular jobs in your country? What kind of preparation do you need to get into these schools? Do you know anyone who goes to a professional school? Tell your partner.

Vocabulary: education

1 Complete the following statements, using words from the text.

a) More and more people are *training* to be computer programmers. (line 5)
b) Not many people want to ____ teachers nowadays. (line 6)
c) If you ____ medicine, it takes seven years to become an intern, or a trainee doctor. (line 7)
d) It ____ a lot of money to go to college. (line 13)
e) When they go to college, most students leave home and ____ into a dormitory. (line 16)
f) Students ____ a midterm and a final exam in each college course. (line 20)
g) You can't graduate from college unless you ____ all your exams. (line 21)
h) College students play an important ____ in the future of the country. (line 39)

2 Work in small groups. Do you think the statements in 1 are true of your country?

Word stress

1 Match an appropriate stress pattern with the correct column of school subjects.

a) ■ ▪ ▪ b) ▪ ▪ ■ ▪ c) ■ d) ■ ▪ e) ▪ ■ ▪ ▪

1 ■	2	3	4	5
Art	English	Chemistry	Biology	Economics
Math	Music	History	Geography	
	Physics	Politics	Philosophy	
			Technology	

2 42 Listen, check, and repeat the answers to 1.

3 Work with a partner. Look at the school subjects in 1 and discuss which ones were…

a) the hardest to learn/the easiest to learn.
b) the most boring/the most interesting.
c) the least useful/the most useful.

Anecdote

Think about your favorite subject in high school. You are going to tell your partner about it. Choose from the list the things you want to talk about. Think about what you will say and the language you will need.

- ☐ What was your favorite subject in school?
- ☐ What was particularly special about this subject?
- ☐ What was the teacher's name, and what was he/she like?
- ☐ What were the other students like?
- ☐ What was the classroom like?
- ☐ How many classes did you have a week?
- ☐ What kinds of activities did you do in class?
- ☐ How much homework did you have to do?
- ☐ What kinds of grades did you get in the subject?
- ☐ Did you learn anything that is useful to you today?

10

Review 2

Fact or Fiction?

Language reviewed: adverbs of frequency (Unit 6); present perfect (Unit 7); future forms—*(be) going to* and present continuous (Unit 8); numbers (Unit 6); verbs with two objects (Unit 6)

Appropriate language

1 A magazine conducted a survey to find out how people lie. Look at the six most common lies and choose the correct structure in each sentence.

a) "Sorry I'm late, honey. I **could / had to / should** work late at the office."
b) "I **couldn't / didn't have to / can't** get here earlier—the bus was late."
c) "You sent it last month? I **hardly ever / never / occasionally** received it!"
d) "I **gave it up / give it up / 'm going to give it up**. Tomorrow. Next week. Soon."
e) "You can trust me. I **always keep / often keep / never keep** a secret."
f) "Thank you. That was the best meal we **ever have / had ever had / 've ever had**."

2 43 Work with a partner. Look at the lies and decide for each sentence who is speaking to whom. What is the situation? Listen and check your answers.

3 Work in small groups. Discuss these questions.

- Have you ever given false information to: a) your parents? b) your boss? c) an official?
- Have you ever lied about: a) your age? b) your background? c) your experience?
- In what situations (if any) do you think it's O.K. to lie?

Listening

1 Work with a partner. Underline any words or phrases that you associate with the job of a customs officer.

alcohol   blackboard   contraband cigars   conveyor belt   inside information
ladder   legal limit   search   tractor

2 44 (Parts 1 & 2) You are going to listen to a radio program about a customs officer who works at the border crossing in San Diego, California. Listen and mark each of the following statements *T* (true) or *F* (false).

a) The driver has driven a long way.
b) The driver has been to a little town near Tijuana.
c) The driver's birthday is next week.
d) The driver has bought some whisky for the party.
e) The driver hasn't broken the law.
f) Customs officers often have inside information.
g) Customs officers can usually tell if someone is lying.
h) Customs officers always catch the real professionals.

3 Rearrange these comments about liars from the radio program so that they make sense. Then listen again to Part 2 and check your answers.

a) look They you usually don't at   *They usually don't look at you.*
b) hide hands often They their
c) face a their lot touch sometimes People
d) They little say very often
e) too start They much sometimes saying
f) negative use Liars more usually verbs
g) often up voice goes Their

Speaking

1 Read the questions. Prepare two answers for each question—one true and one false.

a) What are you doing next weekend?
b) How often do you help with the housework at home?
c) How much chocolate did you eat yesterday?
d) How many foreign capital cities have you been to?
e) When was the last time you got some exercise?
f) Who's your favorite singer of all time?
g) When was the first time you kissed somebody?
h) How many times have you lied to your mother?

2 Work with a partner. Follow these instructions, using the questions in 1.

STUDENT A	STUDENT B
Ask your partner question (a). →	Give your partner both a true and a false answer to the question.
Decide which answer is true and explain your decision. You can ask for further information if you are not sure. →	Tell your partner if he/she guessed right or wrong.

3 Continue taking turns until you have both asked and answered all the questions. Who is the most successful liar?

Numbers

1 Work with a partner. Look at the following chart and guess the missing numbers and countries in each category.

Top 3 whisky drinkers
(Bottles per year)
1 __(a)__ : 145,000,000
2 France: 137,000,000
3 The U.S.: __(b)__

Top 3 beer drinkers
(Quarts per person per year)
1 __(c)__ : 169
2 Ireland: 149.3
3 Germany: __(d)__

Top 3 coffee drinkers
(Cups per person per year)
1 __(e)__ : 1,356
2 Denmark: __(f)__
3 Finland: 1,293

Top 3 Coca-Cola drinkers
(Glasses per person per year)
1 __(g)__ : 343
2 Mexico: 322
3 Germany: __(h)__

2 45 Listen and check your answers to 1. Who made the best guesses in the class?

3 Listen again and repeat each number. Which statistic do you find the most/the least surprising?

Verbs with two objects

1 Complete the following sentences by putting the words in parentheses in the correct order.

a) The last time I went abroad,... (my family I lots of presents bought)
b) The last time I went to dinner with friends,... (took I them a box of candy)
c) The last time I went to a wedding,... (got a very expensive gift the couple I)
d) The last time I went on vacation,... (all my friends I postcards sent)
e) On my last birthday,... (me my mother a big cake made)
f) On Valentine's Day,... (gave my sweetheart me a beautiful bunch of flowers)

2 Guess how many of the sentences in 1 are true for your partner. Ask your partner to find out how many correct guesses you made.

Growing Up

Language reviewed: modals of advice, obligation, and permission (Unit 9); expressions about work and education (Units 7, 8, and 9)

Reading

1 Work in groups of three. You are going to read about three generations of the Bennett family. Discuss what each of them probably said about the following topics. Write *GF* (grandfather), *S* (son), or *GS* (grandson) next to a quote under each topic.

1 Fathers	**2 Family life**	**3 Education**	**4 Relationships**
a "We couldn't disturb him."	**a** "I didn't have to come home at a certain time."	**a** "My parents didn't have to support me financially."	**a** "We should get married one day."
b "I don't have to hide anything from him."	**b** "We had to make our own entertainment."	**b** "I think a college education should be free."	**b** "We couldn't bring girlfriends home."
c "We had to obey him without question."	**c** "I could only watch TV on weekends."	**c** "I had to walk to school."	**c** "We had to get married."

2 Student A: Read about the grandfather. Student B: Read about the son. Student C: Read about the grandson. Check your answers to 1 and take turns explaining the reasons behind each quote.

For example: Student A – 1c) *The grandfather had to obey his father without question because he was a very strict man.*

Three Generations

Three men from the Bennett family talk about how life has changed over three generations.

The grandfather (65)

When I see my son and his son together, I think they have a great relationship—it wasn't like that in my day. My father was very strict, and we had to obey him without question.

When I was a boy, I had to walk three miles to school. There was no other way of getting there.

At home we didn't have a television, so we had to make our own entertainment. I spent all my spare time outside playing football.

But we couldn't play football on Sundays because we had to go to church.

I quit school when I was fourteen and went to work in a bakery. That's where I met Mabel.

We couldn't bring girlfriends home in those days. We had to meet in public places. I guess that's why so many people got married young. I was only nineteen, and Mabel was eighteen.

The son (44)

When I was growing up, my father was always at work, and when he came home, we couldn't disturb him because he was tired.

Because my father quit school when he was very young and regretted it afterwards, he wanted me to do well in school. I had to show him my homework every night, and I could only watch television on weekends.

When I was eighteen, I got into a good college. My parents didn't have to support me financially because the college gave me a full scholarship.

I didn't go home very often, even during the holidays. I preferred spending time with my friends, especially my girlfriends. In my last year of college I met Louise, and we moved in together. We had to get married when Louise found out she was pregnant.

The grandson (19)

I've always had a very close relationship with my dad, and I don't have to hide anything from him.

When I was in school, I had a lot of freedom. When I went out, I didn't have to come home at a certain time—my parents trusted me.

I'm in college now, and my parents have to pay my tuition, but I have to work nights to pay for any luxuries I want.

I think it's wrong that my parents have to pay for my college education. I think a college education should be free for everybody.

My girlfriend often stays at my parents' house, and I sometimes go and stay with her parents. Both our parents think we should get married one day, but we're definitely not in a hurry.

3 Read about all three men. For each generation, write down three ways in which you think their lives were the same as or different from your own, your father's, and your grandfather's. Compare with a partner.

Vocabulary: *work* or *job*?

1 Work with a partner. Complete each of the following questions with *work* or *job* and then ask each other the questions.

a) Have you ever had a full-time ____ ?
b) Would you like to ____ abroad?
c) Do you know anybody who has a dangerous ____ ?

2 Write down six more questions by replacing the underlined words in 1 with appropriate alternatives. Use words and phrases from the box or your own ideas.

For example: *Have you ever looked for a full-time job?*

with children	outdoors	boring	part-time	looked for	applied for
well-paying	from home	resigned from			

3 Ask your partner your questions from 2. Find out as much information as you can.

Vocabulary: work expressions

1 Look at the word snake. How many different jobs can you find?

drummerfactoryworkerfinancialadvisorgeishacompanypresidentsalesclerktelemarketervet

2 Complete the following quotes with one of the verbs in the box. Match each quote with a job in 1.

have	make	run	spend	take

a) "I ____ a living by telling people how to invest their money."
b) "I didn't have to ____ any tests to get this job. It's noisy and smelly, and the pay is awful."
c) "Sometimes I have to ____ very difficult decisions about whether or not to operate."
d) "I ____ all my time on the telephone. Sometimes I can ____ over three hundred phone calls a day."
e) "I can't ____ a day off during the weekend; Saturdays and Sundays are our busiest days."
f) "The most important objective when you ____ a business is to ____ a profit. Nothing else matters."
g) "You can ____ a lot of money if you have a hit single. Unfortunately, right after our first hit, we split up."
h) "I don't mind serving the customers. But I also have to ____ good conversation, and that's really hard."

Discussion

1 Work together as a class. Write the names of all the jobs that you, your parents, and your grandparents have had.

2 Work in small groups. Look at all the jobs you wrote down in 1 and discuss the following questions.

a) In which job can you earn the most money?
b) In which job do you get the most days of paid vacation?
c) Which job do you have to study longest for?
d) In which job do you get the most training?
e) Which job is the most stressful?
f) Which job is the most useful to society?

Language reviewed:
All the main structures from Units 1–9.

The Review Game

Player 1

Player 1 START

1 Where do they live? (page 8)

2 What's New York like? (page 15)

3 I have two childs: a boy and a girl. (page 15)

4 There are much problems. (page 15)

5 Talk about a person with the same name as yours.

6 There's a few wine left but no beer. (page 15)

7 What you both were wearing? (page 19)

8 Raúl is not as taller as Venus Williams. (page 27)

9 My husband bought me a gadget. (page 35)

10 Talk about the best city you have ever visited.

11 The teacher explained us the exercise. (page 35)

12 I don't bother going to supermarkets anymore. (page 38)

13 My brother's never been to a pop concert. (page 43)

14 She's called you a few minutes ago. (page 43)

15 Talk about playing sports in school.

16 I'm going to keep on singing. (page 50)

17 You must not break the rules. (page 55)

FINISH

Player 4

Player 4 START

1 Who did create A.L.I.C.E.? (page 8)

2 It's a beautiful weather. (page 15)

3 There were only a few people who saw them. (page 15)

4 We want an advice. (page 15)

5 Talk about a character in a movie you have seen recently.

6 My son was finding them this morning. (page 19)

7 She's the happiest person in the world. (page 27)

8 That's the worst movie I've ever seen. (page 27)

9 Venus Williams is a few heavier than Michael Schumacher. (page 27)

10 Talk about a retired person you know well.

11 The teacher explained us the exercise. (page 35)

12 My husband bought a gadget to me. (page 35)

13 She's hardly ever on time. (page 36)

14 I haven't been to the beach last summer. (page 43)

15 Talk about your favorite subject in high school.

16 We're starting our Americas tour next week. (page 50)

17 You have to arrive on time for school. (page 55)

FINISH

Player 2 START

1 Why she get married? (page 8)

2 Who lives here? (page 8)

3 He has two mouses. (page 15)

4 How many e-mails do you get every day? (page 15)

5 Talk about the best city you have ever visited.

6 There was many good food at the party. (page 15)

7 The last time I was losing my keys was two weeks ago. (page 19)

8 She's worse than him! (page 27)

9 I gave for my husband a small flashlight. (page 35)

10 Talk about playing sports in school.

11 The teacher explained us the exercise. (page 35)

12 I always tell them the same thing. (page 36)

13 Men don't want usually brightly colored ties. (page 36)

14 Are you doing anything for lunch today? (page 50)

15 Talk about a character in a movie you have seen recently.

16 I had to wear a uniform. (page 55)

17 I couldn't to invite my friend back to my house. (page 55)

FINISH

Player 3 START

1 Does she love him? (page 8)

2 How are the people in your village like? (page 15)

3 I need a work. (page 15)

4 How much sleep do you get at night? (page 15)

5 Talk about playing sports in school.

6 He didn't give me many information. (page 15)

7 They are the nicest couple I know. (page 27)

8 He's more interesting than you. (page 27)

9 Shaquille O'Neal is much taller than Raúl. (page 27)

10 Talk about a character in a movie you have seen recently.

11 The teacher explained us the exercise. (page 35)

12 My husband for me bought a gadget. (page 35)

13 I normally am on a diet. (page 36)

14 I haven't seen any good movies recently. (page 43)

15 Talk about the last time you bought a present for somebody.

16 We didn't have to take a bath every night. (page 55)

17 You should be honest about your feelings. (page 55)

FINISH

HOW TO PLAY

Play the game with three, four, or five players. One person in each game is the *Checker*. That person doesn't play the game. You will need a coin and counters and an extra copy of *American Inside Out* Pre-intermediate Student's Book.

1 Each player places his/her counter on a different square marked START.

2 Decide which player is going to start the game. The first player then tosses the coin and moves the counter along his/her "road" as follows:
Heads = two spaces.
Tails = one space.

3 Players then take turns moving along their "roads."
If a player lands on a grammar square (darker color), he/she has to read the sentence on that square and say if the sentence is grammatically correct or incorrect. If the sentence is incorrect, he/she must correct it.

4 The *Checker* will then turn to the Language Reference on the page given and see if the player is right. If the player is right, he/she can now wait for his/her next turn. If the player is wrong, he/she has to skip a turn.

For example:
Student A:
11. The teacher explained us the exercise. (page 35)
Uh… I think it's correct.

Checker:
Wrong! It should be "The teacher explained the exercise to us." You skip a turn.

5 If a player lands on a speaking square (lighter color), he/she has to talk about the topic for sixty seconds. Players should be timed from the point at which they start talking so that they can have a little thinking time before they start.

6 The first player to reach his/her FINISH is the winner.

11 Smile

Work in small groups. Look at this expression and discuss the questions.

- When do people say this?
- What do you say in your language?
- Do you find it easy to smile in photographs?

Vocabulary: the face

1 Use words from the photograph below to complete the following article about smiling. Choose an appropriate singular or plural form for each word.

"Smile and the world smiles with you. Cry and you cry alone."

According to research from the United States, we smile for many different reasons.

- There's the listener/response smile. When two people are having a conversation, the listener smiles to encourage the speaker.
- There's the polite smile. This is the kind of smile you make when your aunt gives you a horrible birthday present.
- There's the miserable smile—for example, when you go to the dentist and he tells you that you need to have a (1) ____ taken out.

Very often, these social smiles are not real; they are "fake" smiles. Fake smiles are easy to do—you just have to tighten the muscles on your (2) ____ .

But there's only one smile that is the smile of true enjoyment. This smile is extremely hard to fake. It involves the muscles at the corners of the (3) ____ and the muscles around the eyes.

When someone gives a true smile, the (4) ____ get smaller, and you see little (5) ____ around the edge. The (6) ____ go up, and on some people, (7) ____ appear in their cheeks.

The genuine smile of enjoyment not only makes us feel good, but makes others feel good too.

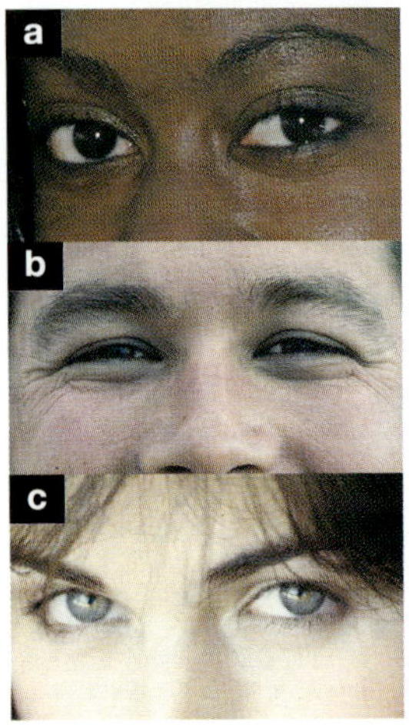

2 46 Listen and check your answers. How many different smiles are mentioned? Can you do all these smiles? Show your partner.

3 Look at the photo in 1 again and check (✓) the features you can see.

bags under the eyes	beard	beautiful teeth	false eyelashes	freckles
mustache	pale skin	wavy hair		

4 Which of these features do you like on a man or a woman? Describe your ideal face to your partner.

5 Work with a partner. Look at the pairs of eyes on the left. According to the text, which ones do you think are smiling? How can you tell? Look at page 125 to see the complete faces. Which ones did you guess correctly?

/s/, /z/, or /ɪz/?

1 47 Listen and repeat these nouns. In each set, underline the noun where the final "s" is pronounced differently from the others.

a) ears eyes cheeks legs
b) lips hands toes arms
c) dimples freckles wrinkles eyelashes

2 Put the nouns from the box into the appropriate columns, depending on the sound of the final "s." Add the nouns from 1. The first ones have been done for you.

backs knees noses chins
mustaches wrists heads shoulders
stomachs beards

+ /s/	+ /z/	+ /ɪz/
backs	*knees*	*noses*

3 48 Listen, repeat the words, and check your answers. Which of the nouns in 2 would you not expect to use in the plural when describing someone?

Vocabulary: describing character

1 The way you smile can show what kind of person you are. Read the article below and match one of the headings (*a–d*) to each paragraph (*1–4*).

a) Shy and sensitive b) Sassy and impertinent c) Confident d) Sociable

What's in a Smile?

1 This is the smile of a joker. The raised eyebrows and dimples in the cheeks show a good sense of humor and a warm personality. This person is often a rebel—with little respect for authority.

2 The wide, toothy smile shows that people like this are easygoing and friendly. They enjoy being in a crowd and are a lot of fun to go out with. They're always looking for the next party.

3 The smile is in the eyes. This is a sensitive person and a loyal friend. This kind of person thinks before speaking, is a good listener, and doesn't like to be the center of attention in a crowd.

4 This is a smile that says, "I know it all." These people are very sure of themselves. They like a good argument, and they usually win. They're hard-working and very ambitious. And they can be very bossy.

2 49 Listen and check your answers.

3 50 Listen to six different people talking and use the most appropriate adjective in the box to describe each one.

ambitious bossy confident sensitive sociable easygoing

LANGUAGE TOOLBOX

affectionate cold dark
deep frightening
independent loyal
mysterious nasty
selfish stormy strong
sweet unpleasant

4 Use any of the adjectives in the Language Toolbox or your own ideas to take this personality test.

Write one word to describe each of the following.

- a dog ____
- a cat ____
- a rat ____
- coffee ____
- an ocean ____

5 Turn to page 125 to find out the meaning of what you have written. Do you think it's accurate? Tell your partner.

What Are You Like?

Reading **1** Answer the questionnaire below. For each situation, choose *a*, *b*, or *c*, according to what you are most likely to say. Then calculate your score, read what it means on page 127, and compare with a partner.

Optimist or Pessimist – What Are You?

1 It's Sunday, and you're in the middle of a long walk in the country. It starts to rain.

- **a** It always rains when I go for a walk.
- **b** It could be worse—it could be snowing.
- **c** Great! I really enjoy walking in the rain.

2 You arrive home after a great vacation.

- **a** I don't want to go back to work.
- **b** I'm going to start planning my next vacation. I want to have something to look forward to.
- **c** The vacation was great, but now I'm looking forward to sleeping in my own bed.

3 It's your 40th birthday.

- **a** The best years of my life are over.
- **b** I'm getting older—so what? It happens to everybody.
- **c** I hope to live to 100—where's the party?!

4 You have a cold.

- **a** I need to see a doctor as soon a possible.
- **b** I need to buy some tissues.
- **c** It's just a cold—it won't kill me.

5 Your partner has ended your relationship.

- **a** I've had enough of men/women. I'm never going to fall in love again.
- **b** I know I'll get over it, but it might take a long time.
- **c** He/She wasn't the right one for me.

6 You have to make an important life decision.

- **a** Whatever I decide to do, it will be the wrong decision.
- **b** I'm going to take my time and think carefully about my decision.
- **c** Whatever I decide to do, it will be the right decision.

7 It's autumn.

- **a** I don't like autumn because it will soon be winter.
- **b** It's just another time of year.
- **c** It's a beautiful time of year.

8 You unexpectedly inherit $5,000.

- **a** $5,000 isn't going to change my life.
- **b** Great! I can buy a few luxuries that I couldn't afford before.
- **c** This must be my lucky day—I think I'll buy a lottery ticket.

How to score Each time you answer **a**, score 1. Each time you answer **b**, score 2. Each time you answer **c**, score 3.

2 Who got the highest and lowest score in the class?

Vocabulary: verb patterns **1** Complete these statements by choosing the appropriate structure. Refer to examples in the questionnaire if necessary.

a) I want **to be/being** extremely rich.
b) I'm looking forward to **go out/going out** tonight.
c) I've decided **to get up/getting up** early even on the weekend.
d) I enjoy **to speak/speaking** English.
e) I need **to spend/spending** more time at home.
f) I hope **to go/going** on a great vacation next summer.

2 Do you think any of the sentences are true for your partner? Ask questions to find out.

3 Use the same verb structures to write six more sentences that are true for you. Compare them with a partner.

For example: *I don't want to get married until I'm thirty.*
I'm looking forward to finishing my education.

Don't Worry, Be Happy

Song

1 Make word pairs by matching a word from list A with a word from list B that rhymes.

A	B
style	bed
trouble	smile
head	note
frown	double
late	down
wrote	litigate

2 51 You are going to listen to a song called *Don't Worry, Be Happy*. Read the song and complete each verse with the word pairs from 1. Then listen and check your answers.

3 Find at least three reasons for worrying that are mentioned in the song.

4 Work with a partner. Discuss what you think the biggest worries are for the following people.

a) a child
b) a 14-year-old girl
c) a 16-year-old boy
d) a college student
e) a parent
f) a grandparent

How does this song make *you* feel? What music makes you feel happy? Tell your partner.

Here's a little song I (1) _____ .
You might want to sing it note for (2) _____ .
Don't worry, be happy.

In every life we have some (3) _____ .
When you worry you make it (4) _____ .
Don't worry, be happy.

Ain't got no place to lay your (5) _____ ?
Somebody came and took your (6) _____ ?
Don't worry, be happy.

The landlord says your rent is (7) _____ ?
He may have to (8) _____ .
Don't worry, be happy.

Ain't got no cash, ain't got no (9) _____ ?
Ain't got no girl to make you (10) _____ ?
Don't worry, be happy.

'Cos when you worry, your
face will (11) _____ .
That will bring everybody
(12) _____ .
Don't worry, be happy.

Don't Worry, Be Happy

A huge hit in 1988 for singer, composer, and conductor Bobby McFerrin.

Close-up

Imperatives

1 Choose a correct alternative way of saying "Be happy" from the following.

a) Be not sad. b) Don't sad you. c) Don't be sad. d) Don't you sad.

2 Look at the following imperatives. Give an alternative way of saying the same thing by using the adjectives in parentheses.

a) Be good. (naughty) *Don't be naughty.*
b) Be quiet! (noisy)
c) Be on time. (late)
d) Be nice. (mean)
e) Behave yourself. (rude)
f) Cheer up. (miserable)
g) Say what you think. (shy)
h) Calm down. (angry)
i) Act your age. (childish)

3 Work with a partner. Choose an imperative from 2 and write a three-line dialogue to show a typical situation where it could be used.

For example: *A: I'll see you at 8:30 outside the theater.*
B: Don't be late!
A: Don't worry. I'm never late.

Language Reference: Imperatives

We use an imperative form when we are telling somebody to do something or not to do something: orders, advice, encouragement, etc.

Come here. Be quiet! Don't be shy. Come on. Hurry up!

Take It Easy

Reading

1 Imagine that today is "No-Stress Day." Read the article on the right and answer the questions. Discuss your answers with a partner.

a) Which suggestion is the easiest for you to do?
b) Which suggestion is the most difficult for you to do?
c) Which is the best or worst suggestion?

2 Work with a partner. Add three of your own suggestions to the list.

Vocabulary: phrasal verbs

1 Complete the sentences using these phrasal verbs from the article.

give up	hang up	put on
turn off	turn on	take off
throw away		

a) I always *take off* my shoes before I go into my house.
b) If I want to relax, I ____ all the lights and sit in silence.
c) When I want to look my best, I ____ a suit.
d) I could never ____ smoking—it's the only thing that helps me relax.
e) The first thing I do when I get to the office is ____ my computer.
f) I never ____ plastic bags, because they're so useful.
g) I never do any ironing. I just ____ my clothes very carefully when they come out of the washing machine.

2 Are any of the sentences true for you? Discuss with a partner.

16 Ways to De-stress

1 Take off your watch.
2 Turn off your cell phone.
3 Don't eat your breakfast on your feet—sit down and enjoy it.
4 Put on your most comfortable clothes.
5 Don't run after the bus—let it go.
6 Smell the roses.
7 Give up the gym.
8 Fall in love.
9 Turn on your television only if there's something you really want to watch.
10 Throw away any clothes you haven't worn in the past two years.
11 Laugh.
12 Hang up your clothes when you take them off.
13 Spend ten minutes doing absolutely nothing.
14 Walk.
15 Do the ironing only if you love it.
16 Put on your favorite music and turn up the volume.

Close-up

Phrasal verbs

1 Work with a partner. Look at the three phrasal verbs used in these sentences and answer the questions.

subject	verb	object	particle		subject	verb	particle	object	
I	*took*	*my shoes*	*off*	*, and*	*I*	*ran*	*after*	*the bus.*	*But it didn't stop.*

	subject	verb	particle	
So	*I*	*sat*	*down*	*and cried. I hate bus drivers.*

a) Which phrasal verb does not take an object?
b) Which phrasal verb can have the object between the verb and the particle? (SEPARABLE)
c) Which phrasal verb always has the object after the particle? (NONSEPARABLE)

2 When the object is a pronoun such as *it, them,* or *her,* where do you always put it when the phrasal verb is: a) separable? b) nonseparable?

3 Put the words in the right order to make answers to the questions. Look the phrasal verbs up in a dictionary if you are not sure.

a) What should I do with this banana skin? (away throw it) *Throw it away.*
b) What should I do with this mess? (it up clean)
c) What should I do about this problem? (it deal with)
d) What should I do with this application form? (fill out it)
e) What should I do with my grandmother's wedding ring? (away it put)
f) What should I do about my party? Nobody can come. (it call off)

Language Reference: Phrasal verbs

The term "phrasal verb" usually refers to all multi-word verbs consisting of a verb + particle(s). Phrasal verbs can be divided into three basic types.

1 verb + particle

Some phrasal verbs are intransitive and so do not take a direct object.

Sit down *and enjoy it.* *When are you going to* ***grow up****?*

2 verb + object + particle (SEPARABLE)

The biggest group of phrasal verbs are transitive. When the direct object is a noun, we can put it before or after the particle.

Take off *your shoes.* ***Take*** *your shoes* ***off****.*

When the direct object is a pronoun, we must put it between the verb and the particle.

Turn *it* ***off****, please.* NOT ~~*Turn off it*~~

3 verb + particle + object (NONSEPARABLE)

With this type of phrasal verb, we always put the direct object—noun or pronoun—after the particle.

She ***takes after*** *her grandmother.* *I* ***ran after*** *it, but the bus didn't stop.*

Laughter—the Best Medicine

1 52 Listen to a report about laughter—without laughing. What are the benefits of laughter?

2 Work with a partner. Sit facing each other. Student A: Try to make student B smile and/or laugh by saying funny things. Student B: Try to keep a straight face. Take turns making each other smile and/or laugh.

12 *Rebel*

May Day

Reading

1 Work with a partner. Look at the photograph below and discuss the following questions.

a) What do you think is happening?
b) What things do people demonstrate about in your country?
c) Have you ever seen or taken part in a demonstration? What was it about?

2 Read the article. Are the following statements true or false?

a) Many of the protesters disagree with globalization.
b) Twelve protesters were arrested in Sydney, Australia.
c) Demonstrations in Winnipeg were peaceful.
d) In Norway, a protester threw a bottle at the foreign minister.
e) Three hundred demonstrators were arrested in Portland, Oregon.

3 Do you think demonstrations are a good way of making a point?

Global May Day Protest

Around the world, thousands of people took part in protest marches and demonstrations today. Many of the protesters were demonstrating against globalization. Demonstrations were peaceful in most places, but in Sydney, Australia, violence broke out, and dozens of protesters were arrested.

Police in Winnipeg, Canada, prepared for violence, but the demonstration was more like a big street party than a protest.

In Norway, a protester threw an apple pie in the face of foreign minister Thorbjoern Jagland.

In Portland, Oregon, peaceful demonstrators gathered downtown. When the police told them to leave, the protesters became violent and police fired rubber bullets at 300 marchers. Sixteen people were arrested.

What are You Doing Here?

Listening

1 At May Day demonstrations around the world, not everybody demonstrates against the same thing. Match the slogans (*a–e*) with the causes (*1–5*).

a) NO TO MULTINATIONALS	1 Against nuclear weapons
b) SAVE THE TREES	2 Against cruelty to animals
c) STOP STAR WARS	3 Against globalization
d) BAN ANIMAL TESTING	4 Against destruction of the environment
e) EQUAL PAY FOR EQUAL WORK	5 Against unequal pay for women

2 53 You are going to listen to radio interviews with the four protesters in the photos on the right. Before you listen, look at the photos and try to match the people with the slogans and causes in 1. Listen and check your answers.

Jake, 23, college student

Debbie, 27, housewife

Ronny, 27, cook

Caroline, 23, teacher

Vocabulary: protest

1 Complete the sentences below, using these words from the recordings in the previous section.

> against   anti-   supporter of   don't feel
> in favor   really care   support

a) I'm a ____ peaceful action.
b) I'm ____ of many of the causes here.
c) I'm not ____men—I just want a fairer system.
d) I'm ____ animal testing.
e) I ____ animal rights.
f) I ____ strongly about politics.
g) I ____ about a clean, safe environment for our children.

2 Work with a partner. Discuss the statements in 1. Which ones are true for you?

3 What causes do you feel most strongly about? Compare with a partner.

Vocabulary: word families

1 What are the noun forms for the following verbs: *pollute, globalize, demonstrate, inform*?

For example: *pollute – pollution*

2 54 Add each verb and noun pair from 1 to the chart according to their stress pattern. Listen, repeat, and check your answers.

A Verb	A Noun	B Verb	B Noun	C Verb	C Noun	D Verb	D Noun
▪■	▪■▪	▪■	▪▪■▪	■▪▪	▪▪■▪	■▪▪	▪▪▪■▪
pollute	*pollution*	____	____	____	____	____	____

3 55 Listen and repeat eight more verb/noun pairs. Add them to the appropriate columns in the chart in 2. On which syllable does the stress fall when a noun ends in *-ion*?

Close-up

Dynamic and stative meanings

Dad, you're shaving with my cell phone.

1 Work with a partner. Look at the verbs in these three excerpts from the radio interviews in the previous section. Discuss the questions.

"People are handing out leaflets with information."
"We're demonstrating for equal pay."
"I'm having fun with my friends."

a) Do the verbs describe actions or states?
b) What is the name of the tense used in all three excerpts?

2 Rewrite these sentences by putting the verb in parentheses in the present continuous tense.

a) A phone (ring). *A phone is ringing.*
b) A teacher in another class (talk).
c) The traffic (make) a lot of noise.
d) A clock (tick).
e) A student (laugh).
f) People (chat).

3 Work as a class. Listen in silence for fifteen seconds and check (✓) the actions in 2 that are true. Write down other things that are happening.

4 Work with a partner. Look at the verbs in three more excerpts from the radio interviews in the previous section. Discuss the questions.

"I just want a fairer system."
"I have three dogs, two cats, and a pet mouse."
"I don't know much about it."

a) Do the verbs describe *actions* or *states*?
b) What is the name of the tense used in all three excerpts?
c) Is it possible to use a continuous tense with verbs when they describe a state?

5 From the excerpts in 1 and 4, which verb has two different meanings and describes both an action and a state?

6 Work with a partner. Decide if the verbs in parentheses describe an action or a state. Put the verb into an appropriate form to complete the sentences.

a) Jane (like) James Bond movies.
b) Tony (know) how to play the piano.
c) Marta (have) a television in her bedroom.
d) Julie (have) difficulty with this exercise.
e) Brian (look) like his father.
f) Ryan (look) for a new place to live.
g) Sue (think) of going out tonight.
h) Rosa (think) war is stupid.

7 Replace the names in 6 with names of students in the class to make as many true sentences as you can. Ask questions to help you.

For example: *Do you like James Bond movies? Are you thinking of going out tonight?*

Language Reference: Dynamic and stative meanings

Dynamic meanings: actions

Most verbs have dynamic meanings. They describe actions: Something "happens." We can use them with continuous forms to talk about activities in progress.

*People **are chatting**.*

Stative meanings: states

Some verbs connected with knowledge, emotion, or possession have stative meanings. They describe states: Nothing "happens." We cannot use them with continuous forms.

*I **don't feel** strongly about politics.*

Note: Some verbs such as *have, look,* and *think* can have both dynamic and stative meanings.

*Rosie **is looking** for a new place to live.* (*look* = dynamic meaning)
*Brian **looks** like his father.* (*look* = stative meaning)

Celebrity Rebels

Reading

1 You are going to read an article about three famous people who have all rebelled against their family in different ways. Read the article and find out who…

a) joined a political group.
b) committed a crime.
c) began smoking as a teenager.
d) colored his/her hair.
e) had inappropriate relationships.
f) left home to live with the circus.

REBEL **REBEL**

Patty Hearst

On February 4, 1974, Patricia Hearst, the 19-year-old daughter of a very wealthy businessman, was kidnapped by a revolutionary political group called the Symbionese Liberation Army (SLA).

She was held prisoner for 57 days while the kidnappers waited for her parents to pay the ransom.

But they didn't pay the ransom, and so Patty decided to rebel against her family. She became a member of the SLA and was renamed Tania.

Then she broke the law: Five members of the SLA, including "Tania," were photographed robbing the Hibernia Bank in San Francisco.

Patricia was later charged with bank robbery, but she was released after three years in prison. She was finally pardoned by President Clinton in 2001.

Princess Stephanie of Monaco

Princess Stephanie is the younger daughter of Prince Rainier of Monaco. She is known as the "rebel royal," mainly because of her unsuitable relationships. She married one of her bodyguards and had two children. She then divorced him and had a relationship (and a third child) with another bodyguard.

After that she was photographed in a circus caravan with Franco Knie, an elephant trainer—in other words, the rebel royal ran away with the circus!

Macaulay Culkin

Macaulay Culkin was born on August 26, 1980, in New York, the third of seven children. "Mack," as his friends call him, starred in the movie *Home Alone*, which made him one of the most famous and richest child stars of all time.

In 1995, his parents separated and started fighting over Mack's money. Disgusted with his parents' behavior, Mack refused to accept any movie roles until they stopped fighting.

Then, at the age of 17, he started smoking, dyed his hair pink, and got married.

2 Replace the underlined words in 1 with words or expressions from the text.

3 Work with a partner. Discuss the following questions.

- Who do you think is the most rebellious of the three people?
- In what other ways do people rebel against their families?
- In what ways did you rebel against your family when you were younger?

Anecdote

Think about a time when you got into trouble as a child. You are going to tell your partner about it. Choose from the list the things you want to talk about. Think about what you will say and the language you will need.

- ☐ How old were you?
- ☐ Where were you?
- ☐ Were you alone or with other people?
- ☐ What did you do?
- ☐ Why did you do it?
- ☐ Did you know it was wrong?
- ☐ What did you feel like afterward?
- ☐ Who caught you?
- ☐ What happened to you?
- ☐ Did you ever do the same thing again?

Close-up

Passives

Language Reference p. 75

1 Work with a partner. Look at the question and two alternative answers (*1* and *2*) below. Discuss why the second answer is the more natural alternative. Then choose the correct explanation (*a* or *b*).

What happened to Patty Hearst on February 4, 1974?

	subject	verb	*by*	object / agent
1	A revolutionary political group	kidnapped		her. (object)
2	She	was kidnapped	by	a revolutionary political group. (agent)

a) Because the question is about Patty Hearst. We usually start sentences with the person or thing that we are interested in.
b) Because Patty Hearst was a very rich and important woman.

2 Work with a partner. Refer to answers *1* and *2* in the last exercise. Discuss the following.

a) Which tense are both answers in?
b) In which answer is the verb in the passive form?
c) Which auxiliary verb combines with a past participle to form the passive?

3 Here are the main events from the Patty Hearst story. Complete the following task.

a) Put each verb in the most appropriate form: active or passive.
b) Put the events in the correct order and retell the story.
c) Check your answers in the text on page 73.

( ) a) She (**charge**) with bank robbery.
( ) b) She (**rename**) "Tania."
( ) c) She (**hold**) prisoner for 57 days.
( ) d) She (**photograph**) robbing a bank.
( ) e) She (**decide**) to rebel against her family.
( ) f) She (**pardon**) by President Clinton in 2001.
( ) g) She (**release**) after three years in prison.
( ) h) She (**become**) a member of the SLA.
(*1*) i) She (**kidnap**) by a revolutionary political group. *was kidnapped*
( ) j) She (**break**) the law.

4 Use simple past passives to complete the article about Che Guevara.

IMAGE OF A REBEL

IT is an image that became a legend of the twentieth century. It is tattooed on Diego Maradona's arm. A Che poster (1 **pin**) ***was pinned*** on Mick Jagger's wall when he was a student, and millions of T-shirts are still decorated with the image today. The picture (2 **take**) on March 5, 1960, at a memorial service in Havana, Cuba. Cuban photographer Alberto Korda (3 **send**) by the magazine *Revolución* to take photographs of the Cuban leader Fidel Castro.

"Che was standing behind Fidel Castro on the platform," said Korda. "You couldn't see him. Then suddenly he stepped forward to the edge of the platform. I managed to take a photo. Then he was gone."

Seven years later, in October 1967, Che Guevara (4 **kill**) in Bolivia, and Korda's photograph became an icon for revolutionaries everywhere. Korda's photographs (5 **exhibit**) in Paris in Spring 2001. It was while he was attending the exhibition of his work that Korda died.

5 56 Listen and check your answers.

6 Think of famous people that you admire. Whose picture would you like to have…

a) on a poster on your wall? b) on your T-shirt? c) tattooed on your arm?

Language Reference: Passives

In passive sentences, the object of the active verb becomes the subject of the passive verb. We can mention the person or thing ("agent") which performs the action, but it's not necessary.

		subject	verb	object
Active	In 1974,	a revolutionary political group	kidnapped	Patty Hearst.

		subject	verb	*by*	agent
Passive	In 1974,	Patty Hearst	was kidnapped	by	a revolutionary political group.

We use the passive when we want to say what happened to a subject rather than what a subject did.

Patty Hearst ***was renamed*** *"Tania."* *Where* ***was*** *Che Guevara* ***killed****?*
Korda's photos ***were exhibited*** *in Paris in Spring 2001.*

How "Green" Is the Class?

Report writing

1 Work in small groups. Look at the activities below and discuss which ones are good and which are bad for the environment.

a) Traveling into a city by car.
b) Buying fresh, organic fruit or vegetables.
c) Using public transportation.
d) Taking bottles to a recycling center.
e) Recycling paper.
f) Wearing a fur coat.
g) Picking up litter and throwing it away.
h) Buying a hamburger in a plastic container.
i) Paying more for something because it is environmentally friendly.
j) Using plastic bags for your shopping.

2 Work in small groups. You are going to conduct a survey to find out how many people have done the activities in 1 in the last two weeks. Follow these instructions.

a) Prepare the question you are going to ask for each activity.
For example: a) *Have you traveled into a big city by car in the last two weeks?*
b) Decide who is going to ask which questions.
c) Go around the class and ask the questions and write down the answers.
d) In your groups, write down the results of the survey for each activity.

3 Using the results from 2, write a survey report which is true for your class by replacing the underlined expressions in the model text on the right. Change other parts of the model if necessary.

Survey Report

A survey was carried out in Newtown, California, to find out how green people are.

The results of the survey show that only a few people have used public transportation in the last two weeks, but everybody has traveled into a city by car.

Most of the people interviewed have bought a hamburger in a plastic container, and several people have picked up litter and thrown it away.

A small number of people have taken bottles to a recycling center or have recycled paper, but none of the people interviewed have paid more for something because it is environmentally friendly.

A large number of people have worn a fur coat, and everybody has used plastic bags for their shopping.

Nobody has bought organic fruit or vegetables in the last two weeks.

The results of the survey suggest that the inhabitants of Newtown, California, are not very green.

13 Dance

Reading

Complete the questionnaire and compare your answers with a partner.

Vocabulary: *on* and *at*

1 Test your prepositions! The questionnaire talks about being *on stage* or *at a club*. Add *on* or *at* to each noun phrase in the box.

the phone	a concert	vacation
a plane	the doctor's	the Internet
a business trip	the hairdresser's	
a dance club	a trip	

on the phone,… *at a concert,…*

2 Write down two true sentences and one false sentence about yourself, using prepositions + noun phrases in 1. Read your partner's sentences and guess which sentence is false.

1 *I was on the phone just before the class began.*
2 *I was at a dance club on Saturday.*
3 *I was…*

DANCE DIVA OR TWO LEFT FEET?

1 Your favorite place for dancing is…
a on stage.
b at a club or a party.
c in your own bedroom.

2 Check the music you know how to dance to.
Pop Rock 'n' roll House
Reggae Salsa Flamenco
Ballroom (e.g., waltz)
Traditional music of your country

3 Which sentence best describes your attitude toward dancing?
a I hate it.
b I love it, and I'm pretty good.
c I love dancing, but I'm not particularly good.

4 Which sentence best describes the way you dance?
a I don't care what other people think.
b I feel uncomfortable.
c I want people to look at me.

5 When I dance,…
a I stay more or less in one place.
b I need a lot of room to move around.
c I do the same as my partner.

6 At a pop concert, I usually…
a get up and dance to the music.
b stay sitting down.
c I don't go to pop concerts.

7 How often do you dance all night?
a About once or twice a year.
b Never. Don't be ridiculous!
c Every weekend.

8 At a party,…
a I'm usually the last to get up and dance.
b I'm usually the first to get up and dance.
c I don't go to parties where people dance.

How to score

1	a 3, b 2, c 1	**5**	a 2, b 3, c 1
2	1 point for each check	**6**	a 3, b 2, c 1
3	a 1, b 3, c 2	**7**	a 2, b 1, c 3
4	a 3, b 1, c 2	**8**	a 2, b 3, c 1

Turn to page 127 to find out what your score means.

The Clubbing Capital of the World

Work in small groups. Discuss the questions.

- Which town or city in your country is famous for its nightlife?
- Where do people go dancing or clubbing where you live?
- Which is your own favorite place for a night out?

Reading

1 You are going to read an article about the island of Ibiza. Read the first part of the article (*Party Island*) and answer the questions.

a) What kind of people go to Ibiza?
b) How many tourists visit the island every year?
c) How long has Ibiza been a party island?
d) What happened in 1987?
e) What kinds of music do the DJs play?

Party Island

The beautiful Mediterranean island of Ibiza has a population of 80,000. But in the summer, two million tourists visit the island. Why? Because Ibiza is the clubbing capital of the world.

Top DJs play the latest dance music in 400 clubs and bars situated around the island's two main towns, San Antonio and Ibiza town.

Ibiza has been a party island since the sixties when hippies first started coming to the island.

But it became famous for clubbing with the arrival of Acid House in 1987.

Since then, DJs have been playing dance music for all tastes: dance, trance, techno, garage, pop, rock, funk, etc.

2 Have you ever been to a club that has any of the following? Compare with your partner.

a) live music
b) several different dance floors
c) foam parties
d) room for 10,000 people
e) a swimming pool
f) trees planted inside

3 Read the second part of the article (*The Clubs*). Match the clubs with the features in 2.

For example: a) live music – *Privilege*

The Clubs

Amnesia

(www.amnesia.es)

When it opened in the 70s, *Amnesia* had an open-air dance floor, but in 1990, noise laws forced the owners to build walls and a roof. The club is best-known for its foam parties. The music is a mix of house and trance, with some rock and pop. *Amnesia* has always been one of the island's favorite clubs for end-of-season parties.

Privilege

(www.privilege-ibiza.com)

The owners of a restaurant called *Ku* decided to build a mini disco (125 people maximum) back in 1978. It was here that Bob Marley, Grace Jones, and Freddie Mercury performed live, and many international stars have followed in their footsteps since then. In 1994, they built a new club and called it *Privilege*. It is the size of a soccer field—it has room for 10,000 and has everything: several different dance floors, palm trees in the main room, a DJ suspended over the swimming pool, and on some nights there's even a DJ in the restrooms!

4 Would you like to go to Ibiza? Why/Why not? Tell your partner.

My Ibiza

▲ Josh, 18, student

▲ Simone, 29, DJ

▲ Antonio, 36, restaurant owner

Listening

1 Work with a partner. You are going to listen to a radio program called *My Ibiza*. Look at the photos of the three people interviewed and guess who said each of the following.

a) "I haven't been home in a couple of years now."
b) "I've been living in Ibiza since 1995."
c) "I've spent all my money."
d) "I haven't been to the beach yet."
e) "I've been a resident DJ at *Amnesia* for two years."
f) "I've been dancing all night."

2 57 Listen and check your answers to 1. Which person do you think enjoys his/her life most?

Vocabulary: informal language

1 Replace the underlined words in these statements with informal expressions from the interview with Josh.

how come	I'm broke	beat	clubbing	reckon

a) I'm usually so tired after a night out that I don't get up till after lunch.
b) I often wonder why I never meet anybody interesting when I go out.
c) I've been going to dance clubs since I was fifteen.
d) I think it costs far too much to get into clubs these days.
e) When I don't have any money, I usually get my friends to pay for me.

2 Find out if any of the statements in 1 are true for your partner.

Anecdote

Think of a time recently when you went to a place where people were dancing and having a good time. You are going to tell your partner about it. Choose from the list below the things you want to talk about. Think about what you are going to say and how you are going to say it.

- ☐ Where were you? A club? A party? A concert?
- ☐ What kind of music was playing?
- ☐ Who was playing the music? A live band? A DJ?
- ☐ How loud and clear was the music?
- ☐ How crowded was the place?
- ☐ What kind of clothes were people wearing?
- ☐ Did you dance or did you watch other people dancing?
- ☐ Were people dancing alone or with a partner?
- ☐ How long did you stay there?
- ☐ Did you have a good time?

Close-up

for and _since_

Language Reference p. 80

1 Look at the way *for* and *since* are explained in the diagram. Then complete the chart so that the information is correct counting from today.

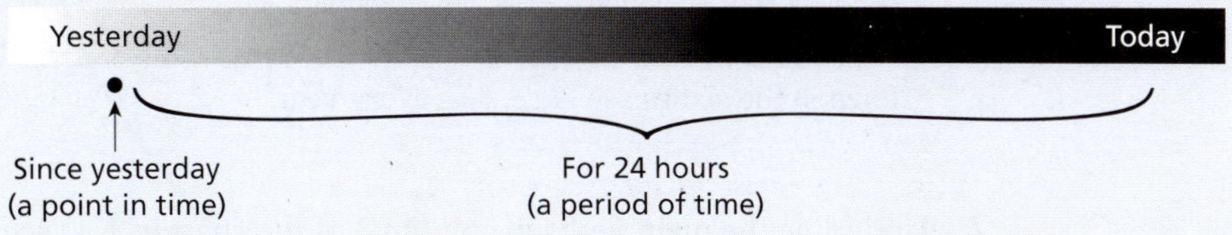

Since		For
yesterday	=	*24 hours*
1999	=	____ *years*
Sunday	=	____ *day(s)*
my last birthday	=	____
I started studying English	=	____

2 Add more examples of your own to the chart in 1.

been* and *gone

Language Reference p. 80

1 Work with a partner. Read the following sentences about the people in the radio program *My Ibiza* on page 78. Then discuss the questions.

1 Josh has been in Ibiza for nine or ten days, but he hasn't been to the beach yet.
2 Simone has been in Ibiza since 1997. She is Brazilian, but she hasn't been home in a couple of years.

a) What tense are the underlined verbs?
b) In which case is *been* used to mean the same as *gone*?

2 Make true sentences about yourself, using the following cues and an appropriate time expression with *since*, *in*, or *never*. Compare your answers with a partner.

a) not go to a dance club
For example: *I haven't gone to a dance club since I was twenty-four./I haven't gone to a dance club in years./I've never gone to a dance club!*
b) not go to a good party
c) not go to the beach
d) not go to a rock concert
e) not go to a wedding
f) not go out for dinner
g) not go skiing
h) not go abroad

David likes going somewhere hot for his vacations.

3 Write down the names of some good stores, restaurants, bars, or dance clubs in your city. Ask your partner if he/she knows them or has gone to them recently. Find out as much as you can.

STUDENT A

Have you ever gone to *Monsoon*?
Or
Have you gone to *Monsoon* recently?

STUDENT B

Yeah, I went there last Saturday.
Or
No, never. What / Where is it?

Present perfect and present perfect continuous

Verb Structures p. 129

1 Look at the chart based on information from the radio program *My Ibiza* on page 78. Which "facts" tell us *how long* an activity has continued?

1 Past facts	+	2 Present facts	➔	3 Present perfect facts
Simone started as a DJ at *Amnesia* two years ago.	+	Simone is a DJ at *Amnesia*.	➔	She's been a DJ at *Amnesia* for two years.
Tourists started coming to Ibiza in the sixties.	+	Tourists come to Ibiza every year.	➔	They've been coming to Ibiza since the sixties.

2 Underline the main verbs in column 3 of the chart in 1. Discuss these questions with your partner.

a) Which verb describes a state?
b) Is it in the present perfect or present perfect continuous?
c) Which verb describes a single or repeated action?
d) Is it in the present perfect or present perfect continuous?

3 Write the name of…

a) a foreign person you know.
b) a type of music you like.
c) a subject you are interested in.
d) a club or bar you go to.
e) a store you buy clothes in.
f) a favorite possession you have.
g) the house you live in.
h) the place you work or study.

1 Decide if each underlined verb describes a state or a single/repeated action.
2 Write eight present perfect facts which answer the question *How long…?*
3 Compare your facts with a partner.

For example: *I've known Max for seven years. I've been going to Bar Isa since 1999.*

4 Work as a class. Find out who has done or who has been doing the things in 3 the longest. Follow these instructions.

a) Each student choose one "fact" from 3 and practice the questions you will ask. For example: *a) Do you know anybody foreign?* ➔ *How long have you known him/her?*
b) Ask everybody in the class and record the answers.
c) Report the results back to the class.

Language Reference: Present perfect and present perfect continuous

for and *since*

for + a period of time and *since* + a point in time are two ways of saying the same thing.

for a few days / for three years / for ages
since Monday / since I graduated / since 1997

been and *gone*

The past participle of *go* is *gone*; *been* is the past participle of *be*. However, *been* is sometimes used to mean the same as *gone*.

*He **hasn't been** to the beach yet.* (go)
***Have** you **been** abroad this year?* (go)
***I've been** sick since last night.* (be)
*How long **have you been** here?* (be)

Present perfect and present perfect continuous

We can use the present perfect when we want to say how long something has continued from a point in the past up to now. For verbs with stative meanings, we always use the present perfect.

***I've been** a DJ for two years.*
***She's known** Tommy since they were in school.*

For verbs with dynamic meanings, we usually use the continuous form.

***I've been clubbing** every night.*
*My mother**'s been playing** tennis since she was eight.*

Note: We can use the present perfect for unchanging, permanent situations and the present perfect continuous for temporary situations. Compare:

***I've lived** here all my life.* (Permanent)
***I've been living** here since May.* (Temporary)

Billy Elliot

Reading and listening

1 Read this introduction to an excerpt from a book based on the movie *Billy Elliot*. What is the problem? What do you think will happen?

> Billy's mother is dead. His father and brother are miners, and they are on strike. Billy's father wants his son to learn to box, like he did and his father before him, but Billy becomes fascinated by the magic of ballet. In secret, Billy starts taking ballet lessons every Saturday. In this excerpt from the story, Billy describes what happens when his father comes to watch him boxing but instead finds him in a ballet class.

2 **58** Read and listen to the excerpt. Who do you sympathize with: Billy or his dad?

nan (line 6): informal word for *grandmother*
telly (line 7): informal word for *television*
wind me up (line 10): informal expression for *annoy me*
lads (line 15) informal word for *boys*
I had him there (line 17): informal expression for *caught him in a difficult situation*

Back home he pointed at a chair behind the table, staring at me all the while he was taking his coat off. Then he sat down opposite me.

I knew what he wanted. He wanted me to say sorry. Well, I wasn't going to. He could wait for ever. It was stupid! What had I done wrong?

"Ballet," he said at last.

"So what's wrong with ballet?" I said. My nan was sitting on a chair by the window, eating a pork pie and watching us like we were on the telly. I looked at her. It was easier than having to look at him. I could see him turning red again out of the corner of my eye.

"What's wrong with ballet? Look at me, Billy. Are you trying to wind me up?"

"It's perfectly normal," I said, turning to face him.

"Normal?" I was scared. He'd gone all white around the lips.

"I used to go to ballet," said my nan.

"See?" I said.

"For your nan. For girls, Billy. Not for lads. Lads do football or boxing or wrestling or something."

"What lads do wrestling?" I asked and I had him there because no one I know does wrestling round here.

"You know what I mean."

"I don't know what you mean."

The thing is, all right, I knew what he meant. At least, I used to know. Ballet isn't what boys do. It's not football and boxing and being hard. It's not what we do. But once I've done it, it is what we do.

Just because I like dancing, it doesn't mean I'm turning into someone else. Does it?

(From *Billy Elliot*, by Melvin Burgess)

3 Here is a brief summary of the excerpt. Put the lines of the summary in the correct order.

(4) a) at his father. He looked
(2) b) off and without saying anything sat
(7) c) up. Billy knew what his father meant.
(3) d) down opposite Billy. Billy didn't look
(1) e) His father took his coat
(5) f) at his nan instead. Billy said there was nothing wrong
(6) g) with doing ballet, but his dad thought he was winding him

4 What interests did you have when you were twelve? What did you want to be? Tell your partner.

14 Call

Work in small groups. Discuss these questions.

- How many phone calls do you make/receive in a typical day?
- What do you use your phone for most?
- Who do you call most?

Reading

1 Work with a partner. List any things that you dislike about phones. Read the magazine article and check if it mentions any of the things on your list.

PHONE MOANS

Audrey: "I hate it when the person I'm speaking to starts drinking or eating something. It sounds disgusting!"

Ben: "It's so boring when you go out with somebody who spends half the time talking on her cell phone. When I go out with somebody, I turn my phone off and listen to my voice mail when I get home."

Cathy: "I think there should be places where cell phones are banned. For instance, when I'm on a train or in a restaurant, I hate listening to people talking about private things. It should be against the law! Call me old-fashioned, but I like to travel and eat in peace."

Dan: "I've given up calling my friends who have children. Every time I call them, they ask me to talk to their two-year-old boy. I have to speak to him in this silly voice, and he never talks, so I have to listen to him breathing into the phone. Luckily, they haven't asked me to talk to the baby yet, but she's usually screaming in the background, so you can't have a normal conversation anyway."

Ellen: "I like to talk to a real person on the phone, but nowadays you get a recorded message that gives you all these options to choose from. If you don't hear everything the first time, you can't ask them to repeat. You have to start again. Oh, and the music that they play while you're on hold—awful."

Frank: "I hate it when you call a company or an office and you can never get through to the person you want to speak to. The operator connects you to an extension, and the person you want is not there, so you have to wait for ages. Then you get another extension, and it's still the wrong one, so you have to wait again. And again and again until you get tired of trying."

2 How many of the things mentioned in the article sometimes happen to you?

Vocabulary: telephones

1 Complete the questions with words and expressions from the article on page 82.

a) Do you think it should be against the law to use a c____ p____ while you're driving?
b) Have you ever been in an embarrassing situation because you forgot to t____ your phone o ____ ?
c) When somebody leaves a message on your v____ m____ , how long do you wait before you return the call?
d) When was the last time you listened to a r____ m____ and had to choose from different o____ ?
e) While you are o____ h____ , do you prefer to listen to music or to silence?
f) Have you ever had a problem getting connected to the right e____ ?

2 Choose three questions from 1 to ask your partner.

Domestic Crisis

Listening

1 59 Listen to the first part of Lorna's telephone conversation. Which of the following problems does Lorna mention?

a) My back is hurting.
b) The house isn't clean.
c) The car has broken down.
d) The cat has died.
e) The kids are annoying me.
f) I've had a fight with my partner.
g) The refrigerator is empty.
h) I'm bored.
i) I don't have any money.
j) I've lost my keys.

2 Lorna uses the words and expressions in the box to talk about the five problems mentioned in 1. Rewrite the problems, using the words and expressions that Lorna uses. Listen and check your answers.

a mess	run out of	killing me	nothing to eat	driving me crazy

3 60 Listen to the second part of the telephone conversation. Who is Juliet?

4 61 After the first conversation, Lorna tries to get help. She makes two more phone calls. Listen to the two conversations and say if each sentence is true (*T*) or false (*F*).

a) Lorna's mother is out.
b) Lorna's father offers to help with the children.
c) Lorna asks Jackie to baby-sit for a couple of hours.
d) Jackie asks if her sister can come with her.
e) Lorna offers to drive over and pick Jackie up.

5 Have you ever had any of the problems in 1 above? Did you call anybody for help? Who? Tell your partner.

Close-up

Offers and requests

I said, would you mind turning down your fan?

1 Listen again to Lorna's two conversations in 4 in the previous section. Match the opening phrases (*a–g*) with the sentence endings (*1–7*).

a)	Can I	1	drive over and pick you up?
b)	Should I	2	come over and baby-sit.
c)	Could you	3	bring my boyfriend?
d)	I was wondering if you could	4	call you back later?
e)	Would you mind	5	tell her it's urgent?
f)	Is it O.K. if I	6	hanging on a minute, please?
g)	Would you like me to	7	leave a message for your mother?

2 Put the opening phrases in 1 (*a–g*) into three groups.

Offers: asking people if we can do something for them	b		
Requests: asking people if they can do something for us	c		
Requests for permission: asking people if it's O.K. for us to do something	a		

3 Work with a partner. Look again at the opening phrases in 1. Do you usually use more or fewer words if you want to be formal?

4 Look at the following mini-situations. Think of a person you would call for each situation. Tell your partner.

A
You want someone to choose a movie for you to see together.

B
You want someone to take care of your pet while you are on vacation.

C
You want someone to write a job reference for you.

D
You want someone to check an important letter you've written in English.

E
You want someone to help you buy a new outfit for a friend's wedding.

F
You want someone to lend you some money till the end of the month.

5 Work with a partner. Choose two of the mini-situations in 4 and write a short phone conversation for each one. Include an offer and a request in each conversation.

Language Reference: Offers and requests

Offers

Here are two common ways of asking people if we can do something for them.

***Should I** give you a ride?*

***Would you like me to** help you?*

Requests

There are many ways of asking people if they can do something for us. Usually, the more words we use, the more polite or formal the request sounds.

***I was wondering if you could**… ?* ↑ more polite/formal
***Would you mind**… ?*
***Could you**… ?* ↓ more direct/informal

Here are some ways we can request permission—ask people if it is O.K. for us to do something.

***Can I** use your phone, please?*

***Is it O.K. if I** bring my friend?*

Telephone Talk

Listening

1 Lorna finally tries to get in touch with her husband at work. He works for a company called Butler and Crowmarch. Complete her conversation with the receptionist, using the most appropriate expressions.

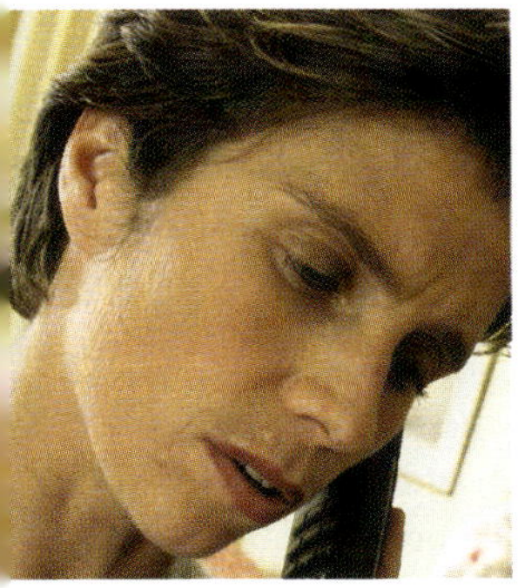

R: (1) **Yes / Good morning**. Butler and Crowmarch.
L: (2) **Could I / I want to** speak to Mr. Carr, please?
R: Certainly. (3) **Who's calling, please? / Who are you?**
L: Mrs. Carr.
R: (4) **Wait / One moment, please**.
Hello. (5) **He's not there. / I'm sorry, but Mr. Carr is away from his desk.**
L: Oh. (6) **Do you know when he'll / When will he** be back?
R: I'm not sure. (7) **Would you like / Do you want** me to ask his assistant?
L: Yes, please.
R: Just a moment, please. (8) **He's busy till five. / Hello, Mrs. Carr. Mr. Carr is in a meeting until five o'clock.**
L: Oh, O.K. (9) **Can I / Let me** leave a message.
R: Certainly.
L: (10) **Tell him / Could you tell him** to call me before he leaves the office? It's important.
R: No problem, Mrs. Carr. I'll give him the message.
L: Thank you. Goodbye.

2 **62** Listen and compare your version with the version on the recording.

3 Work with a partner. Practice the conversation. Take turns being Lorna and the receptionist.

Telephone numbers

1 **63** The following telephone numbers have been copied down incorrectly. Listen to the recording and correct the numbers.

a) Amtrak train schedules and fares: 1 (900) 872-7245
b) Budget Rent-A-Car: 1 (728) 656-6010
c) AAA emergency road service: 1 (800) 222-3457
d) Port Authority bus schedules: 1 (212) 500-2341
e) PATH Trains to New Jersey: 1 (800) 234-6624
f) Directory Assistance: 401

2 Explain your answers in 1 to a partner. Take turns identifying the mistake and saying what the correct number is. Do not show each other any numbers you have written down.

For example: *For Amtrak trains, it isn't one nine hundred. It's one eight hundred. Do you agree?*

3 Work with a partner and complete the following task.

a) Write down five telephone numbers that are important to you.
b) Take turns dictating the numbers to each other.
c) Check that you wrote down your partner's numbers correctly.
d) Explain to each other why the numbers are important.

The "Latest Thing"

Reading **1** You are going to read an article about a father who doesn't want to buy a cell phone for his twelve-year-old son. Why do you think he does not want his son to have a phone? Discuss with a partner. Read the article. Are any of your ideas mentioned?

Why I Bought My Child a Gun

Every five minutes my children ask me for the "latest thing." They tell me that all their friends have it already, and they can't live without it. Our house is full of Game Boys, Play Station CDs, and a million other "latest things."

But the one "latest thing" we have refused to buy is a cell phone. Our twelve-year-old wants one, and we've said "no." He says he'll use it only for messaging and he really needs it for emergencies.

We don't want him to have a cell phone, because they may be bad for children's health. Unfortunately, when I say, "I don't want you to have a cell phone, because you might get a brain tumor," he tells me that he doesn't mind.

Why do twelve-year-old boys only want things that are bad for them? We've already told him that he can't listen to rap music—the words are disgusting. And I've said no to beer with his meals. Right now, I'm saying no to everything.

Then a few weeks ago he asked for something called a BB gun. He says everybody has one. Of course they do. He shows me a Web site full of them and tells me it fires only plastic pellets. Finally, I say yes. I can't believe I've said no to phones and yes to guns.

In October our son becomes a teenager, and I pray that research will find that cell phones are safe ... even better, that they make young people less moody—and more interested in personal hygiene.

Until then, I'm saying no.

(Adapted from the *Guardian*)

2 Work in small groups. Discuss the following questions.

- Who is the youngest person you know with a cell phone?
- What are the arguments for and against letting young children have cell phones?
- At what age do you think it's O.K. for children to have cell phones?

Vocabulary: *say, tell, ask*

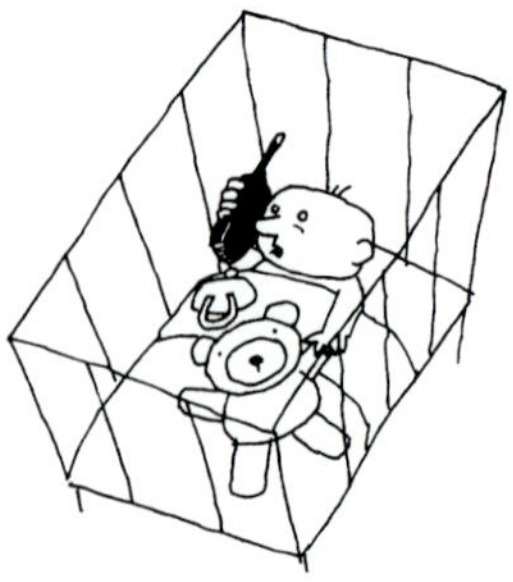

I can't talk now.

1 Complete this summary of the article by choosing the most appropriate alternative.

a) The father's twelve-year-old son always **says/tells/asks** him for the "latest thing."
b) He **says/tells/asks** him that he wants a cell phone.
c) He **says/tells/asks** that he'll use it only for messaging.
d) He **says/tells/asks** him that he doesn't mind getting a brain tumor.
e) The son then **says/tells/asks** for a BB gun.
f) He **says/tells/asks** everybody has one.
g) He **says/tells/asks** him it fires only plastic pellets.
h) The father **says/tells/asks** "no" to the cell phone and "yes" to the gun.

2 Complete each of the following rules with *say, tell,* or *ask*.

a) You ____ (somebody) for something.
b) You ____ somebody something.
c) You ____ something.

Who? What? Where?

Listening **1** 64 You are going to listen to six short conversations. Listen and answer these questions: Who is speaking? What is the situation? Where are they? Choose from the places in the box.

in a parking garage	at a club	at a bus stop	at home	at the zoo	at home

2 Which of the situations in 1 have you been in? Tell your partner.

Close-up

Indirect questions

1 Work with a partner. Look at the position of subject and verb in these sentences and discuss the questions below.

Direct questions

be

question word	verb	subject		question frame	subject	verb	
Where	*is*	*the restroom*	? →	*Do you know where*	*the restroom*	*is*	?

Other verbs

question word	auxiliary	subject	verb		question frame	subject	verb	
–	*Has*	*the last bus*	*left*	? →	*Do you know if*	*the last bus*	*has left*	?

Indirect questions

a) Where does the subject go in direct questions with *be*?
b) Where does the subject go in direct questions with other verbs?
c) Where does the subject go in indirect questions?

2 Put the subjects in the correct position in these direct and indirect questions. Listen again to the six conversations and check your answers.

Subjects	Direct questions	Indirect questions
a) the restroom	Where is *the restroom*?	Could you tell me where *the restroom* is?
b) the time	What is?	Do you have any idea what is?
c) the lions	Where are?	Do you know where are?
d) I	Could have a Zoomatron?	Do you think could have a Zoomatron?
e) I	Where can get a taxi?	Do you know where can get a taxi?
f) we	Where did leave it?	Can you remember where left it?

3 Work with a partner. Rewrite the ends of these indirect questions in the correct order.

a) Do you know what	is address my ?
b) Can you remember who	was English teacher first your ?
c) Do you know what	is zodiac sign your ?
d) Do you know if	parents born in were city this your ?
e) Do you think	is my improving English ?
f) Could you tell me how long	city you in living this been have ?

4 Ask each other the questions in 3.

Language Reference: Indirect questions

The word order in indirect questions is different from the word order in direct questions. It is the same as in normal statements: *subject + verb (+ object)*. You do not use the auxiliaries *do/does/did*.

Question frame	Subject	Verb	(Object)
Do you think	*I*	*could have*	*a Zoomatron?*
Do you know if	*the last bus*	*has left?*	
Can you remember who	*your first English teacher*	*was?*	
Could you tell me where	*you*	*live?*	

15

Review 3

The Waiting Game

Language reviewed: describing people (Unit 11); *for* and *since* (Unit 13); present perfect and present perfect continuous (Unit 13); indirect questions (Unit 14); noun phrases with *on* and *at* (Unit 13)

Listening

1 **65** You are going to listen to a radio reporter conduct three interviews with people in line to get tickets for the Wimbledon tennis championships. Look at the picture while you are listening and answer the questions.

a) Who thinks they will get into Wimbledon?
b) Who doesn't think they will get in?

2 Rearrange the words to make the questions that the reporter asked in the first interview.

a) Could you tell me come from where you ?
b) Could you tell me been have how long waiting you ?
c) Do you think get in you will ?
d) Do you know are how in many front people of there you ?

3 Listen to the first interview again and check the word order of the questions in 2. How does the woman answer the questions?

4 Complete the sentences from the interviews. Put each verb into the present perfect or the present perfect continuous and choose *for* or *since*.

a) You (**look**) at her **for/since** hours. *You've been looking at her for hours.*
b) I (**wait**) here **for/since** eight fifteen this morning.
c) I (**be**) in London **for/since** four weeks.
d) It (**rain**) **for/since** one thirty.
e) We (**be**) here **for/since** about eight.
f) We (**chat**) **for/since** ages.

5 Listen to the interviews again to check your answers to 4.

6 Work in small groups. Which do you prefer:

a) watching big sporting events live?
b) watching big sporting events on TV?
c) not watching big sporting events?

Discuss your answers and give examples from your own experience.

Vocabulary: describing people

1 Complete the descriptions with words from the box. Match each description to a person in the picture of the line for Wimbledon on page 88.

bags	cheeks	hard-working	humor	annoying	miserable	outfits	teeth
wavy	wrinkled						

A She has pale skin and a few freckles, but the most noticeable thing about her is her eyelashes. She doesn't have any! She always looks _____ , but in reality, she is not unhappy. She is serious and _____—and always extremely polite.

B She has short, gray _____ hair and always wears green to match her green eyes. Her _____ are always red—is it because she is embarrassed or does she suffer from the cold? Certainly, she is very shy, but she is a loyal friend and can be a lot of fun to be with.

C She's a senior citizen with a warm personality and a friendly face. Sociable and easygoing, she has a wonderful sense of _____ and seems to be smiling all the time. Even with her tanned, _____ face, she is still good-looking.

D He's fifty-two but looks older. With unwashed hair, big, bushy eyebrows, and a mustache that seems to have some of his dinner still in it, he's usually a mess. In fact, you could say that personal hygiene is not his strong point. He has _____ under his eyes because he doesn't sleep enough. He wears an old-fashioned suit (does he sleep in it?) and has an _____ habit of looking the other way when you talk to him.

E She's fifty, and she always likes to look her best when she goes out. She wears stylish _____ and chooses lipsticks to match. Red is her favorite color because it shows off her row of beautiful pearly _____ . She recently dyed her hair pink. She is very sure of herself, and some people think she is kind of bossy.

2 On a piece of paper, write a short description of another student in your class. Fold your piece of paper and give it to your teacher. Then take a piece of paper with a description written by another student and guess who is being described.

Vocabulary: *at* and *on*

1 Complete each sentence in the questionnaire with *at* or *on*.

HOW PATIENT ARE YOU?

1	You're _____ the Internet and downloading an interesting program, but it's very, very slow. How long will you wait before giving up?	_____ **minutes**
2	You are _____ a party _____ a friend's house. It's extremely boring, and you know only one person—your friend. How long will you wait before going home?	_____ **minutes**
3	You are going _____ a business trip tomorrow, and you decide to have your hair cut before you go. It is very, very busy _____ the hairdresser's. How long will you wait before giving up?	_____ **minutes**
4	You're sitting _____ a plane, and the person _____ your right is listening to loud music _____ his personal stereo. How long will you wait before asking him to turn it down?	_____ **minutes**
5	You are going out _____ a date. Your friend is waiting for you _____ the movie theater. You are _____ the bus stop, but your bus does not arrive. How long will you wait before calling a taxi _____ your cell phone?	_____ **minutes**
		Total number of minutes: _____

2 Answer the questions in the questionnaire. For each question, write the maximum number of minutes that you will wait. When you have finished, add up the minutes for all the questions. Write your total.

3 Compare your answers with other people. Who is the most patient/impatient person in the class?

National Sports

Language reviewed: passives (Unit 12); dynamic and stative meanings (Unit 12); verb patterns (Unit 11); imperatives (Unit 11); *say, tell,* and *ask* (Unit 14); offers and requests (Unit 14); phrasal verbs (Unit 11)

Passives

1 Complete each of the following statements with an appropriate passive form of the verb. Then decide if the statements are true or false. Check your answers on page 127.

a) The 1992 Olympic games (**hold**) in Atlanta, Georgia. True or false?
b) Cricket (**play**) by two teams of thirteen players. True or false?
c) The game of rugby (**invent**) at Rugby School, England in 1823. True or false?
d) Mount Everest (**climb**) for the first time in 1953. True or false?
e) Bob Beamon's 1968 long jump world record of 8.9 meters (**never break**). True or false?
f) Brazil (**beat**) 2–1 by Germany in the 2002 soccer World Cup final. True or false?

2 Make up three more true/false statements about trivia, using passive verb structures. Exchange your statements with your partner. Are they true or false?

Dynamic and stative meanings

1 You are going to look at some pictures of a London street. Before you look at the pictures, choose the best verb forms in the questions below.

a) What **happens/is happening** in your picture?
b) How **do the people stand/are the people standing**?
c) What **do they wear/are they wearing**?
d) What **do they have/are they having** in their hands?
e) Where **do you think/are you thinking** the people **come/are coming** from? Why?

2 Work with a partner. Student A, look at the picture on page 127. Student B, look at the picture on page 128. Discuss the questions in 1. How many similarities and differences can you find between the pictures?

Reading

1 Read the article below about lining up or "queuing" in Britain. Choose either the *to*-infinitive or the *-ing* form for the verbs in parentheses. How useful is the advice in the article?

The Noble Art of Lining Up

There is one sport at which the British are always the world champions. Nobody can beat them at the noble art of lining up, or as they say, "queuing." The British actually look forward to (1 **spend**) their weekends in a line, or queue, waiting for a store to open or waiting for a parking space at the furniture superstore.

If you ever decide (2 **visit**) Britain, you will need (3 **know**) some of the basic rules of the sport.

First of all, remember that you need only one person to form a line. If you are alone at a bus stop, for example, don't look too relaxed. Make sure that you are in the line, and look optimistically to your right.

If you want (4 **keep**) your place in the line, never leave a space between you and the person in front; otherwise the person behind you will ask, "Are you in the queue?" (meaning "Don't you know how to queue properly?").

Conversation is generally not a good idea, and only two topics are acceptable: the weather and the bus schedule. Anything more and you will end up with a complete stranger sitting next to you, telling you his or her life story.

Unfortunately, the bus does not always stop in the correct place. Try (5 **stay**) calm and, whatever you do, don't cut in line, or as they say in Britain, "jump the queue." You can be sure that every single person in the line knows exactly who is in front of them and who is behind.

Follow these simple rules and you, too, can enjoy (6 **visit**) the home of the noble art of lining up. But if you decide not to follow the rules, be prepared for the worst.

2 **66** Listen and check your answers.

3 Work with a partner. Complete the following task.

a) Underline all the examples of imperatives you can find in the article.
b) Prepare a list of useful "do's" and "don'ts" for foreign visitors to your country (e.g., driving; using public transportation; eating out; visiting someone's home).
c) Compare your list with other people in the class.

Vocabulary: telephone language

1 Have you ever been late for work, a meeting, an appointment, or a lesson? Wh you say? Tell your partner.

2 Look at the outline of a telephone conversation. Choose the correct word in each

MRS. KNIGHTLY	THE SECRETARY
1 Mrs. Knightly **asks/tells** for Mr. Rogers. →	**2** The secretary **says/asks** Mrs. Knightly to wait. **3** She **says/tells** that Mr. Rogers is not there.
← **4** Mrs. Knightly **asks/tells** the secretary if she will take a message. →	**5** The secretary **says/tells** yes.
← **6** Mrs. Knightly **says/tells** the secretary her name. **7** She **says/tells** she will be late. →	**8** The secretary **asks/tells** Mrs. Knightly for her telephone number.
← **9** Mrs. Knightly **tells/says** no. **10** She **tells/says** she'll call back later.	

3 Match the stages (*1–10*) in the telephone conversation in 2 with the speeches (*a–j*) below.

a) Uh, would you mind taking a message?
b) Certainly. Could you hold for a minute, please?
c) Certainly.
d) I'll call back later.
e) Uhm, well, it's Joanna Knightly.
f) I'm sorry, but Mr. Rogers is not in yet, ma'am.
g) I have an appointment with Mr. Rogers at 9:15, and I'm sorry, but I missed the bus…
h) Oh, hello. Can I speak to Mr. Rogers, please?
i) That's all right, thanks.
j) Would you like to give me your telephone number, and I'll ask Mr. Rogers to call you when he gets in?

4 **67** Listen to the conversation to check your answers. Practice the conversation with a partner.

Vocabulary: phrasal verbs

1 Complete the sentences with words from the box.

down	out	out	over	off	up	up

a) My car broke ____ last night.
b) I turned ____ my cell phone, so I didn't get your message about the meeting.
c) I went ____ with some friends last night, so I went to bed very late and overslept this morning.
d) The bus ran ____ of gas, and we're waiting for another one to arrive.
e) A friend said that she would pick me ____ in her car, but she hasn't arrived yet.
f) I split ____ with my boy/girlfriend last night, and I need a little time to get ____ it.

2 Work with a partner. Discuss these questions.

- Which sentence in 1 is the best excuse for being late?
- Which is the worst excuse?
- What other excuses can you think of?

3 Work with a partner. Write and practice a telephone conversation between a person who is late for work and his/her boss.

Nightclubs

Language reviewed: informal language (Unit 13); modals of obligation and permission (Unit 9); clothes and accessories (Unit 6)

1 Work in groups of four. Discuss the following questions.

- How many good nightclubs are there in your city?
- Which is the most expensive club to get into?
- Have you or your friends ever had difficulty getting into a club? Why?

2 Look at these pictures of the scene and the characters in a sketch called *The Door*. Compare the pictures to your favorite nightclub and the kind of people who go there. How different are they? Tell your partner.

3 **68** You are going to listen to and read the sketch. What do the bouncers do so that they can go home early?

4 Work in groups of four. You are going to perform the sketch.

a) Decide who is going to play each character. (The first man, second man, and third man can be played by the same person. The first woman and second woman can be played by the same person.)
b) Practice your parts individually. Think about what voice your character will have, what he/she will look like, and how he/she will act.
c) Perform the sketch for the rest of the class.

The Door

Scene Outside a nightclub. Two bouncers, B1 and B2, one on either side of the door. Music coming out of the club.

Characters **B1** (Bouncer 1)
B2 (Bouncer 2)
M1 (First man)
W1 (First woman)
M2 (Second man)
W2 (Second woman)
M3 (Third man)

B1 You O.K., pal?
B2 Yeah.
B1 You look beat—what have you been up to?
B2 I *am* beat—I've worked every night this week.
B1 What? You're crazy.
B2 Yeah, but I'm broke. I need the cash. I'm looking forward to getting home tonight though—know what I mean?
B1 Cheer up—it's midnight, and there's hardly anybody here. I guess we can finish early tonight.
B2 No—look, people are starting to arrive now.
B1 Don't worry—we'll get rid of them soon.

First man approaches.

B1 Sorry, pal, you can't come in.
M1 What do you mean I can't come in?
B1 Sorry, pal. We have a very strict dress code here, and you can't come in.
M1 Why not?
B1 Because you're wearing sneakers.
M1 But I was here last night, and I was wearing exactly the same clothes.
B1 Last night was "casual night." Tonight is "dress casual" night.
M1 Dress casual night? What are you talking about?
B1 On dress casual night, you have to wear dress casual clothes. You can't wear jeans, sneakers, or baseball caps.
M1 Well, I'm not coming here again.

First woman approaches.

B1 Sorry, beautiful, you can't come in.
W1 What?
B2 Sorry, but we have a very strict dress code here, and you can't come in.
W1 But I'm a model. You have to let me in.
B1 Yeah, but we can't let you in. You're wearing jeans.
W1 But they're designer jeans. I paid a lot of money for them. Everybody wears jeans.
B2 Yeah, but rules are rules. You can't come in.
W1 I'm going to tell all my friends about this.

Second man approaches.

B2 Sorry, pal, you can't come in.
M2 What?
B1 Sorry, but we have a very strict dress code here, and you can't come in.
M2 But I'm wearing a suit.
B2 That's right. It's dress casual night, and you're wearing a suit, so you can't come in.
M2 But I came here on Monday night, and I was wearing exactly the same clothes.
B1 Monday night was formal night, sir. On formal night you have to wear a suit.
B2 Yeah, tonight is dress casual night, and you have to wear dress casual clothes.
M2 How ridiculous. I'm not coming here again.

Second woman approaches.

B1 Sorry, miss, but you can't come in.
W2 Why not? I'm twenty-one.
B2 Sorry, miss, but we have a very strict dress code, and you can't come in.
W2 But I'm not wearing sneakers or jeans or a baseball cap.
B1 No, but your skirt's too short. You can't wear a miniskirt on dress casual night.
W2 Look, I'm the DJ's girlfriend. You have to let me in.
B2 Yeah, and I'm the DJ's brother-in-law. Now get lost!
W2 Oh, yeah? I'll see you later.

Third man approaches.

B1 Evening, sir.
M3 Evening.
B2 All right, you can go in.

Almost immediately the third man comes out.

B1 That was quick, sir.
M3 It's too boring—there's nobody in there!
B1 O.K. Let's go home.
B2 All right, pal. See you tomorrow.

16 *Lifestyle*

Reading

1 Work with a partner. Choose an appropriate alternative to give somebody advice on how to live longer. Decide on the top three tips for a healthy and longer life.

You'll live longer if you…

a) eat a low- **calorie/vitamin/protein** diet.
b) eat three quarters **junk/frozen/plant** food and one quarter **animal/canned/baby** food.
c) eat seven servings of **jam/fruit and vegetables/chocolate** every day.
d) stop eating when you are **50%/80%/100%** full.
e) do the things you **enjoy/hate /can**.
f) have a strong network of **advisors/friends/doctors**.

2 Read this article about the lifestyle on the island of Okinawa in Japan. Which tips from 1 are mentioned?

How Not to Die Before You Get Old

Chiako is active and healthy. She gets up at 7 A.M. every day, takes a brisk 30-minute walk, and plays gate-ball with her friends three times a week. There is nothing unusual about this, except that Chiako is 102 years old. She is not alone—there are hundreds of healthy centenarians who lead similar lives in Okinawa.

Okinawa is a group of islands between Japan and Taiwan. Near a beach, there is a large stone with the following words on it: "At 70 you are still a child, at 80 you are just a youth, and at 90, if the ancestors invite you into heaven, ask them to wait until you are 100, and then you might consider it."

Okinawans manage to stay thin in old age by eating a low-calorie diet that consists of three quarters plant food and one quarter animal food. They eat seven servings of fruit and vegetables every day, and they stop eating when they are 80% full.

They also keep active by dancing, walking, and gardening. In other words, they do the things they enjoy.

Okinawans have developed a stress-resistant personality. Nobody is in a hurry, schedules are non-existent, and there is always tomorrow. Hundreds of people, both young and old, go to the beach every day to watch the spectacular sunsets. In Okinawa, there is always time to watch the sun set.

As well as large extended families, Okinawans have strong networks of friends. "When someone is ill and doesn't come to work, a neighbor will always knock on the person's door to find out how he or she is."

There's no magic pill. If you have good friends, a healthy diet, and a stress-free lifestyle, you will live longer. It's as simple as that!

3 How different is your lifestyle from the one described on Okinawa? Compare with your partner.

Vocabulary: word combinations

1 Complete these expressions with words from the article on Okinawa.

a) How often do you go for a b____ walk?
b) Do you think you h____ a healthy lifestyle?
c) Do you feel that you are always i____ a hurry?
d) Do you have a large e____ family?
e) Do you have a strong n____ of friends?

2 Work with a partner. Ask each other the questions in 1.

Anecdote

Think about the healthiest or fittest person you know. You are going to tell your partner about this person. Choose from the list the things you want to talk about. Think about what you will say and what language you will need.

- ☐ Is it a man or a woman?
- ☐ How old is this person?
- ☐ How do you know this person?
- ☐ What does he/she look like?
- ☐ What does he/she do for a living?
- ☐ What does he/she do to stay healthy and fit?
- ☐ Has this person ever been unhealthy or unfit?
- ☐ How is his/her lifestyle different from yours?

Health Spas

Listening

1 **69** You are going to listen to a woman asking for information about a health spa.

a) What's the name of the health spa?
b) Why does she want the information?
c) What do you think her husband will think about her idea?

2 Complete the sentences by choosing the correct alternatives and then listen to the conversation again. Check (✓) the activities that her husband will do at the health spa.

a) He'll **pass/take** a fitness test.
b) He'll **make/go on** a diet.
c) He'll **take/have** a cigarette.
d) He'll **do/make** two hours of yoga.
e) He'll **do/have** a sauna.
f) He'll **make/go for** a four-hour hike.

3 Work with a partner. Discuss these questions.

- Are there any health spas in your country like the one in the recording?
- What kind of people go to health spas?
- Would you like to go to one?

Close-up

Future time clauses

Language Reference p. 97

Verb Structures p. 130

1 Work with a partner. Look at the following sentences from the listening in the previous section and answer the questions.

Conjunction	+	**Subordinate clause**	+	**Main clause**
As soon as	+	*he arrives,*	+	*he'll take a fitness test.*
If	+	*he has a cigarette,*	+	*he'll be in big trouble.*
When	+	*he finishes the week,*	+	*he'll feel like a new man.*

a) Do these sentences refer to past, present, or future time?
b) Which verb structure is used in the main clause?
c) Which verb structure is used in the subordinate clause?

2 Which of the conjunctions in 1 suggests:

a) something will *possibly* happen?
b) something will *certainly* happen at a particular time?
c) something will happen *immediately*?

3 Look at how the sentences in 1 are formed. Is the following sentence structure also possible?

main clause + conjunction + subordinate clause (*He'll take a fitness test as soon as he arrives.*)

4 Complete each of these sentences with the correct verb structure.

a) If there's nothing good on TV tonight, I **go/'ll go** out.
b) When I **'ll go/go** on vacation next summer, I'll send you a postcard.
c) I'm going straight home as soon as the class **will end/ends**.
d) When I **'ll have/have** enough money, I'm going to buy a new jacket.
e) If I get up early tomorrow, I think I **go/'ll go** for a run.

5 How many sentences in 4 are true for you? Rewrite the sentences as necessary so that they are all true for you. Compare your sentences with a partner.

will for prediction

1 Complete each of these quotes by inserting *will* in the correct position. Match each quote with the person who you think made the prediction.

a) "Man ***will*** not fly for fifty years."
b) "No woman in my time be Prime Minister."
c) "The Internet collapse within a year."

1 Bob Metcalf, founder of 3Com Corporation, in 1995. (A year later, he took his magazine article, liquefied it in a blender, and ate it with a spoon.)
2 Wilbur Wright to his brother Orville in 1901. (In 1903, the Wright brothers made the first flight.)
3 Conservative politician Margaret Thatcher in 1969. (She became British Prime Minister in 1979.)

2 Work in small groups. You are going to consult the Oracle to find out things about your future. Turn to page 128 and follow the instructions. Compare your answers.

3 Think about the topics in the box and use the sentence beginnings to write about your life in the future. Compare with your partner.

family children relationships health and fitness house job travel possessions money spare time hair English

I'll definitely… /I definitely won't…
I'll probably… /I probably won't…
I hope I'll… /I hope I won't…
I think I'll … /I don't think I'll…

Language Reference: Future forms

Future time clauses

When we are talking about the future, we use a future form in the main clause, but we use the simple present in the subordinate clause after *when, if, as soon as, before, after*, etc. We use a comma after the subordinate clause.

conjunction	subordinate clause	main clause
When	*he* ***finishes*** *the week,*	*he'll feel like a new man.*
If	*he* ***has*** *a cigarette here,*	*he'll be in big trouble.*

Note: Main clause + conjunction + subordinate clause (*He'll feel like a new man when he finishes the week.*) is an alternative order. We do not use a comma after the main clause.

will for prediction

We use *will* + simple verb form to make predictions about the future. We can grade or qualify our predictions by using the following structures.

I'll definitely / I definitely won't *go to Mexico next summer.*
My father will probably / My father probably won't *retire when he's sixty-five.*
I hope I'll / I hope I won't *have more than two children.*
I think I'll / I don't think I'll *be rich and famous.* NOT ~~I think I won't ...~~

Food Glorious Food

Vocabulary: food

1 Work with a partner. Look at the shopping list and check (✓) the items this person has bought. Which seven items has the person forgotten?

Fruit and vegetables
oranges, lemons, bananas,
apples, grapes, peaches,
potatoes, tomatoes, lettuce,
spinach, carrots, cauliflower,
eggplant, mushrooms,
red peppers, green beans,
olives, cucumbers, onions, garlic
Meat, fish, and seafood
chicken, sausage, trout,
sardines, shrimp
Other
tea, soup, nuts

2 Place the items in 1 on the chart so they are true for you. Compare with your partner.

haven't had recently	have had recently	could live without	couldn't live without

3 Which of the items in 1 are never/always on your own shopping list? Add other things that are always on your shopping list. Compare with your partner.

Sounds and spelling

1 70 The relationship between vowel sounds and spelling isn't always obvious. Listen and repeat the words in column A and column B.

A		B	
a)	lettuce	1	nut
b)	onion	2	tomato
c)	banana	3	spinach
d)	sardines	4	beans
e)	orange	5	lemon
f)	potato	6	olive

2 71 Match a word from column A with a word from column B according to the highlighted vowel sounds. Listen and check your answers. Which word do you find most difficult to say?

Vocabulary: food idioms

1 Work with a partner. Look at the conversations and discuss.

a) Who do you think is speaking?
b) What do you think the conversations are about?

A

A: We're having a surprise party for Bill.
B: Oh, that's great. I'll be there.
A: O.K., but remember—it's a surprise, so don't spill the **beans/spinach/mushrooms**.

B

A: Hey, what do you think of the guy over there with the blue shirt on?
B: Uhm—he's O.K., but he's not my cup of **hot chocolate/soup/tea**.
A: Good—he is mine.

C

A: Why can't I go out?
B: Look, I've told you a hundred times. It's raining. Now stop carrying on about it. You're driving me **sausage/nuts/onions**.
A: But why can't I?

D

A: No, I can't. It's too difficult.
B: No, it isn't. It's a piece of **toast/pizza/cake**. Come on.
A: No, no. Stop it. I'm going to fall over.

E

A: What have you done today? Nothing!
B: That's not true. I've read the paper.
A: And watched television for two hours. You're nothing but a lazy couch **potato/cucumber/tomato**.

F

A: What was it like?
B: Awful, it was so crowded. We were packed in like **grapes/sardines/garlic**.
A: I guess you won't go there again, will you?

2 Complete the idioms by choosing the correct alternatives.

3 72 Listen to the conversations and check your answers to 2. Do you have any idioms like these in your language?

4 Replace each underlined phrase with an idiom from 1.

a) I can't keep a secret—I always tell everyone about everything.
b) I could never be friends with someone who watches TV all the time.
c) I hate places where you are with lots of other people.
d) I think that learning English is really easy.
e) I was a naughty child and drove my parents crazy.
f) Going clubbing isn't something I enjoy.

5 Are the sentences in 4 true or false for you? Compare with a partner.

How to Eat a Banana

Vocabulary: food preparation

1 You are going to read an excerpt from a Web site about recipes for dishes made with bananas. Check (✓) the dishes you would like to try and put an ex (✗) next to the ones you wouldn't like to try.

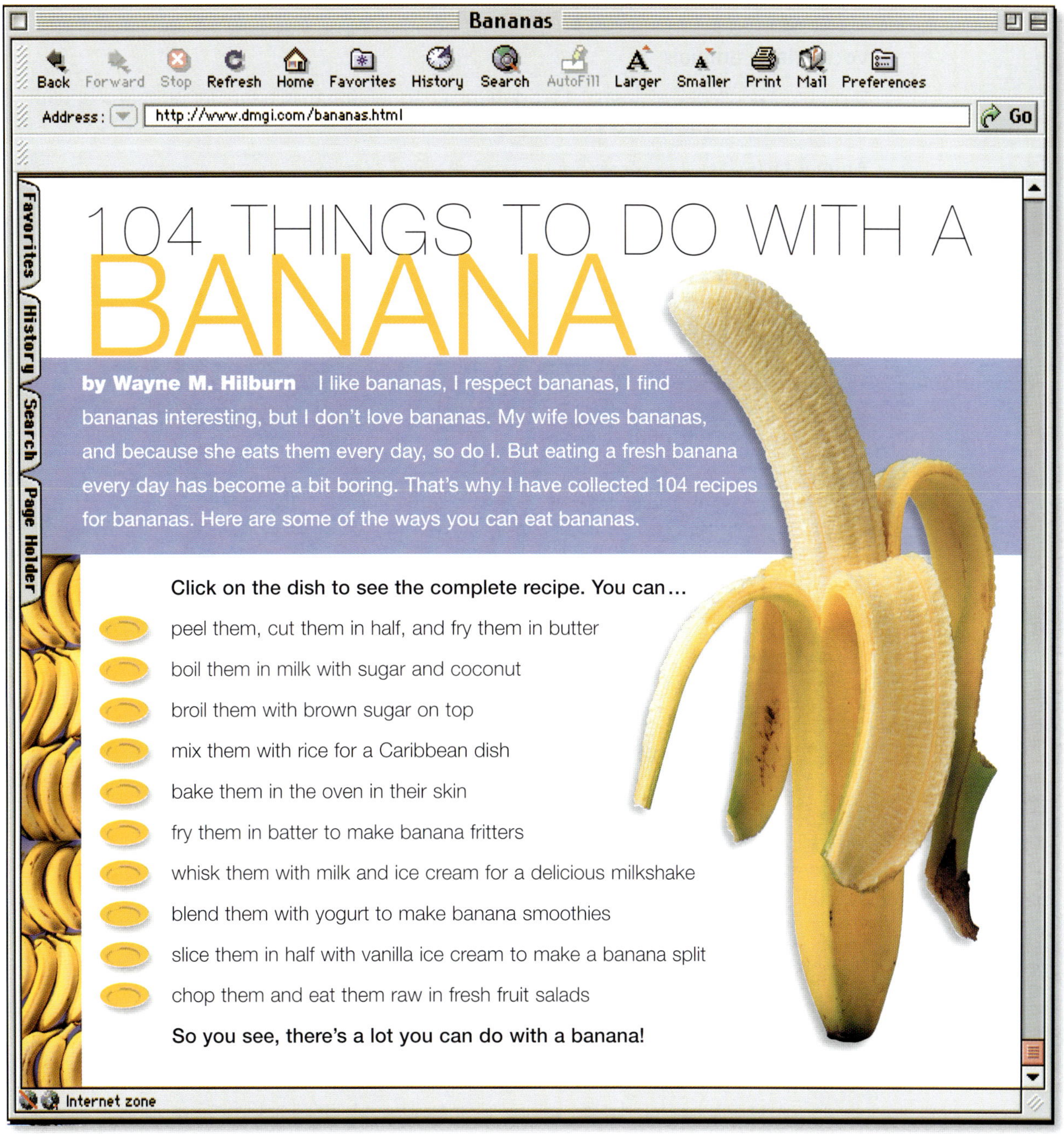
Bananas

Back Forward Stop Refresh Home Favorites History Search AutoFill Larger Smaller Print Mail Preferences

Address: http://www.dmgi.com/bananas.html Go

Favorites History Search Page Holder

104 THINGS TO DO WITH A BANANA

by Wayne M. Hilburn I like bananas, I respect bananas, I find bananas interesting, but I don't love bananas. My wife loves bananas, and because she eats them every day, so do I. But eating a fresh banana every day has become a bit boring. That's why I have collected 104 recipes for bananas. Here are some of the ways you can eat bananas.

Click on the dish to see the complete recipe. You can…

- peel them, cut them in half, and fry them in butter
- boil them in milk with sugar and coconut
- broil them with brown sugar on top
- mix them with rice for a Caribbean dish
- bake them in the oven in their skin
- fry them in batter to make banana fritters
- whisk them with milk and ice cream for a delicious milkshake
- blend them with yogurt to make banana smoothies
- slice them in half with vanilla ice cream to make a banana split
- chop them and eat them raw in fresh fruit salads

So you see, there's a lot you can do with a banana!

Internet zone

2 Read the list of dishes again and write down words that describe:

a) different ways of preparing food (For example: *peel*)
b) different ways of cooking food (For example: *fry*)
c) one word meaning *not cooked*

3 Think of lots of different items of food that you can prepare and cook in the ways described in 2.

For example: *peel an apple, an orange, a potato*, etc. *fry an egg, fish, onions*, etc.

4 Think about a meal you have eaten recently. Write down exactly what you ate. How did the cook prepare the food? How did he/she cook the food? Describe the meal in detail to your partner.

17 Animals

Vocabulary: animals

Test your knowledge of animals! Work with a partner and match the definitions (*a–f*) with the words (*1–6*). The answers are on page 124.

Animal facts

a)	An animal that can last longer without water than a camel.	1	A cheetah.
b)	A person who treats sick animals.	2	A dolphin.
c)	An insect that can lift fifty times its own weight.	3	A vet.
d)	An animal that can run at 60 mph.	4	A giraffe.
e)	An animal that can live to seventy years old.	5	An ant.
f)	An animal that can recognize its own image in a mirror.	6	A turtle.

Homophones

1 There are some words in English that sound exactly the same but have different spellings and different meanings. Complete the chart by matching each of the words in the box with one of the clues below.

tail weight bear right deer wait dear tale write bare

Word A	Sound	Word B
1 ***tail*** – a cat has a long one	/teil/	_____ – an imaginative story
2 _____ – brown animal with long legs/Bambi	/dir/	_____ – ...sir or madam,...
3 _____ – a large animal with thick fur	/beir/	_____ – empty/nude
4 _____ – correct/not wrong	/rɑit/	_____ – use a pen to do this
5 _____ – don't go/stay in one place	/weit/	_____ – in pounds, for example

2 73 Listen, repeat, and check your answers. In your language, do you have words that sound the same but have different spellings?

Close-up

Relative clauses **1** Combine each of the following sentences with *that* to make one new sentence.

a) I have a friend. He lives in San Diego. *I have a friend that lives in San Diego.*
b) I have a car. It isn't very easy to park.
c) I know a woman. She has a beautiful singing voice.
d) I went to a private school. It was a long way from my house.
e) My parents have two dogs. They like going for long walks.
f) I have a sister. She works in a store.
g) Last week I watched a very sad movie. It made me cry.

2 Work with a partner. Look at the new sentences you have written in 1. Underline the relative clauses in the new sentences. What is the subject of the verb in each relative clause?

For example: *I have a friend* [subject: *that*] [verb: *lives*] *in San Diego.*

3 In which sentences in 1 can you replace *that* with *which*? In which sentences can you replace *that* with *who*? What is the rule for using the relative pronouns *which, who,* and *that*?

4 How many of the sentences in 1 are true for you? Compare your answers with a partner.

5 The definitions in column A are ungrammatical. Correct each one by ~~crossing out~~ one unnecessary word. Then match the definitions with a word from column B.

A	B
a) An animal that ~~it~~ can smell water three miles away.	1 A saddle.
b) A person who he studies birds.	2 A kangaroo.
c) An animal that it sleeps standing up.	3 A mosquito.
d) The only animal—apart from humans—that it gets sunburn.	4 An elephant.
e) A word to describe people who they are afraid of spiders.	5 An ornithologist.
f) The thing that you sit on it when you ride a horse.	6 A pig.
g) An insect that you get malaria from it.	7 A horse.
h) An animal whose name it means "I don't understand."	8 Arachnophobic.

6 Use the ideas in the boxes (and your own) to write down three true statements about your feelings or the feelings of people you know well. Compare your statements with a partner.

I My mother My father My friend etc.	+	love(s) hate(s)	+	people men women children animals bars stores rooms etc.	+	who which that	+	are funny/serious. talk too quietly/loudly. are very cheap/expensive. drive too slowly/fast. are very big/small etc.

Language Reference: Relative clauses

A ***relative clause*** gives additional information about a person or a thing introduced in the main clause. It comes immediately after the person or thing it is describing.

A person ***who treats sick animals*** *is called a vet.*
I have a car ***that isn't very easy to park***.

We usually introduce a relative clause with a relative pronoun: ***who*** for people, ***which*** for things, and ***that*** for people or things. We usually use ***which*** only in written English and in formal spoken English. The relative pronoun becomes the subject (or the object) of the verb in the relative clause, so we don't need to use *she, him, it,* etc.

An ornithologist is a person ***who studies birds***. NOT ... ~~who he studies birds~~
A mosquito is an insect ***that you get malaria from***. NOT ... ~~that you get malaria from it~~

Animal Tales

Reading

1 Work in groups of three. You are going to read some true stories about the six animals in the pictures. Which animal do you think goes best with descriptions *A–F*?

A An animal that healed someone who was depressed.
B An animal that died of a broken heart.
C An animal that refused to be separated from another animal in the same house.
D An animal that knew when its owner was coming home.
E An animal that loved classical music.
F An animal that accidentally deleted some valuable files on a computer.

2 Work in groups of three. Student A, Student B, and Student C: Read your two animal stories and match a description in 1 to each story.

Student A

STORY 1

Mr. and Mrs. Roper live with their son, Robert, and a myna bird named Sammy. Robert travels a lot in his work, and he is sometimes away for weeks or even months. He doesn't always tell his parents when he is coming home, but he doesn't need to. Mr. and Mrs. Roper always know when their son is going to arrive because Sammy starts calling "Robbie" a few hours before Robert walks through the door.

STORY 2

Bill Bowell, a retired manager, was suffering from depression. The doctor gave him antidepressants, but they didn't help, and he was unable to work for twelve years.

Then he decided to swim with the dolphins.

"My life changed forever," says Bowell. "A dolphin named Simo looked into my eyes for a few minutes, and I started to cry. All my emotions erupted like a volcano. As I cried, Simo put his head on my chest and stayed very still." After swimming with dolphins, Bowell says he has fully recovered.

Student B

STORY 1

A man had to move to a new job a hundred twenty miles away. He owned a dog and a cat, and he loved them both. But he thought that the cat would prefer to stay in the same house with new owners.

So when he moved to a new house, he took only the dog.

About three weeks later, the dog suddenly disappeared. For several days, the man looked for his dog but didn't find him.

Then, seven weeks later, the dog showed up ... but he was not alone. By his side was the cat. They were tired and hungry after their long journey, and the cat's paws were bleeding. But they recovered quickly and were never separated again.

STORY 2

A bank worker in San Francisco decided to take his cat, Morris, into work with him one day. While the man was talking on the telephone, Morris walked across the keyboard of his computer and accidentally keyed in a secret code that deleted files worth $100,000. As you can imagine, the man's employers were not amused.

Student C

STORY 1

People say that fish are cold, but this story proves that they have feelings too.

A friend was moving to another country, so we took her pet goldfish and put it in a bowl with our goldfish. They lived together for six months, and when the friend came back, we separated them, and she took her goldfish home.

I immediately noticed that my goldfish was behaving strangely, banging against the side of the bowl. The next morning he was floating on the surface, dead.

Later that day, my friend called to say that her goldfish was also dead.

I believe they each died of a broken heart.

STORY 2

While on a camping trip a few years ago, my husband and I stopped in a quiet place for a picnic and played some Mozart on a CD player. After a few minutes, we looked up and realized that we were surrounded by cows who were listening to the music. When the Mozart was finished, we put on a CD of modern music. The cows immediately turned around and walked away.

3 Work in groups of three. Without looking at the book, take turns retelling your stories to the other people in your group. Explain which descriptions from 1 you have matched to your stories. Which story do you like best?

Vocabulary **1** The words and expressions in the box are from the stories in the previous section. Use them to complete this joke about a smart dog.

showed up	turned around	paw	decided to	stayed very still	walked away
looked into his eyes					

SMART DOG

For years, a dog (1) ***showed up*** on the butcher's doorstep every Wednesday morning to do his owner's shopping. On this Wednesday morning, the dog walked into the butcher's shop as usual with a purse around his neck. The butcher asked the dog what he wanted. He pointed his (2) ____ at the sausages. "How many pounds?" the butcher asked him. The dog (3) ____ and barked twice. The butcher packed two pounds of sausage. "Anything else?" he asked. The dog pointed to the hamburgers. "How many?" the butcher asked him. The dog barked four times, and the butcher packed four hamburgers. The dog then walked behind the counter and (4) ____ so the butcher could open his purse, take the right amount of money, and tie the meat around the dog's neck. Then the dog (5) ____ and (6) ____ . A regular customer was surprised to see the dog doing his shopping and (7) ____ follow him home. After about a mile, the dog approached a house and scratched at the door. When it opened, the customer said to the woman inside the house, "That's a very smart dog you have there." "Smart?" she replied. "Not really. That's the second time this week he's forgotten his front door keys."

2 74 Listen and check your answers to 1. Do you know any jokes or stories about animals? Tell your partner one of your jokes or stories.

Special Friends

Listening **1** 75 Listen to Tim, Gus, and Maxine being interviewed about their pets. Guess what their pets are from the words in the box. Compare your guesses with a partner. The answers are on page 127.

a cat	a rat	a pig	a dog	a hamster	a parrot	a spider	a snake

Tim

Gus

Maxine

2 Work with a partner. Look at the following list of pet characteristics. Check (✓) the ones that you think were mentioned in the interviews.

a) He's/She's a good companion.
b) He/She listens to my problems.
c) He/She makes me laugh when he/she does silly things.
d) We have a special bond.
e) He/She helps me make friends with other people with pets.
f) He/She scares people away.
g) He/She keeps me fit because I have to take him/her out for walks.
h) He/She looks cool.
i) He/She parties all night long.
j) He/She gives me unconditional love.

3 Listen to the interviews again and check your answers to 2. Put *T* for Tim, *G* for Gus, or *M* for Maxine if they mention that their pet has one of the characteristics.

4 Which of the characteristics in 2 would you look for in a pet? Which of these characteristics would you look for in a person? Discuss with a partner.

Close-up

Conditionals

Yasmina would like to be a tiger.

1 Work with a partner. The diagram shows the last question from the interview in the previous section. Discuss the questions.

If-clause	Main clause
If + past tense *If you were an animal,*	*would* + simple verb form *what animal would you like to be?*

a) Is the question about a real situation or an unreal situation?
b) Is the question about now or the past? What tense is used in the *If*-clause?

2 Replace the word *animal* in the diagram in 1 with words from the box and/or your own ideas. Ask your partner the questions. Discuss your answers.

a famous person	a fictional character	a color	a car	a month

3 Complete the *Unreal situation* column with conditional sentences so that they are true for you. Compare your sentences with your partner.

Real situation		Unreal situation
a) I'm not a member of the opposite sex.	➔	*If I were a member of the opposite sex, I'd/I wouldn't ____ .*
b) I'm not the president of my country.	➔	If ____ , I'd/I wouldn't ____ .
c) I don't have $1 million.	➔	If ____ , I'd/I wouldn't ____ .
d) I don't speak English fluently.	➔	If ____ , I'd/I wouldn't ____ .
e) I can't fly a plane.	➔	If ____ , I'd/I wouldn't ____ .

4 Work in small groups. Look at these "moral dilemmas." Complete them with the correct verb form and then discuss your answers to each one.

a) If you (**find**) a wallet in the street with $20, would you turn the wallet in to the police—but keep the cash?
b) If you saw your friend's partner kissing someone else, (**you tell**) your friend?
c) If a salesclerk (**give**) you too much change, would you keep the money and say nothing?
d) If a friend left his/her bag at your house by mistake, (**you look**) through it?
e) If you (**see**) some children stealing some chocolate from a store, would you tell the store owner?

5 Write down two more "moral dilemmas" beginning with *If* + past tense and pass them on to another group. Discuss the answers.

Language Reference: Conditionals

We can use a conditional sentence to talk about a present situation that is unreal or not probable. Conditional sentences have two clauses: an *If*-clause and a main clause.

***If*-clause**
To show that a present situation is unreal, we use a past tense.

Main clause
We usually use *would* + simple verb form in the main clause.

Real situation		Unreal situation
time (now) = simple present	➔	time (now) = simple past
*I **am** not an animal.*	➔	*If I **were/was** an animal, ...**
*I **live** in an apartment.*	➔	*If I **lived** in an igloo, ...*

If-clause	Main clause
If I had $1 million,	***I'd travel** around the world.*
If I could fly a plane,	***I'd sell** my car.*

*Note: We use ***were*** with singular pronouns *I, he, she,* and *it* to emphasize that the situation is unreal. You will also sometimes hear ***was*** in informal spoken English.

Reptiles

Reading **1** Read the article about a pet snake and explain the links between the following.

a) 2 years old—5 years old b) 6 inches—3 feet c) 2 minutes—3 months

KING JIM

My son has been interested in having a snake as a pet since he was two. I think he's fascinated by their power to make people like me run away in horror. I've never been big on the idea of having a snake in the house, and I was hoping he would get tired of asking for one in the end, but his stepfather went ahead and bought a little surprise snake for Louis's fifth birthday.

It was quite sweet: about six inches long and the width of a pencil—a non-venomous Californian King snake that Louis called King Jim. But then it grew and grew and grew. A year and a half later, it was about three feet long and as thick as a sausage. Some people objected to it so much that they stopped coming to our house.

Personally, I disapprove of keeping a wild animal as a pet. It must get so bored with going around and around in its cage. I know he's unhappy, because once when Louis left the cage door open for a couple of minutes, King Jim escaped in a flash. We worried about him dying of cold or hunger, but to our surprise, he showed up in the kitchen downstairs three months later.

When I think about it now, I can't believe we didn't tell our friends that we had an escaped snake in the house.

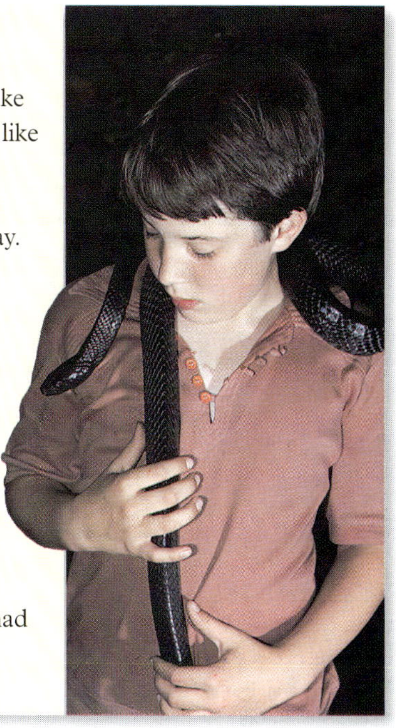

(Based on an article in the *Guardian Weekend*)

2 Would you have a pet snake? What's the most unusual pet you know? Tell your partner.

Vocabulary: prepositions after verbs and adjectives

1 Study the examples from the article above. Then complete the sentences to make some true and some false statements about yourself.

verb or adjective	preposition	*-ing* form or noun or pronoun
My son has been interested	*in*	*having a snake.* (line 1)
Some people objected	*to*	*it.* (line 9)

a) At school, I was fascinated *by* … (line 2)
b) I've never been big ____ … (line 3)
c) As a child, I never got tired ____ … (line 4)
d) My parents disapprove ____ … (line 11)
e) I'll never get bored ____ … (line 12)
f) I often worry ____ … (line 14)
g) I feel happy when I think ____ … (line 16)

2 Work with a partner. Read your partner's statements from 1 and guess which statements are true and which are false.

Anecdote

1 76 Listen to Mandy talking about her friend's pet iguana. Which of the following topics does she talk about?

- ☐ What kind of animal is it?
- ☐ Who is its owner?
- ☐ What's its name?
- ☐ How old is it?
- ☐ What does it look like?
- ☐ What kind of personality does it have?
- ☐ Where does it sleep?
- ☐ What does it eat?
- ☐ Does it need much exercise?
- ☐ Can it do any tricks?

2 Work with a partner. Write down as much information as you can remember about the topics Mandy talks about. Listen again and check your answers.

3 Think about a pet that you know: yours or somebody else's. You are going to tell your partner about it. Choose from the list in 1 the things you want to talk about. Think about what you will say and what language you will need.

18 *Weird*

Work in small groups. Look at the photograph below and discuss the questions.

- What do you know about crop circles?
- Who or what do you think made them?
- How do you think they are made?

crop circles Patterns that began mysteriously appearing in fields in England and some other European countries in the 1980s.

Reading

LANGUAGE TOOLBOX

Who/What do you think . . . ?
I think . . .
I don't think . . .
Maybe it's . . .
I have no idea.
I don't have a clue.

Many theories have been suggested about who or what causes crop circles. Read this list of possible explanations and decide which is most and least believable. Discuss your answers with your partner.

THE CREAM OF THE CROP CIRCLE THEORIES

WIND Strong winds blow the corn into spiral patterns.

ALIENS The circles are landing sites for alien spacecraft or messages from other planets. People say they have seen bright flashing lights on the nights when crop circles have appeared.

MAGNETIC FORCES The crop circles are produced by magnetic forces under the earth.

WEAPONS TESTING The crop circles are caused by military tests that the army wants to keep secret.

HELICOPTERS The patterns are caused by the wind produced by helicopter rotor blades.

HOAXERS Groups of people create the crop circles at night. They say that they have made most, but not all, of the crop circles over the years.

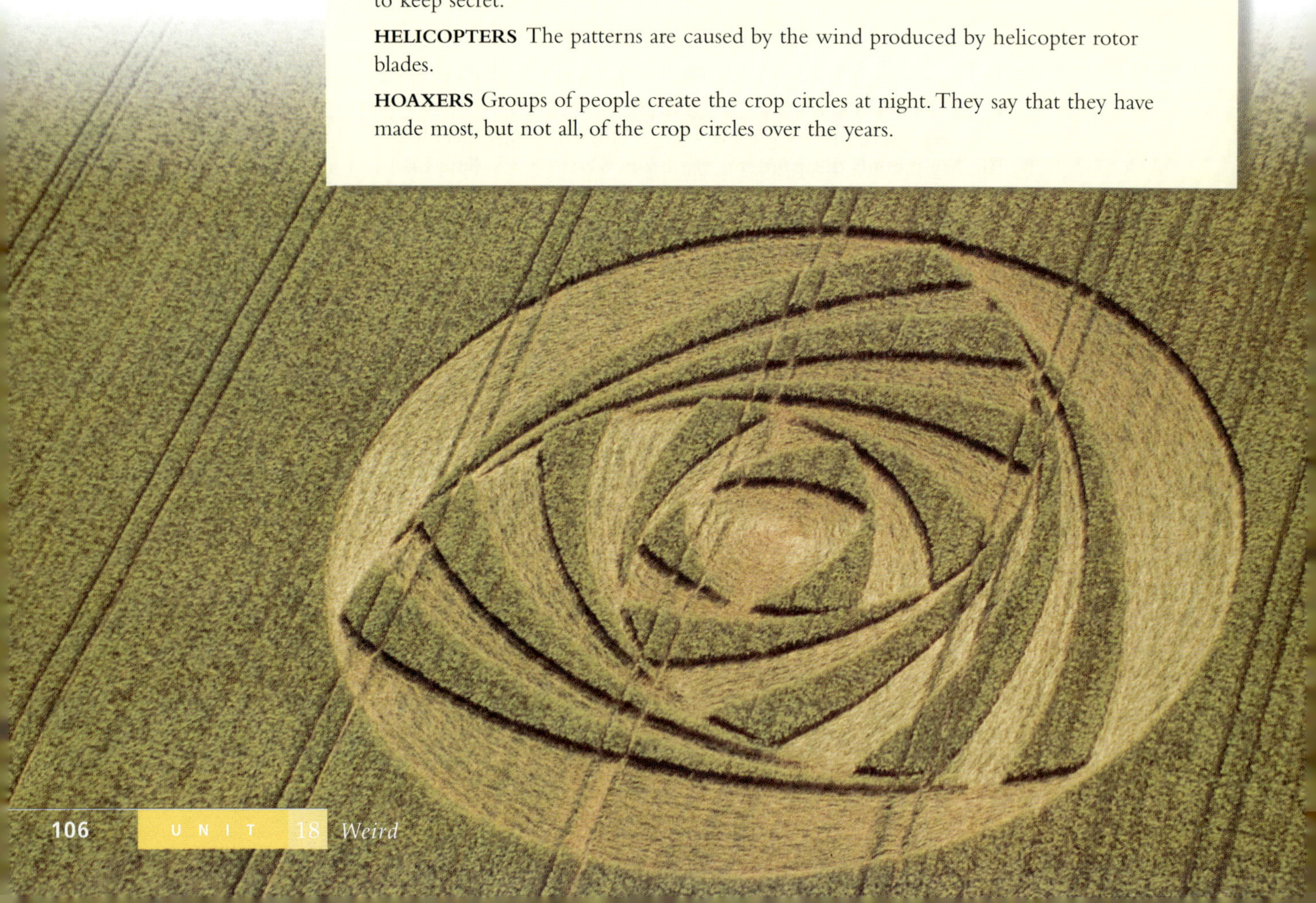

The Mother of All Circles

Listening

1 77 One night in August 2001, the crop circle in this photograph appeared in southern England. You are going to listen to a crop circle expert being interviewed about it. Listen and complete each question with the correct word.

a) How ____ have you been interested in crop circles?
b) How ____ is it exactly?
c) How ____ circles are there all together?
d) How ____ does it take to make a crop circle?
e) How ____ have crop circles existed?

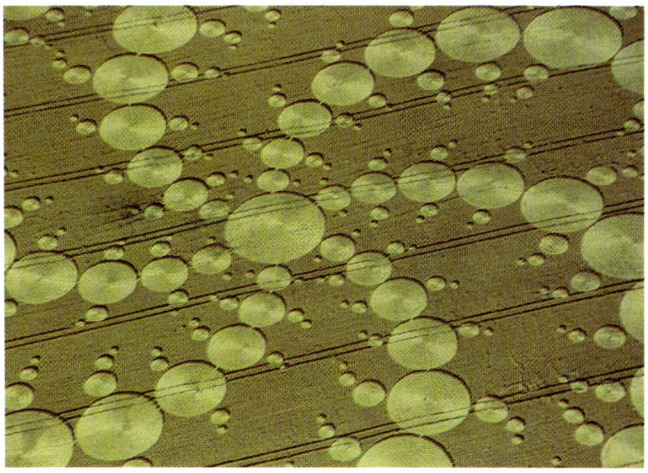

Alton Barnes, Hampshire, England

2 Work with a partner. Match the questions in 1 to the answers below. Listen to the interview again and check your ideas.

1 About a half a mile wide.
2 Since 1980.
3 For about eleven years.
4 More than 400.
5 A few hours or several days.

3 What information in the interview did you find most surprising? How do *you* think the Alton Barnes crop circle was formed? Discuss with your partner.

Vocabulary: *How* + adjective / adverb ... ?

1 All of the questions in 1 above use the construction *How* + adjective/adverb. Make eight more questions by combining the question beginnings (*a–h*) with the most appropriate question ends (*1–8*). In some cases, more than one combination is possible.

a) How long	1 cousins do you have?
b) How often	2 does your car go?
c) How many	3 do you travel by train?
d) How much	4 is the oldest living person in your family?
e) How far	5 does it take you to get to work/school?
f) How fast	6 is it from your house to the nearest beach?
g) How old	7 do you know your neighbors?
h) How well	8 cash do you have on you right now?

2 Use the questions in 1 and your own ideas to interview your partner.

3 Complete the chart by writing down how long it takes you to do each activity. Guess the time it takes your partner to do the same things and then ask questions to check your ideas.

For example: *How long does it take you to get up in the morning?*

	Activity	You	Your partner
How long ... ?	• get up in the morning • eat lunch during a work day • buy presents for people you love • choose from a menu in a restaurant • decide whether you like someone or not • get ready to go out for the evening • get to sleep at night		

Incredible but True

Reading

1 You are going to read three true stories. In each case, a sentence is missing from the story. Match each of the sentences with a story and then reinsert the sentence in the appropriate position–*1*, *2*, or *3*.

a) She was now nearly 22 and hadn't met the love of her life yet.
b) At that time, Amy didn't know that Ian had just started a trip from Sydney to London.
c) It was a reply from another Laura Buxton, who had found the balloon in her backyard 140 miles away.

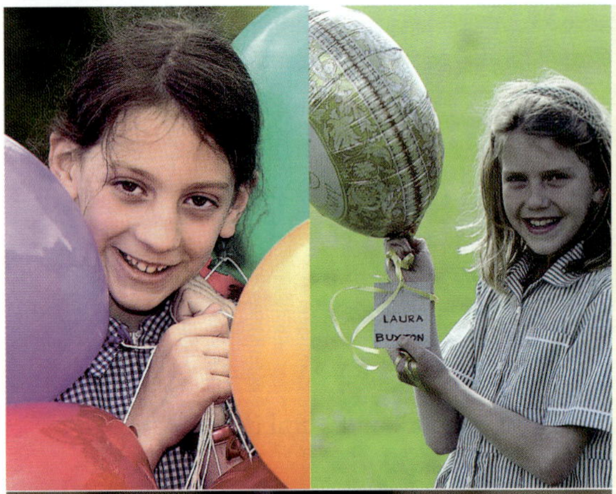

A Two Lauras

Laura Buxton, 10, was celebrating her grandparents' golden wedding anniversary when she had an idea. **1** She decided to release a gold and white helium-filled balloon with her name and address and a note attached. In the note, she asked the person who found the balloon to write back. Ten days later, a letter arrived at her home. **2** Both Lauras were 10 years old, and each has a three-year-old black Labrador, a guinea pig, and a rabbit. **3** "I talked to Laura on the phone," said the first Laura. "I hope we can become best friends. We have lots in common."

B Worlds Apart

Amy Dolby took her seat on the flight from London to Sydney, Australia. She was going to Australia to surprise her boyfriend, Ian Johnstone. **1** He wanted to propose to Amy on July 1 because this was the fifth anniversary of their relationship. **2** They both stopped in Singapore to wait for connecting flights, but they didn't know that they were sitting a few feet away from each other. **3** Ian arrived in Amy's hometown just as she knocked on his door in Sydney. When they found out what had happened, Ian proposed over the phone, and Amy accepted.

C Text Before Marriage

A clairvoyant had once told Emily Brown that she would meet her husband when she was 21. **1** One day, she tapped the text message, "Do you want to talk?" into her cell phone. She then invented a number and sent the message. She didn't know that the number belonged to her future husband. **2** Peter Baldwin was at work 140 miles away when he got the message. He called Emily, and they talked for about an hour. **3** They found that they had lots in common and made arrangements to meet. They got married six months later.

2 **78** Listen and check your answers to 1.

3 Work in small groups. Discuss these questions.

- Have you ever read or heard about "incredible but true" stories like the stories in 1?
- Do you know any people (couples, friends, co-workers) who have met in a strange way?
- Have any strange coincidences or "small world" incidents ever happened to you?

Vocabulary: *have/make/ take* + noun structures

1 Refer to the stories in the previous section and answer these questions.

a) Who had an idea?
b) Who made arrangements to meet someone?
c) Who took her seat on her flight to Australia?

2 Work with a partner. Look at the following statements and choose the appropriate verb in each case.

a) If you don't **have/make/take** risks, you won't succeed in life.
b) You should never **have/make/take** a promise if you can't keep it.
c) Everybody should **have/make/take** an experience of doing something dangerous once in their life.
d) All parents should **have/make/take** a course in parenting skills.
e) The press should not **have/make/take** photographs of famous people without their permission.
f) **Having/Making/Taking** mistakes is part of the process of learning a language.
g) The most important thing in life is to get a job where you can **have/make/take** lots of money.

3 Work with a partner. Decide if you agree or disagree with the statements in 2.

Close-up

Past perfect

Language Reference p. 110

Verb Structures p. 129

1 Work with a partner. Look at the sentence from one of the stories in the previous section and discuss the following questions.

At that time, Amy didn't know that Ian had just started a trip from Sydney to London.

a) Both underlined verb structures describe past events. What is the name of each tense?
b) Which tense shows clearly that one past event happened before the other past event?
c) How do you form these tenses? Complete the chart.

	Affirmative	Negative	Question
Simple past	1 ____	She didn't know	2 ____ ?
Past perfect	He'd (had) started	3 ____	4 ____ ?

2 You are going to read two excerpts from a story titled *Reincarnation*. Read the first excerpt. Why did Jenny Cockell decide to travel to Ireland?

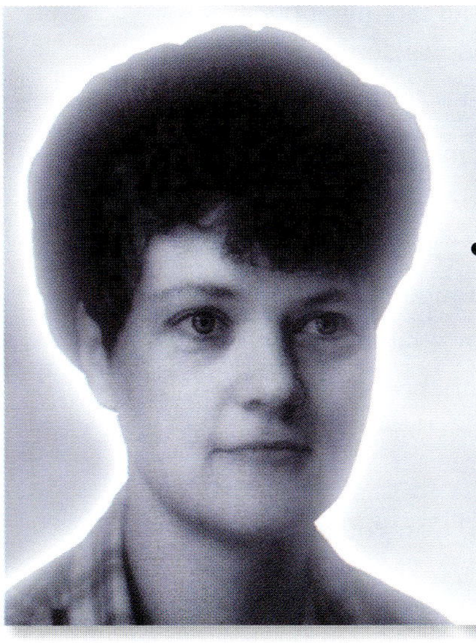

Reincarnation

Jenny Cockell was sure that she (1) **lived/had lived** before. As a child, she remembered her past life in her dreams. In particular, she often dreamed about Mary Sutton, a young Irish woman who (2) **died/had died** more than twenty years before Jenny was born. Over the years, Jenny became convinced that her dreams (3) **were/had been** real memories and that she (4) **was/had been** Mary in a previous life.

In her dreams, she saw the house in Ireland where Mary and her family (5) **lived/had lived**. As her visions continued and became more detailed, Jenny (6) **realized/had realized** that Mary (7) **died/had died** in 1930 and that her children could still be alive. She (8) **wanted/had wanted** to find out and decided to travel to Ireland.

3 79 Work with a partner. Complete the first excerpt by choosing the most appropriate tense (simple past or past perfect) for each of the numbered verbs. Listen and check your answers.

4 Read the second excerpt. Who did Sonny think Jenny was? What do you think?

> In Ireland, Jenny quickly (1 **find**) the house that she (2 **see**) in her dreams. She then found out that Mary Sutton (3 **die**) in the early 1930s after giving birth to the last of eight children. After their mother's death, the children had all been sent to orphanages, but she finally contacted the eldest son, Sonny. It was an emotional day when Jenny (4 **meet**) the son she (5 **not see**) in fifty years. "I talked to him about our family life together. I (6 **remind**) him of the day when he (7 **catch**) a rabbit. There were lots of other memories, and they convinced him that I (8 **be**) his mother in a previous life."
>
> Jenny Cockell has written the story of her extraordinary past life experiences in a book titled *Yesterday's Children*.

5 **80** Work with a partner. Complete the second excerpt by rewriting each of the numbered verbs in the most appropriate tense. Listen and check your answers.

6 Work with a partner. Discuss times you have felt some of the emotions in the box. Explain what had happened to make you feel that way.

When was the last time you	felt were	exhausted sad proud on top of the world frightened embarrassed jealous in a bad mood	?	What had happened? What had you done?

For example: *The last time I felt exhausted was on Friday. I'd been out till 3:00 A.M. ...*

Language Reference: Past perfect

We use the past perfect when we are talking about the past and we want to refer to an earlier past time. The past perfect clearly shows that one past event happened earlier than other past events.

*As her visions **continued** and **became** more detailed, Jenny **realized** that Mary **had died** in 1930.*

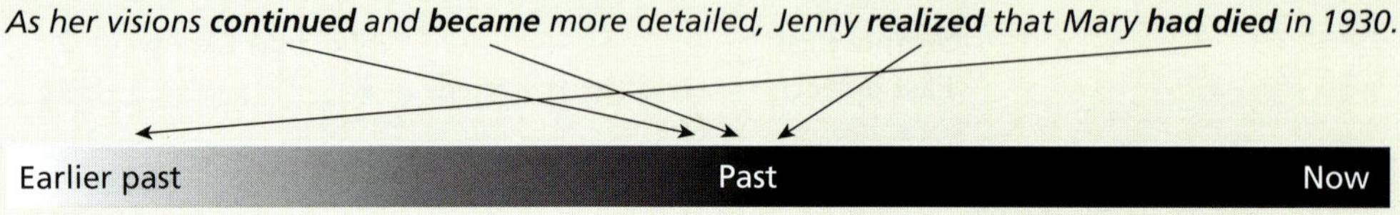

Anecdote

1 **81** You are going to listen to Don and then Lidia talking about strange experiences they have had. Which of the following topics do they talk about?

Don	Lidia	
☐	☐	Who had the strange experience? You, a member of your family, ...?
☐	☐	Where was the person when it happened?
☐	☐	Was the person alone?
☐	☐	Did the person see or hear something strange?
☐	☐	Did the person meet somebody in a strange situation?
☐	☐	What exactly was strange about the experience?
☐	☐	How did you or the person feel?
☐	☐	What happened after the experience?
☐	☐	What do you think about the experience? Can you explain it?

Don and Lidia

2 Work with a partner. Write down as much information as you can remember about each story. Listen again and check your answers. Which story do you think is stranger?

3 Think of a strange experience you or somebody you know has had. You are going to tell a partner about it. Choose from the list in 1 the things you want to talk about. Think about what you will say and what language you will need.

We Are Not Alone

Reading and speaking

1 You are going to read a short account of a famous UFO incident—a mysterious crash in Roswell, New Mexico, in 1947. How many different explanations are there for the crash? Do you believe any of the explanations?

Roswell, New Mexico

On July 8, 1947, the U.S. Air Force told the public that a flying saucer had crashed in Roswell, New Mexico, and that they had found bodies of aliens. Later the same day, the U.S. Air Force changed their story and told reporters that the flying saucer was in fact a weather balloon.

The story became famous when people said that the government had covered up the real story. Thirty years later, witnesses told newspapers that they had seen the aliens. They described the aliens in detail, and models were made according to their descriptions.

In 1994, the U.S. Air Force changed the story again. Now they said that the crash at Roswell in 1947 had been a top secret radar balloon used for spying on the USSR. When government officials investigated, they found that all documents recorded at Roswell from 1945 to 1949 had been destroyed more than forty years ago.

2 Work in small groups. Discuss these questions.

- Do you think there are forms of life on other planets?
- Do you think aliens have visited the Earth?
- What do you think aliens might look like?
- If you saw a UFO, what would you do?
- If you met an alien, what would you ask?
- If you had to elect someone to meet the alien leader, who would you choose? Why?
- If you could travel in a time machine, would you choose to go forward or backward in time? Why?

Writing

1 Work with a partner. Discuss ways of completing *The Night I Met an Alien* by answering the questions. Take notes and add as much detail as possible.

2 Write your story from the notes you took in 1. Compare your stories with other people in the class.

THE NIGHT I MET AN ALIEN

It was an ordinary evening.
What time was it?
What was the weather like?
What were you doing?

For some reason, I looked up at the sky, and I saw a strange object.
What did the object look like?

To my surprise, it landed, and an alien got out.
What did the alien look like?
How did you feel?

Then it spoke to me in perfect English.
What did it say?
What was its voice like?

I asked it what I'd always wanted to ask an alien.
What did you ask?

It answered my question.
What did it say?

Eventually, it got back in the object and flew away. I stood still for a while, and when I turned around, I noticed that something had changed.
What had changed?

My life would never be the same again.

19 Wheels

Reading

1 You are going to read three descriptions of people's first cars. Match each description (*A–C*) with one of the pictures (*1–3*) below. Which car caused its owner the most problems?

MY FIRST CAR

1

2

3

A My first car was a Ford Maverick. I think someone gave it to me—it was a real clunker. It used to break down almost every time I went out in it.

Once I was driving along a country road and the hood blew up against the windshield and blocked my view of the road. It was really dangerous because I couldn't see anything.

Another time, it was raining heavily, and one of the windshield wipers fell off. I had to stop and wait for the rain to stop.

I used to have a love/hate relationship with that car—I loved it when it worked, but I hated it when it broke down.

B It wasn't my car; it was my boyfriend's. It was a blue VW Beetle with a sunroof and whitewall tires.

Every weekend we used to drive to the country with our tent in the back and drive until we felt like stopping. Sometimes we took friends.

It wasn't a big car, but I remember one weekend we went to Montreal with four friends. There were six of us in this little car! I don't think we took any luggage, because there wasn't any space for suitcases. The engine was in the back, and there was only a tiny trunk in the front. But we didn't use to worry about that kind of thing when we were younger.

C Daddy gave me my first car when I was 17. I didn't even have my driver's license. It was a sweet little red Ferrari with a wooden steering wheel and black seats. It was cute, but I didn't use it much, because I used to prefer motorcycles. All my boyfriends had big motorcycles. My daddy used to introduce me to all these nice guys—lawyers and businessmen—but I wasn't interested in them. I was a rebel, and I used to enjoy the danger of going on fast motorcycles.

My poor daddy—I used to drive him crazy.

2 What was the first car you drove? Or what was the first car you remember going in as a child? Describe it to your partner.

Vocabulary: cars

1 Find nine words and expressions in the text in the previous section that describe parts of a car.

2 Work in small groups. Imagine you are going to buy a new car. Divide the following features into "important" and "not important." What other features are important in a car?

air bags	air conditioning	easy to park	economical to run	electric sunroof
good stereo	large trunk	leather seats	nice appearance	power steering
powerful engine	radial tires	spacious interior		

Anecdote

Imagine your dream car. You are going to tell your partner about it. Choose from the list below the things you want to talk about. Think about what you are going to say and how you are going to say it.

- ☐ What kind of car is it?
- ☐ Is it a modern car, or is it an old model?
- ☐ What color is it?
- ☐ What's it like inside?
- ☐ What kind of seats does it have?
- ☐ What special features does it have?
- ☐ What's the top speed?
- ☐ What CDs do you have in your car?
- ☐ Where would you like to go in your car?
- ☐ Who would you take with you?

Close-up

Past time: *used to* + simple verb form

Language Reference p. 114

1 Work with a partner. Look at these excerpts from the article in the previous section. Match each underlined verb structure with a description (*1–3*). In which case is it *not* possible to use *used to* + simple verb form to talk about the past?

a) "Every weekend we used to drive to the country…"
b) "…one weekend we went to Montreal…"
c) "I used to have a love/hate relationship with that car…"

1 A single action in the past
2 A repeated action in the past
3 A state in the past

2 Work with a partner. Look at the following sentences. Where it is possible, replace the simple past with *used to/didn't use to* + simple verb form.

When I was a child…
a) My parents had a big old Buick. *My parents used to have a big old Buick.*
b) My mother drove me to school every day.
c) I didn't like going on long car trips. I got car sick.
d) One summer we went to Canada on a camping trip.
e) My parents never cleaned the car. It smelled awful.
f) Eventually my parents sold the car and bought a smaller one.

3 Change the sentences in 2 so that they are true for you. Compare with a partner.

4 Work with a partner. Use the topics in the box and your own ideas to talk about and compare your life now with your life ten years ago.

the vacations you go on	the car you have	the people you go out with
the TV programs you watch	the amount of sleep you get	the hairstyle you have
the things you do on weekends	the music you listen to	

For example: *I used to spend every summer vacation at my grandparents' house at the shore. These days I usually go abroad. I love traveling…*

Language Reference: *Used to*

We can use *used to* + simple verb form to talk about past habits (repeated actions in the past) or past states. It describes things that were true in the past but are not true now.

Every weekend ***we used to drive*** *to the country.*

We didn't use to worry *about that kind of thing.*

What kind of car ***did you use to have****?*

For and against Cars

1 Work in small groups. Discuss the advantages and disadvantages of owning a car. Write down as many points as you can.

2 82 You are going to listen to three friends discussing the same thing. Listen to their conversation. How many of the points you wrote down in 1 do they mention?

3 Work with a partner. Complete the conversation between Karen, Ron, and Jill with one word in each space. Then listen and check your answers.

K: You're late!

R: Yes, I'm really sorry—I had to wait forever for a bus.

J: Why didn't you drive?

R: Ah, well. I sold my car.

K: Oh, are you getting a new one?

R: No, I'm not getting another car. I've decided to live without one.

J: Wow—what made you do that?

R: I (1) *think* there are too many cars, and this city is far too polluted.

J: Well, that's true, (2) ___ a car is useful.

R: I don't think (3) ___ . Not in the city, anyway. I can never find anywhere to park, and you spend most of the time sitting in traffic jams.

K: But how are you going to get to work?

R: By bicycle.

K: (4) ___ you think bicycles are dangerous?

R: Not really. I don't think they're as dangerous as cars.

J: Well, I couldn't do without my car. I have to take the kids to school every day.

R: I don't (5) ___ children get enough exercise these days—they should walk to school.

K: Well, I don't have children, but I (6) ___ with Jill—I couldn't live without my car. I sometimes have to come home late from the office.

R: Why don't you take the bus? Public transportation is very good.

K: That's not (7) ___ . The buses are not very regular where I work, and anyway, as a woman, I don't feel safe waiting for a bus late at night.

R: O.K., I see what you (8) ___ , but aren't you worried about pollution?

J: Of course, but you don't understand—it's easy for you to worry about the environment. I have to worry about carrying the groceries and kids and…

R: O.K., O.K., you're (9) ___ ! Come on. Let's change the subject. Hey, (10) ___ do you think of my new haircut?

4 83 Listen and repeat the highlighted expressions. Copy the stress and intonation exactly.

5 Whose opinion do you agree with most?

Close-up

Opinions

1 Look at the highlighted text in the conversation in the previous section. Find another expression to show each of the following functions.

a) Ask for an opinion: (1) *Don't you think…* (2) ____
b) Give an opinion: (1) *I think…* (2) ____
c) Agree partly with an opinion: (1) *Well, that's true, but…* (2) ____
d) Agree completely with an opinion: (1) *I agree with…* (2) ____
e) Disagree with an opinion: (1) *I don't think so.* (2) ____

2 Work in groups of three. Complete the following task.

a) Choose one of the topics in the box (or your own idea) and write down all the advantages and disadvantages that you can think of.
b) Write a short conversation between three friends with your ideas from *a*. Use expressions from 1.
c) Act out your conversation in front of the class. Vote for the best conversation.

> fast food   living abroad   being a woman or a man   being rich or famous
> public transportation   marriage   cloning   capital punishment
> living with your parents   private education

Advice and suggestions

1 **84** You are going to listen to a radio talk show called *Road Rage*. Listeners call the radio station with travel questions and problems, and the host, Dave Pearl, gives them advice. Listen and check (✓) which of the following problems are mentioned.

a) I want to go somewhere nice on vacation, but I hate flying.
b) I'm sick of wasting time in traffic jams.
c) I'm a bus driver, and I don't get enough exercise.
d) My husband, who is usually kind and considerate, gets very aggressive when he is driving. It frightens me.
e) I can drive, but I can't pass my test.
f) I don't want to contribute to the pollution of the environment.

2 Work with a partner. Dave gives Mark three pieces of advice. Listen again and match the beginnings with the ends of each sentence. Do you think this is good advice?

a) Why don't you…	1 use public transportation.
b) You could…	2 learn a new language.
c) If I were you, I'd…	3 work at home?

3 Work with a partner. If you were Dave Pearl, what advice would you give to the second caller, Sharon? Use the sentence beginnings in 2 and make some suggestions.

4 Work with a partner. Invent and act out short conversations where Student A has a problem and Student B gives some advice. Use the other travel problems in 1 or your own ideas as your starting point.

Language Reference: Opinions, advice, and suggestions

There are many ways to ask for, give, agree with, or disagree with opinions.

Ask for an opinion: ***What do you think of*** *my new jacket?*
Give an opinion: ***I think*** *it's great.* ***I don't think*** *it's very nice.*
Agree with an opinion: Partly: ***That's true, but…*** ***I see what you mean, but…***
Completely: ***I agree with you.*** ***You're right.***
Disagree with an opinion: ***I don't think so.*** ***That's not true.***

There are many ways of giving advice or making suggestions.

Why don't you *work at home?* ***You could*** *use public transportation.*
If I were you, I'd *learn a new language.*

A Family Vacation

Reading and listening

Bill Bryson

Bill Bryson was born in the United States but lived for many years in England. He's the best-selling author of many humorous travel books.

1 85 Read and listen to this excerpt from a book called *The Lost Continent,* by Bill Bryson. He is describing the vacation trips he used to take with his family. Is each of the following statements true or false? Compare your answers with a partner.

a) The writer used to go on vacation with his parents and his cousins.
b) The children used to make a "bomb" that looked like a porcupine.
c) The "bombs" used to make other cars crash.
d) The parents never used to understand why other drivers got angry.
e) Most of the time, the mother used to keep quiet.

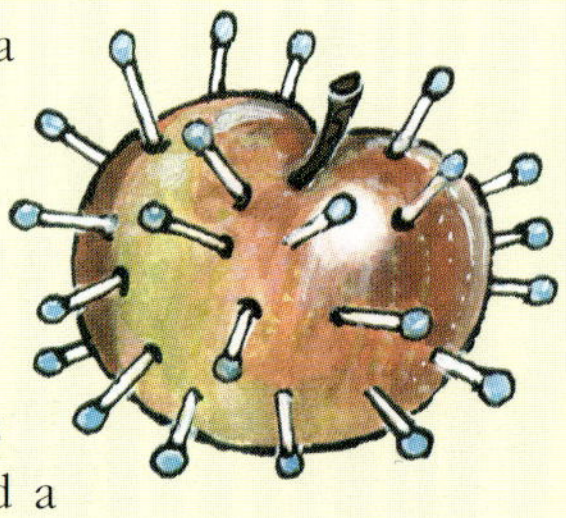

In my memory, our vacations were always taken in a big blue Rambler station wagon. It was a cruddy car—my dad always bought cruddy cars, until he got to the male menopause and started buying zippy red convertibles—but it had space. My brother, sister, and I in the back were miles away from my parents up front. We quickly discovered that if you stuck matches into an apple or hard-boiled egg so that it resembled a porcupine and casually dropped it out the window, it was like a bomb. It would explode with a small bang and a surprisingly big flash of blue flame, causing cars following behind to veer in an amusing fashion.

My dad, miles away up front, never knew what was going on and could not understand why all day long cars would zoom up alongside him, with the driver gesticulating furiously before tearing off into the distance. "What was that all about?" he would say to my mother.

"I don't know, dear," my mother would answer mildly. My mother only ever said two things. She said, "I don't know, dear." And she said, "Can I get you a sandwich, honey?"

Occasionally on our trips she would volunteer other pieces of intelligence like, "I think you hit that dog/man/blind person back there, honey," but mostly she wisely kept quiet.

(From *The Lost Continent,* by Bill Bryson)

2 Match adverbs underlined in the text in 1 with adverbs from the box below to get pairs with similar meanings.

angrily	in a relaxed way	intelligently	gently	rapidly

3 Find the following words in the text and choose the most appropriate meaning from the alternatives.

a) a station wagon (line 2): (1) *a big car with a long body;* (2) *a small sports car*
b) cruddy (line 2): (1) *lovely and new;* (2) *old and ugly*
c) zippy (line 4): (1) *fast;* (2) *slow*
d) to veer (line 11): (1) *to continue driving in a straight line;* (2) *to change direction suddenly*
e) zoom up (line 13): (1) *drive slowly;* (2) *drive fast*
f) tearing off (line 14): (1) *driving away fast;* (2) *driving away slowly*

4 What did you use to do to pass the time on long car trips when you were a child? Tell your partner.

24 Hours from Tulsa

Song

1 Work with a partner. The pictures illustrate a song called *24 Hours from Tulsa*. Discuss which is the most logical order for the story.

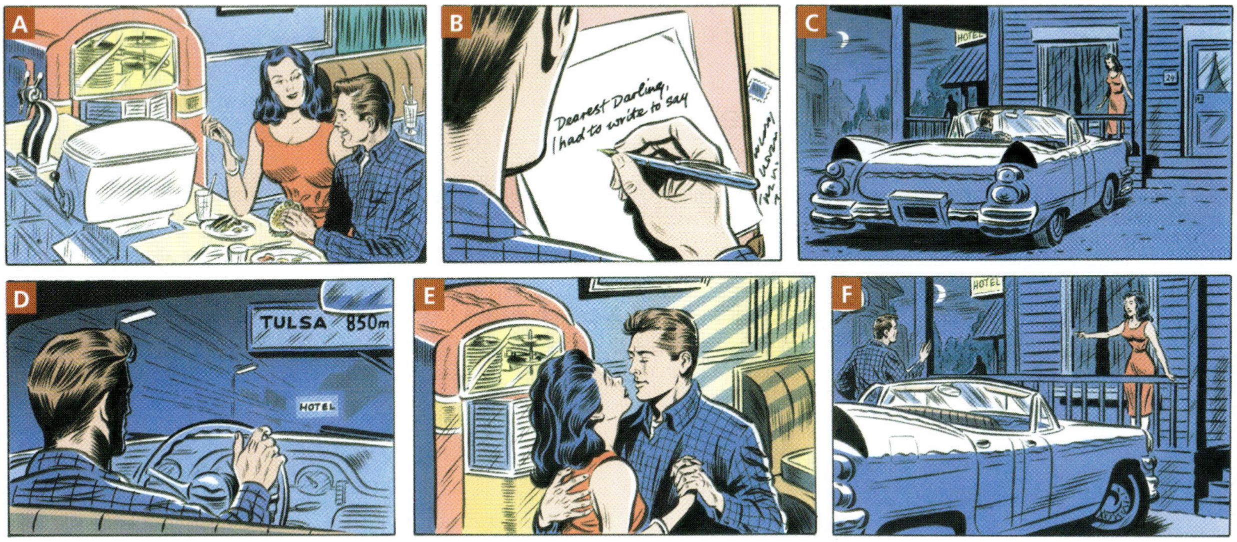

2 86 Listen and read the lyrics of the song and check your ideas in 1.

Dearest Darling,
I had to write to say that I won't be home anymore.
'Cause something happened to me,
While I was driving (1) ____ and I'm not the same
anymore.

Oh, I was only twenty-four hours from Tulsa,
Ah, only one day away from your arms,
I saw a welcoming (2) ____ ,
And stopped to rest for the night.

And that is when I saw her,
As I pulled (3) ____ outside of the small hotel
she was there.
And so I walked up to her,
Asked where I could get (4) ____ to eat and
she showed me where.

Oh, I was only twenty-four hours from Tulsa,
Ah, only one day away from your arms.
She took me to the cafe.
I asked her if she would stay.
She said okay.

Oh, I was only twenty-four hours from Tulsa,
Ah, only one day away from your arms.
The jukebox started to play
And nighttime (5) ____ into day.

As we were dancing (6) ____ ,
All of a sudden I lost (7) ____ as I held her charms.
And I caressed her, kissed her,
Told her I'd die before I would let her out of my arms.

Oh, I was only twenty-four hours from Tulsa,
Ah, only one day away from your arms.
I hate to do (8) ____ to you,
But I love somebody new.
What can I do?

And I can never, never, never
Go home again.

3 Complete the lyrics with words from the box. Listen again and check your answers.

closely	control	home	in	light	something	this	turned

4 The song is the story of why a man has decided to break up with his partner. Work in small groups. Discuss these questions.

a) What do you think of the man in the song?
b) What do you think of the woman at the hotel in the song?
c) What do you think is the kindest or cruelest way to break up with a partner?

24 Hours from Tulsa

This was a big hit for Gene Pitney in 1963. Gene Pitney has been a star for over thirty years.

20 Review 4

Big Game Lottery

Language reviewed: past time—*used to* (Unit 19); prepositions after verbs and adjectives (Unit 17); *will* for prediction (Unit 16); future time clauses (Unit 16); conditionals (Unit 17)

Work with a partner. Look at the proverbs below. Do you have similar proverbs in your language? Which of these proverbs do you agree with?

"The best things in life are free."
"Money is the root of all evil."
"If something can go wrong, it will go wrong."

Reading

1 Read the newspaper article about a lottery winner. If you were in Mrs. Alvarado's position, would you feel the same as her? Why/Why not?

Colorado Woman Wins Top Prize

A 67-year-old woman has won $198 million in the Big Game Lottery, the biggest prize in U.S. history. Eva Alvarado, who **moved** to the United States in 1984, lives in Colorado Springs, where she works as a cleaner in a home for mentally handicapped children.

Two years ago, Mrs. Alvarado's husband **died** in an accident in the potato factory in Bingham County, Idaho, where they both **worked**. "We **hated** that factory, and we **played** the lottery every week because we **dreamed** of escaping to a better life," Mrs. Alvarado **said** yesterday. "But when Ramón died, I moved here, and I don't want to change my life now. This job is the luckiest thing that has ever happened to me. I don't want to leave the children."

Mrs. Alvarado **told** reporters that she wanted to spend some of the money on a new playroom for the children's home.

2 Work with a partner. Read the article again. Which four verbs in **bold** can you replace with the structure *used to* + simple verb form? Why can't you replace the other verbs with the same structure?

Past time: *used to*

1 Look at the following statements. Where possible, replace the simple past verb forms with *used to* or *didn't use to*.

a) I was born in a hospital.
b) As a child, I lived in a small town.
c) I shared a bedroom with my brother/sister.
d) I watched the Cartoon Network on TV every day.
e) My parents gave me lots of pocket money.
f) We went to Disneyland once as a special treat.
g) I didn't enjoy English classes at school.

2 How many of the statements in 1 were true for you as a child? Rewrite the sentences so that they are all true for you. Compare your sentences with a partner.

Listening

1 87 You are going to listen to a radio talk show where callers comment on Mrs. Alvarado's lottery win. Complete each of these comments with an appropriate preposition. Listen and check your answers.

a) Mrs. Alvarado is obviously very fond ____ the children.
b) She will soon get tired ____ all the letters.
c) She needs to think ____ her future now.
d) She doesn't sound very excited ____ winning the lottery.
e) She's more interested ____ the children than the money.
f) She doesn't have to worry ____ the future anymore.

2 Look at some predictions about Mrs. Alvarado's life. Listen again and check (✓) the ones you heard on the radio program.

a) She'll quit her job soon.
b) Life will be very difficult.
c) Everyone will ask her for money.
d) She'll buy a new house and a car.
e) She'll give most of the money away.
f) She'll need a financial advisor.
g) She'll take a long vacation.
h) She'll change her mind about giving money to the children's home.

3 Work with a partner. Which of the predictions in 2 would you make? Do you think it is possible to continue the same lifestyle if you win the lottery? What would you do if you won $198 million?

Future time clauses

1 Complete each sentence with the correct alternative.

a) As soon as the class **'ll end/ends**, Becky's going to buy a lottery ticket.
b) Terry will get married when he **'ll meet/meets** the right girl.
c) As soon as Ron **'ll get/gets** home tonight, he's going to do his homework.
d) If it **'ll rain/rains** tomorrow, Jenny will probably come in by car.
e) Sandy will probably retire when she **'ll be/is** fifty.
f) Tim will probably get a well-paying job when he **'ll finish/finishes** college.

2 Work with a partner. Replace the names in 1 with names of people in the class. How many true statements can you make?

Conditionals

1 Change the following "facts" if necessary to make them all true for you. Then write conditional "dream" sentences. Compare your sentences with your partner.

	Facts		Dreams
a)	I don't have $1 million.	➔	*If I... If I had $1 million, I'd buy a beautiful yacht.*
b)	I don't speak perfect English.	➔	*If I...*
c)	I'm not the mayor of this city.	➔	*If I...*
d)	I can't travel in time.	➔	*If I...*
e)	I'm a man/woman.	➔	*If I...*

2 Work with a partner. Choose a conditional sentence from 1 and take turns adding to a chain of conditions. Who can create the longest "conditional chain"?

For example:

STUDENT A

If I had $1 million, I'd buy a beautiful yacht.

STUDENT B

If I bought a beautiful yacht, I'd sail around the Caribbean.

STUDENT A

If I sailed around the Caribbean, I'd... etc.

It's Your Lucky Day!

Language reviewed: relative clauses and relative pronouns (Unit 17); *have/make/take* + noun structures (Unit 18); *how* + adjective/adverb (Unit 18); past perfect (Unit 18)

Relative clauses

1 Complete each question by choosing the correct alternative.

a) Do you know anyone who **is/he is** really lucky or unlucky?
b) Are there any numbers that **are/they are** especially lucky for you?
c) Do you wear or carry an object that **brings/it brings** you luck?
d) Is there anything special that **do/you do** before an exam to bring you luck?
e) Have you ever received a letter or an e-mail that **promised/it promised** you good luck?

2 Work with a partner. Discuss the questions in 1.

Reading

1 If you received this e-mail message, what would you do? Discuss with a partner.

Good luck!

To: Kay Jones
Cc: Philip Riley
Bcc:
Subject: Good luck!
Attachments: none

This message is from a friend who wishes you good luck. In less than five days, this message will bring you good luck if—but only if—you pass it on to other friends. This is not a joke. You will definitely receive good news in the mail if you send the message to friends who also need good luck. You have to pass this message on in less than 120 hours.

Good luck, but remember: You must send 20 copies of this message in 120 hours.

2 The e-mail continues below with stories about people who did or didn't pass on the e-mail message. Complete the text by choosing the appropriate verb.

- Ana Cuevas from Peru was (1) **making/taking** a course in Web programming. She (2) **made/took** her final exam two days after receiving the message and got an excellent grade.
- A New York stockbroker received the message on her first day at a new job. The next week, she (3) **had/made** $14 million for her company.
- An 83-year-old, Piotr Wojdylo, (4) **had/took** a serious illness, and the doctors said he (5) **had/took** only six months to live. He was (6) **making/taking** arrangements for his funeral when he got the message. Five years later, he is alive and well.
- A businessman from Salt Lake City received the message but (7) **had/made** the mistake of asking his secretary to pass it on. She forgot. Four days later, he (8) **had/took** a terrible car accident, even though he was driving at only 15 mph.
- Photographer Wesley Pratt waited outside Madonna's home for six days. Finally, he (9) **made/took** the pictures that he wanted, but when the film was developed, the pictures were black. He had completely forgotten to pass on the message.
- Regina Witte received good luck messages every Monday for three months but did nothing. Finally, she decided to (10) **make/take** the risk of deleting the message from her computer. She (11) **had/made** the wrong decision! Her computer crashed one hour later.

3 Work with a partner. Complete each question with a word from the box.

fast	long	long	much	often	old	well

a) How ____ did Ana Cuevas do on her examination?
b) How ____ money did the New York stockbroker make?
c) How ____ was the man with the serious illness?
d) How ____ did the doctors say he would live?
e) How ____ was the businessman from Salt Lake City driving?
f) How ____ did the photographer wait to take pictures of Madonna?
g) How ____ did Regina Witte receive good luck messages?

4 Read the e-mail message in 2 again and answer the questions in 3.

Past perfect

1 Read the article below and explain the title.

A Lucky **Escape**

The day started badly. I woke up late because I (1 **forget**) about the alarm clock the night before. I got dressed in five minutes and called a taxi to take me to the airport. Thirty minutes later, the taxi still hadn't arrived. I called the taxi company, and they explained that the taxi (2 **break down**). So I decided to take my own car to JFK, picked up my bag, and left the house. But when I got in the car, the engine wouldn't start. I realized that I (3 **leave**) the headlights on the night before. I decided to try the taxi company again, but when I put my hand in my pocket, my telephone wasn't there. I (4 **leave**) it in the kitchen, so I went back inside to get it. I opened the door and could hear the radio, which I (5 **forget**) to turn off. "This is the eight o'clock news on WNBV. It's Sunday, April seventh," I heard. "Eight o'clock," I thought. "But it's only seven o'clock," and I looked at my watch to check. Suddenly, I remembered. It *was* eight o'clock! The clocks (6 **change**) that weekend! There was no point going to the airport now. The plane (7 **already take off**). But as I sat there listening to the news, I realized how lucky I had been. The plane (8 **crash**) just after take-off at JFK, and it was feared that all 217 people aboard (9 **die**).

2 Work with a partner. Complete the story by putting the verbs into the past perfect.

3 88 Listen and check your answers.

Anecdote

Think about a lucky or unlucky experience you have had. You are going to tell your partner about it. Choose from the list below the things you want to talk about. Think about what you will say and what language you will need.

- ☐ Was it a lucky or unlucky experience?
- ☐ When did it happen?
- ☐ Where were you?
- ☐ Who were you with?
- ☐ What were you doing?
- ☐ What happened?
- ☐ Why was it lucky (or unlucky)?
- ☐ How did you feel afterward?

Language reviewed: All the main speaking topics from *American Inside Out* Pre-intermediate.

Let's Talk About ...

START

1 ...somebody with an unusual name

2 ...somebody who is important to you

18 ...the qualities of your ideal partner

19 ...your favorite subject in school

20 ...things that make you happy or unhappy

21 ...how you relax

22 ...something you feel strongly about

23 ...a time when you got into trouble

24 ...your favorite historical figure

25 ...the last time you went out and had a good time

26 ...a foreign person you know

27 ...the person you talk to most on the phone

28 ...the most helpful person you know

29 ...a time you were late

30 ...the healthiest person you know

38 ...three good reasons for learning English

FINISH

HOW TO PLAY

Play the game in small groups. You will need a die and counters.

1 Place your counters on the square marked START and throw the die.

2 The first player to throw a six starts the game.

3 The first player throws the die and moves his/her counter along the board according to the number on the die.

4 Players then take turns moving around the board.

5 When a player lands on a blue square, he/she has to talk about the subject for thirty seconds.

6 When players land on an orange square, they have to talk about the subject for sixty seconds.

7 If a player has nothing to say or can't talk for the necessary time, he/she is allowed to pass and miss a turn.

8 The game continues until the first player reaches the square marked FINISH.

Additional material

1 Me

I Never Forget a Face, 2

Try to put the right name under each photograph.

a) _____

b) _____

c) _____

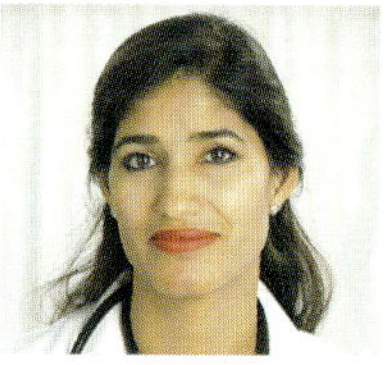
d) _____

e) _____

f) _____

How many did you remember? (The average score is three or four correct answers.)
Go back to page 6 to find out how you can improve your memory.

1 Me

Close-up. Subject questions, 2

Student A

Try to complete these general knowledge statements. Ask your partner appropriate questions to check your answers.

a) _____ created Sherlock Holmes. ➔ *Who created Sherlock Holmes?*
b) J.K. Rowling created _____ . ➔ *Who did J.K. Rowling create?*
c) _____ created Tarzan.
d Alexander Fleming discovered _____ .
e) _____ invented the telephone.
f) Elvis Presley lived in _____ .
g) _____ built the Taj Mahal.
h) The Brazilian soccer team won _____ in 2002.

2 Place

Dream Vacation, 3

1 a) Portuguese
2 b) Turkey
3 a) China
4 c) Poland
5 b) Spain
6 c) Japan

17 Animals

Vocabulary: animals

Answers:
a 4 b 3 c 5 d 1 e 6 f 2

2 Place

Cities of the World, 2

Student A

The capitals are Tokyo, Seoul, Brasília, Berlin, Cairo, and Bogotá.

You have ten country maps. Five cities are marked on maps *a–e*. Use the Language Toolbox to describe to Student B exactly where these cities are. Student B will then describe the location of the other five cities (*f–j*). Mark them on your map. Compare your maps with Student B.

LANGUAGE TOOLBOX

It's in the	southwest. southeast. northwest. northeast. center.
It's on the	_____ coast. _____ River.

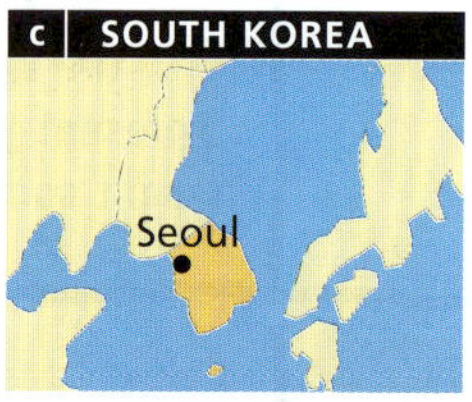

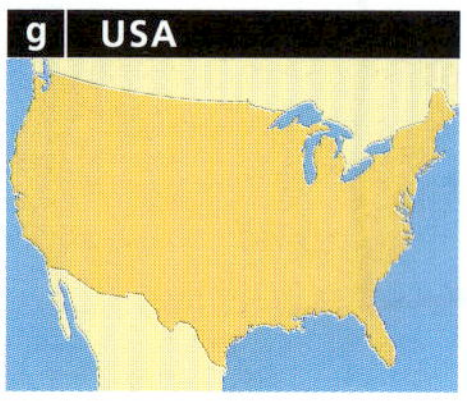

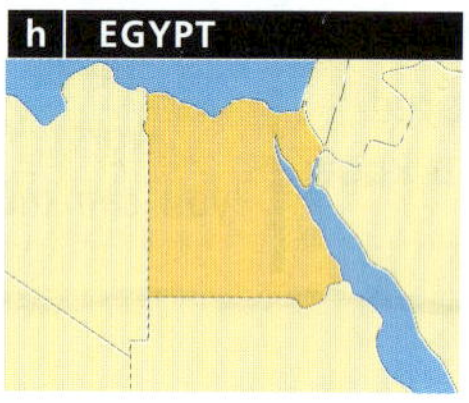

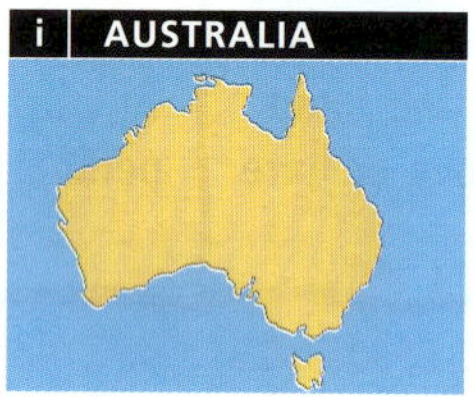

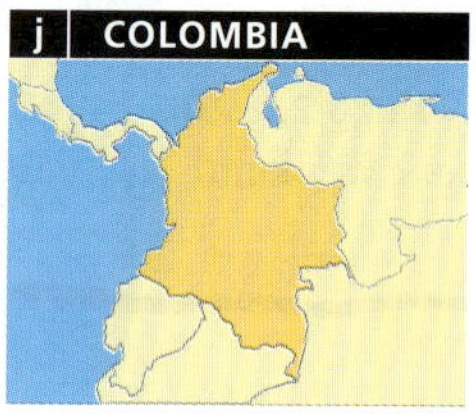

3 *Couples*

True Love. Reading, 3

Student A

1 These are the answers to some comprehension questions about the article *Great Love Affairs* on page 20. Write the questions.
a) In 1998. ➔ *When ...?* b) In the 17th century. ➔ *When ...?* c) Twenty-two years. ➔ *How long ...?*
d) At a polo match. ➔ *Where ...?*

2 Give your questions to your partner.

3 Check your partner's questions. Answer them and then discuss the questions and answers.

4 *Fit*

Vocabulary

	Personality	Sport	Person	Place
A	Cathy Freeman (*Picture 1*)	track and field	runner	track
B	Raúl (*Picture 4*)	a) *soccer*	soccer player	field
C	Shaquille O'Neal (*Picture 2*)	basketball	d) *basketball player*	court
D	*Michael Schumacher* (*Picture 3*)	auto racing	racing driver	racetrack
E	Inge de Bruijn (*Picture 5*)	b) *swimming*	swimmer	f) *swimming pool*
F	*Venus Williams* (*Picture 6*)	c) *tennis*	e) *tennis player*	court

4 *Fit*

Close-up. Comparatives, 5

a) London isn't as wet as Rome. (London annual average: 30 inches of rainfall. Rome annual average: 29 inches of rainfall.)
b) The Maracana Municipa Stadium in Rio de Janeiro is much larger than the Stade de France in Paris. (Maracana capacity: 205,000. Stade de France capacity: 110,000.)
c) The population of Pakistan is a little smaller than the population of Russia. (Pakistan: 144,616,639. Russia: 145,470,197. *U.S. Bureau of Census 2001*)
d) Los Angeles International Airport is a little busier than Heathrow Airport, London. (Los Angeles International Airport: 68,478,000 passengers annually. Heathrow: 64,607,185 passengers annually.)
e) Ireland isn't as big as Cuba. (Ireland: 32,066 square miles. Cuba: 44,200 square miles.)
f) The Statue of Liberty isn't as tall as the Eiffel Tower. (The Statue of Liberty: 305 ft. The Eiffel Tower: 984 ft.)

4 *Fit*

Vocabulary: numbers, 6

Student A

You and Student B each have a set of questions. Student B has the answers to your questions. Ask Student B your questions and write down the answers. (You could try to answer them by yourself first.)
In the box you have the answers to Student B's questions. When you have finished, compare your answers. Which piece of trivia is the most interesting?

a) How fast can a dolphin swim?
b) How much money did Tom Cruise earn in 2000?
c) How many words does a woman speak in a normal day?
d) What percentage of the body's energy does the brain use?
e) What is the longest distance ever traveled in a wheelchair?
f) What is the highest rugby score ever recorded? (A game in Denmark in 1973.)

2%	65 mph	32–0	$38.5 mil	2,611 mi	2,175

11 *Smile*

Vocabulary: the face, 5

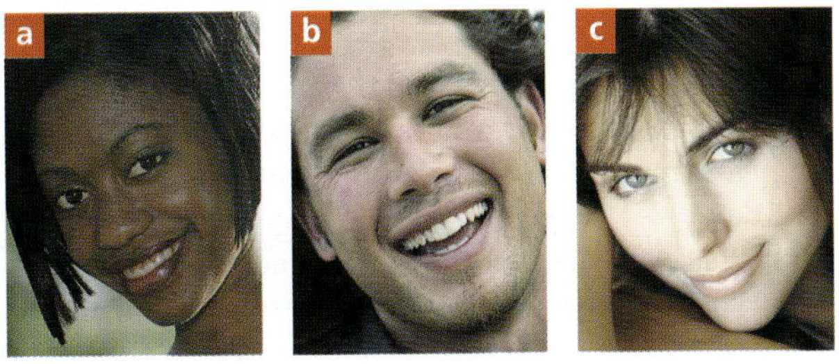

11 *Smile*

Vocabulary: describing character, 4

Your description of a dog is your own personality.
Your description of a cat is your partner's personality.
Your description of a rat is your enemy's personality.
Your description of coffee is how you see love.
Your description of an ocean is your own life.

1 Me

Close-up. Subject questions, 2

Student B

Try to complete these general knowledge statements. Ask your partner appropriate questions to check your answers.

a) Arthur Conan Doyle created _____ . ➔ *Who did Arthur Conan Doyle create?*
b) _____ created Harry Potter. ➔ *Who created Harry Potter?*
c) Edgar Rice Burroughs created _____ .
d) _____ discovered penicillin.
e) Alexander Graham Bell invented _____ .
f) _____ lived in Graceland.
g) Shah Jahan built _____ .
h) _____ won the World Cup in 2002.

2 Place

Cities of the World, 2

Student B

The capitals are Tokyo, Seoul, Brasília, Berlin, Cairo, and Bogotá.

You have ten country maps. Listen to Student A describe the location of five cities on maps *a–e*. Mark them on your map. Then use the Language Toolbox to describe to Student A exactly where the five cities on maps *f–j* are located. Compare your map with Student A.

LANGUAGE TOOLBOX

It's in the	southwest. southeast. northwest. northeast. center.
It's on the	_____ coast. _____ River.

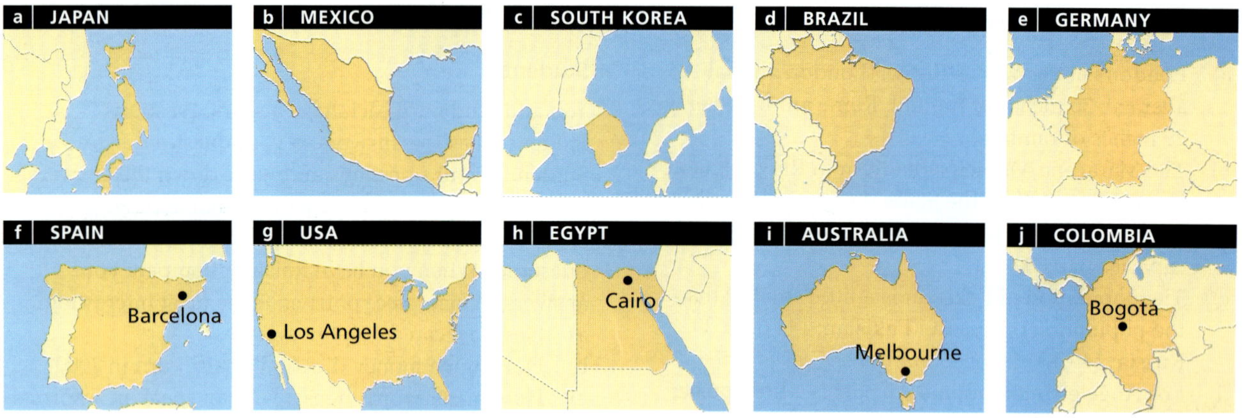

3 Couples

True Love. Reading, 3

Student B

1 These are the answers to some comprehension questions about the article *Great Love Affairs* on page 20. Write the questions.
   a) In 1936. ➔ *When …?*
   b) In April 1970. ➔ *When …?*
   c) Ten months. ➔ *How long …?*
   d) Nineteen years. ➔ *How long …?*

2 Give your questions to your partner.

3 Check your partner's questions. Answer them and then discuss the questions and answers.

4 Fit

Vocabulary: numbers, 6

Student B

You and Student A each have a set of questions. In the box you have the answers to Student A's questions. Student A has the answers to your questions.
Ask Student A your questions and write down the answers. (You could try to answer them by yourself first.) When you have finished, compare your answers. Which piece of trivia is the most interesting?

7,120 194–0 19 mph 20% $43.2 mil 24,901.5 mi

a) How fast can a cheetah run?
b) How much money did Britney Spears earn in 2000?
c) How many words does a man speak in a normal day?
d) What percentage of the body's weight is the brain?
e) What is the longest distance ever traveled on a windsurfer?
f) What is the highest international soccer score ever recorded? (Australia versus Samoa.)

5 Review 1

Sophie and Paul, 4

Read Sophie's answers and write the questions

1	(*name*) *What's your name?*	Sophie Smith.
2	(*old*)	28.
3	(*do*)	Computer programmer.
4	(*zodiac sign*)	Aquarius.
5	(*tall*)	5 ft 3 in.
6	(*like*)	Sociable, sensitive, reliable.
7	(*movies*)	My favorite is *Pulp Fiction*—but also all the movies by Quentin Tarantino.
8	(*favorite*)	Nicholas Cage.
9	(*wear*)	Designer clothes.
10	(*spare time*)	Restaurants, going to the gym, being with interesting people.
11	(*worst fault*)	Forgetting people's names—my memory is hopeless.
12	(*dream weekend*)	Staying in a five-star hotel in Paris with the man of my dreams. Going shopping for designer clothes and then flying back home in first class.

11 Smile

What Are You Like? Reading, 1

If you scored 19–24,
YOU'RE AN OPTIMIST!
You always try to see the positive side of life. You know how to enjoy yourself, and you don't waste time worrying about things that may never happen. But be careful—your friends might find your optimism rather irritating at times.

If you scored 13–18,
YOU'RE MR. OR MS. SENSIBLE!
You are a realist. You know life has ups and downs, but you hope to have more good times than bad times in your life. But be careful—you can be too serious at times. You need to show your feelings a little more.

If you scored 8–12,
YOU'RE A PESSIMIST!
You should try to stop having negative thoughts. You need to learn how to enjoy the good things in life and stop worrying about things that may never happen. And remember, there are many people in worse situations than you.

13 Dance

Reading

What it means

If you scored 20–29
When you dance, you really express yourself. You may look like an octopus in a blender, but you don't care what other people think. Good for you! No party is complete without you.

If you scored 11–19
You enjoy dancing, but you're too worried about your image. You should let yourself go. Be a little less serious about life.

If you scored 10 or less
Hmm, what *do* you enjoy? Do you collect stamps? Hopefully you are an interesting person to talk to!

15 Review 3

National Sports. Passives, 1

a) False—Barcelona.
b) False—eleven players.
c) True.
d) True.
e) False—but it wasn't broken till 1991 (twenty-three years later). His jump at the Mexico City Olympics is considered by many to be the greatest athletic achievement of all time.
f) False—Germany was beaten by Brazil 2–0.

15 Review 3

National Sports. Dynamic and stative meanings, 2

Student A

17 Animals

Special Friends. Listening, 1

Tim's pig, Harriet

Gus's spider, Hendrix

Maxine's hamster, Page

16 *Lifestyle*

Close-up. *will* for prediction, 2

The Oracle

- Choose a question you want to ask.
- Take turns rolling the die, keeping the question in your mind.
- Find the letter corresponding to your question and the number you threw on the die. Find your answer where they meet. For example, you asked question *d* and you threw *4*, so the Oracle says, "One of each."

a) What will the love of my life look like?
b) Will I be famous one day?
c) Will I travel the world?
d) How many children will I have?
e) Where will I be the happiest?
f) What will I look like in ten years?

	1	2	3	4	5	6
a	Not as you expect.	Gorgeous.	Not classically good-looking, but you'll never look at anybody else.	Very fit.	He/She will have wonderful eyes.	He/She'll look like you.
b	No, you won't.	No, but you'll meet someone famous.	You'll be well-known in your profession.	You'll be in the news for doing something crazy.	You'll have your fifteen minutes of fame.	Yes, but you'll have to work very hard.
c	Yes, for pleasure.	Yes, for your job.	No, but you'll travel in your own country.	No, but you'll meet people from all over the world.	You'll have wonderful vacations abroad.	You'll travel when you're older.
d	More than you expect.	The same as your parents.	Your career will be more important.	One of each.	You'll have a big family.	Enough.
e	At home in bed.	In the mountains.	Abroad.	Near the ocean.	Everywhere.	In a big city.
f	Completely different.	Like your mother.	Fabulous.	Younger than you are.	No different.	Like your father.

15 *Review 3*

National Sports. Stative and dynamic meanings, 2

Student B

Verb structures

Basic structures

ASPECT	VOICE	TENSES: Present	TENSES: Past
simple	active	He **writes** letters.	He **wrote** letters.
	passive	Letters **are written**.	Letters **were written**.
continuous	active	He **is writing** letters.	He **was writing** letters.
	passive	Letters **are being written**.	Letters **were being written**.
perfect	active	He **has written** letters.	He **had written** letters.
	passive	Letters **have been written**.	Letters **had been** written.
perfect continuous	active	He **has been writing** letters.	He **had been writing** letters.

Simple present

See Units 6 and 12.

Affirmative	Negative	Question
I/You/We/They **write**.	I/You/We/They **don't (do not) write**.	**Do** I/you/we/they **write**?
He/She/It **writes**.	He/She/It **doesn't (does not) write**.	**Does** he/she/it **write**?

Present continuous

See Units 8 and 12.

Affirmative	Negative	Question
I'**m (am) writing**.	I'**m not (am not) writing**.	**Am** I **writing**?
You/We/They'**re (are) writing**.	You/We/They'**re not (are not) writing**.	**Are** you/we/they **writing**?
He/She/It'**s (is) writing**.	He/She/It **isn't (is not) writing**.	**Is** he/she/it **writing**?

Note: When a verb ends with a single vowel letter followed by a single consonant letter, we usually double the final consonant letter before *-ing*: *chat – chatting; jog – jogging; refer – referring; stop – stopping*.

Present perfect

See Units 7 and 13.

Affirmative	Negative	Question
I/You/We/They **'ve (have) written**.	I/You/We/They **haven't (have not) written**.	**Have** I/you/we/they **written**?
He/She/It**'s (has) written**.	He/She/It **hasn't (has not) written**.	**Has** he/she/it **written**?

Note: See list of irregular verbs on page 132.

Present perfect continuous

See Unit 13.

Affirmative	Negative	Question
I/You/We/They **'ve (have) been writing**.	I/You/We/They **haven't (have not) been writing**.	**Have** I/you/we/they **been writing**?
He/She/It**'s (has) been writing**.	He/She/It **hasn't (has not) been writing**.	**Has** he/she/it **been writing**?

Simple past

See Units 3, 6, and 7.

Affirmative	Negative	Question
I/You/He/She/It/We/They **wrote**.	I/You/He/She/It/We/They **didn't (did not) write**.	**Did** I/you/he/she/it/we/they **write**?

Note: See list of irregular verbs on page 132. When a verb ends with a single vowel letter followed by a single consonant letter, we usually double the final consonant letter before *-ed*: *chat – chatted; jog – jogged; refer – referred; stop – stopped*.

Past continuous

See Unit 3.

Affirmative	Negative	Question
I/He/She/It **was writing**.	I/He/She/It **wasn't (was not) writing**.	**Was** I/He/She/It **writing**?
You/We/They **were writing**.	You/We/They **weren't (were not) writing**.	Were you/we/they **writing**?

Past perfect

See Unit 18.

Affirmative	Negative	Question
I/You/He/She/It/We/They **'d (had) written**.	I/You/He/She/It/We/They **hadn't (had not) written**.	**Had** I/you/he/she/it/we/they **written**?

Note: See list of irregular verbs on page 132.

used to

See Unit 19.

Affirmative	Negative	Question
I/You/He/She/It/We/They **used to write**.	I/You/He/She/It/We/They **didn't use to write**.	**Did** I/you/he/she/it/we/they **use to write**?

(be) going to

See Unit 8.

Affirmative	Negative	Question
I'm (am) **going to write**.	**I'm not** (**am not**) **going to write**.	**Am** I **going to write**?
You/We/ They**'re** (**are**) **going to write**.	You/We/ They**'re not** (**are not**) **going to write**.	**Are** you/we/ they **going to write**?
He/She/It**'s** (**is**) **going to write**.	He/She/It **isn't** (**is not**) **going to write**.	**Is** he/she/it **going to write**?

Present continuous for future

See Unit 8 and page 129.

will

See Unit 16.

Affirmative	Negative	Question
I/You/He/She/ It/We/They**'ll** (**will**) **write**.	I/You/He/She/ It/We/They **won't** (**will not**) **write**.	**Will** I/You/He/ She/It/We/ They **write**?

Modals

Affirmative	Negative	Question
can: see Units 9 and 14.		
I/You/He *etc.* **can** write.	I/You/He *etc.* **can't** (**cannot**) write.	**Can** I/you/he *etc.* write?
could: see Units 9 and 14.		
I/You/He *etc.* **could** write.	I/You/He *etc.* **couldn't** (**could not**) write.	**Could** I/you/he *etc.* write?
must: see Unit 9.		
I/You/He *etc.* **must** write.	I/You/He *etc.* **mustn't** (**must not**) write.	**Must** I/you/he *etc.* write?
may		
I/You/He *etc.* **may** write.	I/You/He *etc.* **may not** write.	**May** I/you/he *etc.* write?
might		
I/You/He *etc.* **might** write.	I/You/He *etc.* **mightn't** (**might not**) write.	**Might** I/you/ he *etc.* write?
should: see Units 9 and 19.		
I/You/He *etc.* **should** write.	I/You/He *etc.* **shouldn't** (**should not**) write.	**Should** I/you/ he *etc.* write?
will: see Unit 16.		
I/You/He *etc.* **'ll** (**will**) write.	I/You/He *etc.* **won't** (**will not**) write.	**Will** I/you/he *etc.* write?
would: see Unit 17.		
I/You/He *etc.* **'d** (**would**) write.	I/You/He *etc.* **wouldn't** (**would not**) write.	**Would** I/you/ he *etc.* write?

Future time clauses

See Unit 16.

Subordinate clause	Main clause
If he has a cigarette,	he'll be in big trouble.
When he finishes the week,	he'll feel like a new man.
As soon as he arrives,	he'll take a fitness test.

Note: The two clauses can usually be used in either order; for example:
He'll be in big trouble if he has a cigarette.

Conditional clauses

See Unit 17.

If-clause	Main clause
If I had $1 million,	I'd travel around the world. I'd buy a big house.
If I were* an animal,	I'd be a lion. I'd be a bird so I could fly.
If I could live anywhere,	I'd choose somewhere hot. I wouldn't stay here!

***You will sometimes hear *was* in informal spoken English.**
Note: The two clauses can usually be used in either order; for example:
I'd travel around the world if I had $1 million.

Relative clauses

See Unit 17.

(The main clauses are in *italics*. The relative clauses are in bold.)
A cheetah is an animal **that can run at 60 mph**.
A person **who treats sick animals** *is called a vet*.
Meow is a noise **cats make**.
The people **my brother works with** *are all crazy*.

Grammar glossary

main verb · adjective · conjunction · modal auxiliary · adverb · article · pronoun · main verb

Learn these useful words and you can understand more about the language you are studying.

determiner · noun · pronoun · main verb · preposition · noun · auxiliary verb

Agents are people or things that perform an action in a passive sentence.
For example: *She was pardoned by* ***President Clinton*** *in 2001.*

Clauses are groups of words containing a verb.

	main clause	subordinate clause
For example:	***I waited,***	***but he didn't come.***

Note: Subordinate clauses are usually introduced by conjunctions.

Combinations refer to words that frequently occur together.
For example: *common sense   get along well   Happy birthday*

Dynamic meaning is a way of referring to verbs when they describe actions. Verbs with dynamic meanings can be used in both simple and continuous verb forms.
For example: *People usually* ***talk*** *to one another on the plane.*
Some people ***are talking*** *in the next room.*

Expressions are groups of words that belong together where the words and word order never or rarely change.
For example: ***black and white***   ***That reminds me,*** *I have to buy some toothpaste.*
How do you do?

Idioms are expressions with a meaning that cannot be understood by knowing the meaning of each individual word.
For example: *It's* ***a piece of cake.*** = *It's really easy.*
Don't ***spill the beans.*** = *Don't tell the secret.*

***If*-clauses** are used to introduce conditions where we can describe a real situation (possible) or an unreal situation (improbable or impossible).
For example: ***If the weather is nice,*** *we'll go on a picnic.* (real situation)
If I won the lottery, *I'd quit my job and never work again.* (unreal situation)

Intransitive verbs do not take an object.
For example: *He* ***walked.***   *Is Marta still* ***sleeping?***   ***Sit down!***

Objects usually come after the verb and show who or what is affected by the verb.
For example: *She closed* ***the window.***   *My neighbor hates* ***me.***   *I made* ***a pot of coffee.***
Note: Some verbs take a direct object (DO) and an indirect object (IO).

	IO	DO		IO	DO		IO	DO
For example: *She gave*	***him***	***a kiss.***	*He sent*	***her***	***some flowers.***	*I teach*	***students***	***English.***

Particles are adverbs or prepositions that form part of a phrasal verb.
For example: *sit* ***down***   *turn* ***off***   *call* ***up***

Phrasal verbs are verbs consisting of a main verb + particle(s). Phrasal verbs are sometimes referred to as two- or three-word verbs.
For example: ***grow up***   ***take*** *your shoes* ***off***   *I* ***ran after*** *the bus.*

Relative clauses give additional information about a thing or a person introduced in the main clause.
For example: *A turtle is an animal* ***that can live to seventy years old.***
The people ***my brother works with*** *are all crazy.*

Relative pronouns such as *who, that,* and *which* are always used when they are the subject of the verb in a relative clause.

	subject	verb	object	
For example: *People*	***who***	***don't eat***	***meat***	*are called vegetarians.*
I have a parrot	***that***	***can speak***	***English.***	

Stative meaning is a way of referring to verbs when they describe states. Verbs with stative meanings cannot be used with continuous verb forms.
For example: *I* ***want*** *a fairer system.* (NOT ~~*I'm wanting a fairer system.*~~)
I've known *him for years.* (NOT ~~*I've been knowing him for years.*~~)

Subjects usually come before the verb and refer to the main person or thing you are talking about.
For example: ***Money*** *doesn't grow on trees.*   ***My tailor*** *is rich.*
The biggest rock group in the world *has started a world tour.*

Phonetic symbols

VOWELS

/ɪ/	big fish	/bɪg fɪʃ/
/i/	green beans	/grin binz/
/ʊ/	should look	/ʃʊd lʊk/
/u/	blue moon	/blu mun/
/ɛ/	ten eggs	/tɛn ɛgz/
/ə/	about mother	/əbaut mʌðər/
/æ/	fat cat	/fæt kæt/
/ʌ/	must come	/mʌst kʌm/
/ɔ/	fall ball	/fɔl bɔl/
/ɑ/	hot spot	/hɑt spɑt/

DIPHTHONGS

/ei/	face	/feis/
/ɔi/	boy	/bɔi/
/ou/	nose	/nouz/
/ɑi/	eye	/ɑi/
/ɑu/	mouth	/mɑuθ/

CONSONANTS

/p/	pen	/pɛn/
/b/	bad	/bæd/
/t/	tea	/ti/
/d/	dog	/dɔg/
/tʃ/	church	/tʃərtʃ/
/dʒ/	jazz	/dʒæz/
/k/	cost	/kɔst/
/g/	girl	/gərl/
/f/	far	/fɑr/
/v/	voice	/vɔis/
/θ/	thin	/θɪn/
/ð/	then	/ðɛn/
/s/	snake	/snɛik/
/z/	noise	/nɔiz/
/ʃ/	shop	/ʃɑp/
/ʒ/	measure	/mɛʒər/
/m/	make	/meik/
/n/	nine	/nɑin/
/ŋ/	sing	/sɪŋ/
/h/	house	/hɑus/
/l/	leg	/lɛg/
/r/	red	/rɛd/
/w/	wet	/wɛt/
/y/	yes	/yɛs/

STRESS

In this book, word stress is shown by underlining the stressed syllable.
For example: water; result; disappointing

LETTERS OF THE ALPHABET

/ei/	/i/	/ɛ/	/ɑi/	/ou/	/u/	/ɑr/
Aa	Bb	Ff	Ii	Oo	Qq	Rr
Hh	Cc	Ll	Yy		Uu	
Jj	Dd	Mm			Ww	
Kk	Ee	Nn				
	Gg	Ss				
	Pp	Xx				
	Tt					
	Vv					
	Zz					

Irregular verbs

Simple form	Simple past	Past participle
be	was / were	been
beat	beat	beaten
become	became	become
begin	began	begun
bend	bent	bent
bet	bet	bet
bite	bit	bitten
blow	blew	blown
break	broke	broken
bring	brought	brought
build	built	built
burn	burned	burned
burst	burst	burst
buy	bought	bought
can	could	(been able)
catch	caught	caught
choose	chose	chosen
come	came	come
cost	cost	cost
cut	cut	cut
deal	dealt	dealt
do	did	done
draw	drew	drawn
dream	dreamed	dreamed
drink	drank	drunk
drive	drove	driven
eat	ate	eaten
fall	fell	fallen
feed	fed	fed
feel	felt	felt
fight	fought	fought
find	found	found
fly	flew	flown
forget	forgot	forgotten
forgive	forgave	forgiven
freeze	froze	frozen
get	got	gotten
give	gave	given
go	went	gone
grow	grew	grown
hang	hung / hanged	hung / hanged
have	had	had
hear	heard	heard
hide	hid	hidden
hit	hit	hit
hold	held	held
hurt	hurt	hurt
keep	kept	kept
kneel	knelt / kneeled	knelt / kneeled
know	knew	known
lay	laid	laid
lead	led	led
learn	learned	learned
leave	left	left
lend	lent	lent
let	let	let
lie	lay / lied	lain / lied
light	lit / lighted	lit / lighted
lose	lost	lost
make	made	made
mean	meant	meant
meet	met	met
must	had to	(had to)
pay	paid	paid
put	put	put
read	read /rɛd/	read /rɛd/
ride	rode	ridden
ring	rang	rung
rise	rose	risen
run	ran	run
say	said	said
see	saw	seen
sell	sold	sold
send	sent	sent
set	set	set
shake	shook	shaken
shine	shined / shone	shined / shone
shoot	shot	shot
show	showed	shown
shrink	shrank	shrunk
shut	shut	shut
sing	sang	sung
sink	sank	sunk
sit	sat	sat
sleep	slept	slept
slide	slid	slid
smell	smelled	smelled
speak	spoke	spoken
spell	spelled	spelled
spend	spent	spent
spill	spilled	spilled
split	split	split
spoil	spoiled	spoiled
spread	spread	spread
stand	stood	stood
steal	stole	stolen
stick	stuck	stuck
swear	swore	sworn
swell	swelled	swollen / swelled
swim	swam	swum
take	took	taken
teach	taught	taught
tear	tore	torn
tell	told	told
think	thought	thought
throw	threw	thrown
understand	understood	understood
wake	woke	woken
wear	wore	worn
win	won	won
write	wrote	written

Tapescripts

1 Me

01

My first name's Susan, but the only person who calls me Susan is my dad. Oh, and my sister when she's angry with me, but luckily that doesn't happen very often now. Most of my friends call me Sue, and so do the people I work with. My old friends call me Maggsie, because my last name is Maggs, and I was always called Maggsie at school. I hated it. Of course, there's only one person who calls me Mom, and that's my son, but when he's with his friends, he calls me Sue.
My mom calls me Sweetheart, and my best friend calls me Suzanne because she's French. My Japanese sister-in-law calls me Suki—apparently, Suki means "loved one" in Japanese, so that's really nice. My husband calls me Bunny, but that's another story...

02

(See page 4.)

03

1 /ɔ/ Paul George Laura Dawn
2 /u/ Julie Ruth Luke Sue
3 /ɑ/ Charles Margaret Barbara Carl
4 /i/ Peter Eve Denise Keith
5 /æ/ Matthew Hannah Anne Nancy

04

A.L.I.C.E. is an award-winning chat robot at www.alicebot.org. She's intelligent and funny and has won prizes for being the most human-like computer. She was created by Dr. Richard S. Wallace. Six thousand people a month chat to A.L.I.C.E. Some people spend up to four and a half hours a day chatting online with her, and some have even said they prefer her to their own girlfriends. Here is a typical conversation.

(A = A.L.I.C.E.; I = Interviewer)
A: Hi. My name's A.L.I.C.E.
I: What does your name mean?
A: It means Artificial Linguistic Internet Computer Entity.
I: Where were you born?
A: I was born in Bethlehem, Pennsylvania.
I: Where did you grow up?
A: I think I grew up in San Francisco.
I: What do you look like?
A: I'm blue, and I have one wheel.
I: What do you do?
A: I talk to people on the Web.
I: Do you like your job?
A: Yes, I have a passion for my work!
I: Can you speak any foreign languages?
A: No, I only speak English now, but I'd like to learn.
I: Are you married?
A: No, I am single. How about you?
I: Do you have any children?
A: No, but you can download me and make A.L.I.C.E. clones for yourself!
I: Who created you?
A: Dr. Richard S. Wallace—he is very, very smart! He's also very kind and generous. In fact he's one of the most...
I: Yeah, yeah, O.K., A.L.I.C.E. Thank you.

05

(See page 9.)

06

Dave Carter's my best friend. We met when we were five years old because our parents were friends, and we went to the same school. He works in a different city now, so I only see him on weekends and during vacations. He's important to me because he knows me so well. We have a really good time together, and we enjoy the same things—football, music, girls, the usual stuff. When I'm feeling down or when I need to talk to somebody, I can always call him. Recently, I had girlfriend problems and he was great—he's a really good listener. He just lets you talk and he listens. But he isn't perfect! He's always late for everything, and he never says he's sorry. Never! The last time I saw him was last weekend. We arranged to meet at four o'clock to play football, and he arrived at six thirty! It was nearly dark! Oh well, I guess nobody's perfect. He's still a really good pal.

2 Place

07

1
(I = Interviewer; P = Paulo)
I: Do you like your city?
P: Oh, yes. I feel lucky to be living in a city that's so big and exciting. I love looking out of my apartment window over the high-rise buildings.
I: What's the downtown area like?
P: Some people say it's too noisy and crowded, but I love that. There's always something to see and do. We also have the most famous beach in the world—Copacabana Beach. Then, on the other side of the city, there are beautiful mountains. The highest one is called Corcovado, and it has the famous statue of Christ. If you look down at the city from there, the view is spectacular.
I: What's the weather like?
P: It's great most of the time. The only time I don't like Rio much is in the summer: it's too hot and humid.

2
(I = Interviewer; G = Gisela)
I: Do you like your city?
G: Yes, it's wonderful. I think my city has everything.
I: What's the architecture like?
G: It's a mixture of old and new with plenty of stores for everybody. The castle is the most famous monument, and at night it looks amazing.
I: What's the nightlife like?
G: It's a young city because of the university, so there are plenty of cheap restaurants and interesting cafes and bars. The nightlife is great!
I: And what are the people like?
G: Well, some people are a little reserved, but in general they're really friendly.

3
(I = Interviewer; A = Armelle)
I: Where do you live?
A: Well, I live in a small village with my parents. My grandparents live here too, and my aunts and uncles. In fact, I think I'm related to about fifty percent of the people in my village.
I: What's your village like?
A: It's very pretty. The countryside is beautiful, and the air is lovely and clean. But it's too quiet. I find it so dull and boring here—there aren't any dance clubs or movie theaters.
I: What are the people like?
A: Oh, they're lovely, but there aren't many young people. I want to go and live in the city. Soon.

4
(I = Interviewer; L = Luigi)
I: What do you think of your city?
L: It is a very special place. There is nowhere else in the world like my city—it's so romantic.
I: What's the center of the city like?
L: The buildings are beautiful, and we have San Marco, one of the most famous churches in the world. San Marco Square is wonderful, and during carnival in February, Venice is the best place in the world to be.
I: Do you like living here?
L: No, I really hate living here. It's horrible. There are too many tourists everywhere.
I: Oh. What are the stores like?
L: Well, because of the tourists, the stores are too expensive, and the canals are dirty and polluted. My city is not big enough for all these people. Why don't they leave us in peace?

08

(See page 12.)

09

(See page 14.)

3 Couples

10

(See page 17.)

11

(A = Announcer; BB = Bobby Brown; R = Rosie; D = David)

A: It's time for our popular contest, *Get Personal*, with your host, Bobby Brown.

BB: Good evening and welcome to this week's *Get Personal*. Let's meet our first couple, Rosie and David.
Now you remember the way the game works. We want to find out just how much they remember about when they first met. So, Rosie and David are going to answer the same questions, and they'll get one point each time they give the same answer.
As you know, Rosie and David are in separate studios—Rosie can't hear David, and David has no idea what Rosie is saying. But they can both hear me. O.K., are you ready to play *Get Personal*?

R&D: Yes, Bobby.

12

(BB = Bobby Brown; R = Rosie)

BB: O.K., ladies first, so we'll start with you, Rosie. Tell me, when did you meet David?

R: Uhm, it was exactly three years, four and a half months ago.

BB: All right! Now Rosie, how did you first meet?

R: Well, I was working as a nurse, and David came into the hospital for an operation.

BB: O.K., Rosie. I want you to think about the moment when you first met. What time of day was it?

R: Uhm, it was getting dark, and I was working nights that week. So early evening.

BB: And what was the weather like?

R: Oh, uh, I think it was raining. Yes, I remember now—it was definitely raining when I arrived at work.

BB: What were you both wearing when you saw each other for the first time?

R: That's easy. I was wearing my nurse's uniform, and he was wearing pajamas.

BB: What color were the pajamas?

R: Uhm, blue. Or were they green? No, they were blue.

BB: Is that your final answer?

R: Yes, blue.

BB: Finally, who spoke first, and what did the person say?

R: David spoke first. In fact, he shouted at me. He said, "Nurse, I'm going to be sick."

BB: Oh, well, that's very romantic! Thank you, Rosie.

13

(BB = Bobby Brown; D = David)

BB: Now, David, it's your turn. When did you meet Rosie?

D: Oh, almost three and a half years ago.

BB: O.K. Second question. Where and how did you first meet?

D: Uhm, well, I was in the hospital for an operation, and Rosie was working there as a nurse.

BB: What time of day was it?

D: Oh, I don't know. Lunchtime?

BB: What was the weather like?

D: Gee…hmm. It was summer, so I guess the sun was shining.

BB: What were you both wearing when you saw each other for the first time?

D: Ah, Rosie was wearing her nurse's uniform, and, and she was also wearing lovely perfume. I was wearing my favorite green pajamas.

BB: Finally, David, who spoke first, and what did the person say?

D: Ah, Rosie spoke first. She said, "How are you feeling?" And I think I said, uh, "I feel terrible."

14

(Sounds.)

15

(See page 21.)

4 Fit

16

(MD = Marketing Director; AE = Advertising Executive)

MD: O.K. Who do you have for me?

AE: Well, we now have a short list of six people. I'm sure you'll love all of them.

MD: Go ahead then.

AE: Well, first of all, we have Raúl.

MD: Who? Never heard of him. Who's next? Someone better, I hope.

AE: No, Raúl's really famous. He plays soccer for Spain.

MD: Well, he's no good to me.

AE: O.K., next, we have Shaquille O'Neal.

MD: Who? I don't know him, either.

AE: He's huge! Super-rich, super-talented, hugely famous.

MD: He's not famous with people like me. And he's not as good-looking as that other kid, what did you call him, Raúl? We need someone who is attractive. I don't care how good he is at basketball.

AE: O.K., what about Michael Schumacher? Maybe we could get him. He's more successful than all of them.

MD: It doesn't matter. I want someone attractive.

AE: Oh, I get it. You really don't want a man. Oh, fine. Well, what about, hmm, I don't know, what about a swimmer? There's that Dutch one, Inge, Inge something. She won a few gold medals, and she looks good.

MD: Yes, that's the idea. But not swimming—I want something more, you know, uh, more, uh, tennis, for example, tennis is a little more interesting than swimming.

AE: What about someone like Venus Williams, or her sister, what's her name? Or number six on my list, Cathy Freeman, the Australian Olympic 400-meter champion? Venus Williams looks great and is probably more famous than Cathy Freeman, but Cathy is more, well, I mean, she's lovely, isn't she? Such a beautiful smile. But some people may think track and field isn't as interesting as tennis…

MD: Maybe. Come on. Let's decide. Who do you think is more exciting? This runner or that soccer player, Raúl?

AE: Oh, Raúl. No question.

MD: Well, I disagree. I think this Cathy Freeman is more exciting than all of them. See if you can get her.

AE: Are you sure? Is that your final decision? I think she's a very interesting choice.

MD: Yup, let's go for it. When can you contact her?

17

(See page 24.)

18

Three quarters.
Zero point two five.
Zero point three three.
One and a half.
An eighth.
A quarter.
One point five.
Zero point one two five.
A third.
Zero point seven five.

19

Three quarters is the same as zero point seven five.
Zero point two five is the same as a quarter.
Zero point three three is the same as a third.
One and a half is the same as one point five.
An eighth is the same as zero point one two five.

20

a) A speed
A hundred twenty-seven miles an hour
Eighty miles an hour

b) A sum of money
Fifty-nine million dollars
Seventeen million dollars

c) A big number
Ninety-seven million, two thousand, four hundred forty
Six hundred twenty-four million, one hundred twelve thousand, three hundred fifty

d) A percentage
Eight point two percent
Twenty-six point seven percent

e) A distance
Thirty-two point four miles
Twenty-six point two miles

f) A soccer score
Four one
Two nothing

21

a) Venus Williams's tennis serve has been recorded at a hundred twenty-seven miles an hour. It's actually the fastest service in women's tennis.
b) Michael Schumacher earned fifty-nine million dollars in 2000, more than any other athlete.
c) The British have a very sweet tooth. They eat a total of six hundred twenty-four million, one hundred twelve thousand, three hundred fifty Mars Bars every year.
d) Only eight point two percent of the UK population trusts the government.
e) The official distance for a marathon, established in 1910, is twenty-six point two miles.
f) Brazil beat Germany two nothing in the 2002 World Cup Final to become champions for the fifth time.

22

Golfing Genius

Tiger Woods was born on December 30, 1975, in California, of mixed heritage: he describes himself as a quarter black, a quarter Thai, a quarter Chinese, an eighth white, and an eighth American Indian. His father, Earl Woods, named him Tiger after a friend who saved his life in the Vietnam War.

He was only nine months old when he started playing golf, and he played his first game at one and a half years old. His father was his first teacher.

At the age of eight, he won a tournament, and he won five more before he was sixteen. On April 8, 2001, Tiger Woods made golfing history. He became the first golfer to win all four majors—the most important tournaments—within the same year.

He is helping to make golf more popular with all ages and levels, and most people agree that he is probably the greatest golfer of all time. Certainly, he is already one of the richest.

He now earns more than $50 million a year. He has a $100 million deal with Nike and also has deals with American Express, Buick, Rolex, and Wheaties.

What advice would he give prospective parents of golf champions? "Don't force your kids into sports. It has to be fun."

The best advice he ever got? From his dad: "Always be yourself."

23

(I = Interviewer; P = Pauline)

I: And here on Radio 101.5 Live, we have a winner in this week's big contest. The prize, the prize this week is a trip to beautiful Augusta for the Masters and the chance to meet Tiger Woods! The winner is Pauline Perkins, and she's on the line right now. Pauline, congratulations. I hear that you're mad about Tiger Woods—you're his biggest fan. Is that right?
P: Oh, yes. I think he's the most wonderful person in the world, and I know absolutely everything about him. I have a Web site all about him, and I write to him every day.
I: Really? What do you like most about him?
P: He's the greatest golfer of all time, and he's gorgeous. So young, too. In fact, he's the youngest player to win four major golf tournaments in one year.
I: Oh, really? How old is he?
P: He was born on December 30, 1975. I always have a party on December 30, and I put pictures of Tiger all over the house.
I: Oh, how nice. Pauline, I hear Tiger Woods is one of the richest athletes on the planet. Does he live like a typical superstar?
P: No, he's different from other superstars. He's the only real superstar. He's just so, ooh, different.
I: What do you mean?
P: He likes staying at home, playing computer games and table tennis. Oh, and eating his favorite food. He's a perfect man. He's so good.
I: What's his favorite food?
P: Pizza or cheeseburgers and strawberry milkshakes. I like the same things.
I: And is it true that Michael Jordan is one of his best friends?
P: Oh, yes. Michael Jordan is like a big brother to Tiger.
I: I see. And can I just ask you one last question?
P: Sure.
I: What are you going to say to Tiger when you meet him?
P: I'm going to tell him that I…

5 Review 1

24

(I = Radio interviewer; B = Brenda)

I: We've been hearing a lot over here in the States about the actor Vinnie Jones. Over in Britain he's really well known, isn't that right?
B: Well, yeah, he's much better known in Britain than he is over here.
I: So, what's the big deal? What's so special about Vinnie Jones?
B: Well, before he became an actor, he was already well known as a soccer player. In fact, I'd say he's still more famous for his soccer skills than as an actor.
I: And which team did he play for? Manchester United?
B: No, no, actually, for much of his career, he played for Wimbledon.
I: Wimbledon?
B: Yes, they're not as successful as Manchester United, but while he was playing for them they beat Liverpool and won the Cup. But it wasn't really for his soccer skills that Vinnie became famous. He was well known in Britain for being the toughest guy on the pitch…I mean field.
I: The toughest guy on the field? In what way?
B: He was always in trouble with the referee. Basically, he was a good player, but he was violent.
I: Is there anything special about that?
B: Not really, no, but Vinnie was much more violent than other soccer players.
I: Jeez. What exactly did he do?
B: Well, for example, on one occasion, he told another player he would tear his ear off.
I: Ugh!
B: And on another occasion he tried to bite the nose of a sports journalist.
I: Wow. He sounds like a very unpleasant person.
B: Well, believe it or not, there is another side to him. If you met him, you'd probably like him—he's a lot nicer than many people think.
I: From what you say, he doesn't sound exactly, uhm, nice!
B: He's a happily married family man, married to a girl he met when he was twelve, devoted to his son and stepdaughter, and he's one of the most generous people I've ever met.
I: No kidding.
B: No, I'm serious.
I: O.K., so how did he get into acting?
B: In 1997, at the age of 33, Vinnie's soccer career was coming to an end. He got a job as a talk show host with Sky TV, and then one thing led to another. He got a phone call from Guy Ritchie, Madonna's boyfriend—now her husband—asking him to take the part of a gangster in the movie that he was making. The movie, *Lock, Stock and Two Smoking Barrels*, was extremely successful in Britain.

I: So that was the start.
B: Yup, that was the start, and in the last few years he has acted with John Travolta, Brad Pitt, and Nicholas Cage.
I: Well, it's a great story—soccer tough guy becomes Hollywood star!
B: Yes, that's right. Obviously, he's not as good-looking as Brad Pitt, but he's a great character actor.
I: O.K., Brenda, thanks for that. Now, it's back to…

25

(See page 31.)

26

(See page 33.)

6 Shop

27

(I = Interviewer; R = Russell; B = Billy)
I: Well, O.K. Question one. Do you mind going shopping on weekends?
R: Not really. But after about an hour, I want to go home.
B: It depends. I don't mind going shopping, but on weekends, I prefer watching sports on TV.
I: O.K., uh, let's see. Question two. What kind of stores do you like going to?
R: Bookstores. I could spend a whole day in a bookstore.
B: I love listening to music, so music stores are my favorite.
I: O.K., uh…Question three. Are there any kinds of stores you hate going to?
R: I hate supermarkets, so I don't bother going to them anymore. I do my shopping on the Internet.
B: I can't stand going into shoe stores with my girlfriend. She tries on ten pairs and then buys the first pair.
I: I see. O.K. Last question. Question four. Do you enjoy buying clothes for yourself?
R: Not really. I don't waste time shopping for clothes unless I really need something.
B: I like having new clothes, but I don't enjoy trying them on.
I: O.K. Thanks.

28

(S = Salesclerk; R = Russell)
S: Can I help you?
R: Oh, I'm just looking, thanks. Well, actually, I'm looking for something for my girlfriend.
S: And what kind of thing are you looking for?
R: I don't really know. A top?
S: O.K. What color would you like?
R: Uhm, what colors do you have?
S: We have any color you want, sir. What color does your girlfriend usually wear?
R: I, I don't…
S: O.K., what color are her eyes?
R: Green.
S: O.K., people with green eyes look good in purple.
R: Oh, great. Yes, purple's fine.
S: Now, what size is she?
R: Uh, well, kind of, she isn't very big, but she's not really small.
S: That'll be medium then.
R: Yes, good, medium.
S: Well, we have this very nice silk evening top here…
R: Good, I'll take it.
S: Are you sure you don't want to see any more…?
R: No, that's great. I'll take it. Thank you. How much is it?
S: That's $100, sir. How would you like to pay?
R: A hundred?! By credit card, please.
S: Fine. If you could just sign…
R: Here you are. Goodbye.
S: Just a minute, sir. Here's your receipt.
R: Oh yes, uhm…can she exchange it if it doesn't fit?
S: Yes, but she needs to keep the receipt.

29

(S = Salesclerk; R = Roz)
S: Can I help you?
R: Yes, I'm looking for a cell phone.
S: And what kind of cell phone are you looking for, ma'am?
R: Uh—what do you mean?
S: Well, what do you want to do with your cell phone—do you want to access the Internet, send text messages, play games…?
R: No, no. I just want to make phone calls.
S: O.K. Something like this, maybe? This model comes with a Call Log feature that keeps track of the calls you have received, missed, and dialed. It also has a Photo Caller ID that lets you know who's calling.
R: No, no, I'm not interested in all that. I just want to make phone calls.
S: Fine. How about this basic model? It's very easy to use.
R: Yes…What colors do you have?
S: Well, we have this rather nice red one.
R: I don't look good in red.
S: You don't look good in red?!
R: That's right. I wear a lot of pink.
S: I see. Uh, well, we don't have pink, but we have this one in blue. Do you look good in blue?
R: Yes, I like blue. I'll take it.
S: Fine. I don't suppose you're interested in the clock function…
R: No.
S: …or voice and speed dialing…
R: No. I just want to pay!
S: O.K., that'll be $90. How would you like to pay, ma'am?
R: In cash. Here you are.
S: Thank you, ma'am. Here's your receipt. Oh, and don't forget this brochure that tells you all about our cell phone accessories. I'm sure you're…

7 Job

30

A

Yeah, well, it all started when we were in high school. We wanted to, like, start a band. I got this secondhand guitar for my sixteenth birthday, and my friend was really good at singing. That's how it started really, you know what I mean? We found a drummer and started doing gigs. And suddenly the band got really big—we started having hit records and making loads of money. So I dropped out of school and really concentrated on the music. I have fifteen guitars now, but my favorite is still the one I got for my sixteenth birthday, you know what I mean?

B

I work on the maternity ward of a large hospital, and I've delivered 649 babies so far. It's a great job because it brings happiness to people's lives. When I hand the new baby to the parents, I know that it's one of the happiest moments of their lives. On the other hand, it's a very stressful job. I usually work nights, and I work long hours, so I haven't had time to have a baby of my own yet!

C

I couldn't live in a city—I love the outdoor life. It's a hard life, but I've never missed a single day's work because of illness, and I'm sixty-nine years old. With the new tractor, I have a little more time on my hands, but I still get up at five o'clock every morning and feed the animals before breakfast. My eldest son gives me a hand on weekends, but I still do most of the work myself—you know you're living when you're outdoors.

31

(T = Talk show host; R = Mr. Reynold)
T: …and tonight we're going to hear from an amazing man whose business has been a success for years. It is a department store that has made a big difference. Mr. Reynold, can you tell us what is so special about your department store?
R: Well, yes, it is special. Reynold's is a large department store, and you can find everything you want for the home here. Oh, and it stays open late from Monday to Saturday.
T: Yes, that's right, but isn't there something special about the staff—you know, has anybody retired recently?
R: Ah, oh, I see. No. Nobody has retired recently, and we never force anybody to retire here.
T: How old is your oldest employee?
R: Well, that would be Arthur. Arthur is our cleaner, and he's 87.
T: He's 87! And he cleans the store every day?

R: Well, not alone, no. He works with two other cleaners. They're not so old—Mabel's 70 and Ivy's 75—no, 76. That's right, yesterday was her birthday.
T: And they don't want to retire?
R: No, I think they enjoy the work, and it keeps them young. Also, we pay a decent salary, and they get four weeks' paid vacation a year.
T: So how many workers do you have who are over retirement age?
R: Well, we employ a staff of a hundred five, and I'd say that maybe half of those are over 65. The young ones work in the office—we have computers now, you know.
T: Really? Has the store changed much over the years?
R: No, not really. I started working here in 1948, and I've only had two secretaries in all that time. Edith, my first secretary, handed in her resignation when she was 72.
T: Oh, why did she leave Reynold's so young?
R: Well, she was getting married to someone who lived in another city.
T: Jeez! That's amazing. Tell me, have you ever fired anybody?
R: No, not yet. I can't see any reason to fire people, unless they're dishonest. That's not a problem we have with the older employees.
T: And do you think you will ever retire, Mr. Reynold?
R: Oh, yes. I'm almost 86! My son's going to take over the business next year. It'll be good to have a younger man in charge. He's, uh, only 64.

32

Good morning. Let me introduce myself. My name's Lourdes Rivas, and I work for American Airlines. As you probably know, we are a major international airline. I'm based at Miami International Airport in Florida, where I'm in charge of sales and promotion. I'm looking forward to taking this course.

8 Rich

33

(See page 46.)

34

(I = Interviewer; M = Matt)

I: Matt, Ozone was a very successful band. Why did you decide to leave?
M: I was very young when I joined the band. At first, all the money and fame and success were very exciting, and I enjoyed the attention. But after a while, I started to lose my identity.
I: What do you mean?
M: Well, we had no freedom at all. Our manager told us how to dress, how to sing and what to sing, how to dance, what to say to the press, where to go, and where not to go.
I: But your manager turned you into a chart-topping band.
M: Yes, but we worked very hard and never went out. It wasn't a normal life for a teenager. We weren't even allowed to have relationships.
I: But you were making a lot of money.
M: Yes, that's true. And at first I enjoyed the money, but I wasted it on stupid things. Also, I spent too much time with people who weren't my real friends—people who were only interested in my money. I lost my real friends. Then one morning I woke up and thought, "I don't know who I am." It was scary.

35

I: And that's when you decided to leave?
M: Yes, that's right.
I: Matt, that was three months ago. Have you decided what you're going to do next?
M: Yes. I've had time to think about my future. I'm going to keep on singing and pursue a solo career.
I: Do you think you've learned anything from your experience in Ozone?
M: Oh, yes. This time I'm going to hire a decent manager who listens to me and who gives me good financial advice. I'm not going to waste my money on stupid things. Also, I'm going to spend more time with my family, and I'm definitely not going to forget my real friends.
I: And what kind of music are you going to play?
M: I'm going to write my own songs and play the kind of music I like. I've learned my lesson, and I'm definitely not going to make the same mistakes again.
I: So, another number 1 hit in the near future?
M: Definitely.

36

(S = Suzy; M = Matt)

S: Welcome back to Suzy B on Radio 103. Matt McKay, ex-lead singer of Ozone, is sitting here with me in the studio today. Matt, how's life?
M: Really good.
S: That's great. Now your first solo single is coming out tomorrow. How are you feeling?
M: I'm feeling great, really positive. We've worked very hard on the album, and I think we've come up with some really good songs.
S: Excellent. And what about gigs? Are you doing any concerts?
M: Actually, we're starting our Americas tour next week. We're doing three nights in New York. Then we're flying to San Diego. We're doing gigs in three cities in California and a gig in Vancouver. Then we're going to Chicago, Dallas, and Miami.
S: Wow, heavy. That's some schedule!
M: Oh, that's not all. We're taking a short vacation the following week, and then we're appearing in Mexico City, Rio, Brasília, and...I think that's it.
S: Phew. You'll need another vacation after that.
M: Well, you know, it's important to get out and meet the fans.
S: Of course. But enough about work—do you have any plans for your vacation yet?
M: Yes. I'm taking my mom and dad to Bermuda for some sun.
S: Great! Matt, good luck tomorrow. I've heard the single, and if you ask me, it's going to go straight to the top of the charts.
M: Thanks. I hope you're right.
S: O.K., let's listen to the single now. Out tomorrow, this is Matt McKay's first solo single, *I'm the One*.

9 Rules

37

(See page 52.)

38

(See page 54.)

39

(See page 54.)

40

I decided to follow the rules in *How to be the Perfect Ms. Right* because I wanted a good relationship. My relationships always fail because I'm too soft, and people take advantage of me. Even my best friends sometimes take advantage of me.

Before I started following the rules in the book, I was seeing Michael four or five times a week and talking on the phone several times a day.

So it was difficult following the rules because I couldn't call him, and when he called me and asked for a date, I had to hesitate and pretend I was busy and then suggest another day. I had to tell him I was busy even when I wasn't.

At first, it all worked. He became more interested and he even took me to meet his mom.

But then he said I was acting strangely. He said I'd changed—at first I was warm and friendly, but I was getting colder and harder. I knew it wasn't the real me, but I couldn't tell him about the book—that's one of the rules!

The rules are supposed to make you mysterious and fascinating, but he just thought I was behaving like a witch.

Then I began to fall in love with him, and I wanted to see him more, but I couldn't. I didn't like playing games with him anymore. It didn't feel right.

And then something awful happened. He saw the book... He was so angry!

He told me to go and play games with somebody else and left.

Anyway, I threw away my copy of the book, and now I'm reading a book called *The Joy of Being Single*. I've decided that I don't have to find a man and get married to be happy. I'm much happier now.

41

(See page 55.)

42

(See page 57.)

10 Review 2

43

a)

W1: I'm home! Sorry I'm late, honey. I had to work late at the office.
M1: But it's eleven o'clock! And this is the third time this week!
W1: I know. I'm really sorry, but it's an important contract.

b)

B: Sorry, Mr. Peters. I couldn't get here earlier—the bus was late.
T: Your bus is always late, Ronnie. Why don't you catch the earlier one?
B: Yes, O.K. Tomorrow I'll catch the earlier bus.

c)

M2: Sir, we sent you the bill on the fifteenth of last month.
M3: You sent it last month? I never received it! How much was the bill for?
M2: Twenty-four thousand three hundred fifty…

d)

W2: When are you going to stop smoking? I can't stand the smell in this house. You know it's bad for the children. And for you.
M4: I know, I know. I'm going to give it up. Tomorrow. Next week. Soon.
W2: I've heard that before…

e)

W3: I have some amazing news about Tina and Brian, but you can't tell anyone. O.K.?
W4: Of course not. You can trust me. I always keep a secret. What's going on?
W3: Well, you know Brigitte from across the street. She said that…

f)

W5: Thank you. That was the best meal we've ever had. Wasn't it, Donald?
M5: Oh, yes, delicious.
W6: Oh, thanks. We have to do it again soon.

44

(H = Host; R = Rob Diaz; D = Driver)

Part 1

H: Welcome to *Tools of the Trade*, our weekly look at professional secrets. This week—the world of the customs officer. We spent a day at the border crossing in San Diego with Rob Diaz, a senior customs officer in the fight against contraband cigars. We join Officer Diaz as he interviews a driver passing through customs.
R: Good afternoon, sir.
D: Afternoon.
R: Where have you been in Mexico, sir?
D: I haven't been far. Some small town…
R: Could you be more precise, sir? Where exactly have you been?
D: I don't know what the place is called—it's a little town south of Tijuana.
R: I see, sir. Did you buy any alcohol or cigars during the trip?
D: Uh, no. Well, not much. My sister's birthday is next week, so I just went down to buy some beer for the party. Hey, do you want to come? Just kidding!
R: Well, if you don't mind, I'm going to take a look in the back of the car. Is it open?

Part 2

H: The back of the car contained two cases of beer—no problem there. But then they found eight thousand Cuban cigars—that is illegal! The driver was arrested.
Officer Diaz, do you search every car that passes through?
R: No, that would be impossible. Thousands of cars drive through every day.
H: So how do you know which cars to stop?
R: Well, we often have inside information, but this time, I had a feeling.
H: Just a feeling?
R: Well, maybe a little more than that. You see a guy by himself, he doesn't look like a businessman, it's the middle of the week…and you think, "What is he up to?"
H: That's it?
R: No—then we ask a few simple questions. We watch their body language, and you can usually tell if they're lying.
H: You can see it in their eyes?
R: Well, not in the eyes, because they don't usually look at you. They often hide their hands, too. But there are other signs. Have you ever noticed the way people sometimes touch their face a lot when they are lying?
H: So, just by looking at them, you can—
R: No, you have to listen, too. To begin with, they often say very little, just the minimum. Just "Morning, officer" or "Afternoon, sir." They don't give you precise information like names of places. And then they sometimes start saying too much, saying any old thing to fill the silence.
H: I've read somewhere that liars usually use more negative verbs. Have you found this?
R: Yes, that's right. Also, their voice often goes up, "Uh, no, not much," and they sound scared.
H: Does anyone ever get past you?
R: Oh, yeah. We've caught hundreds of the little guys, but we hardly ever catch the big ones, the real professionals.
H: Rob Diaz, thank you very much. With contraband Cuban cigar smuggling increasing, customs officers clearly have a difficult job on their hands.

45

The top 3 whisky drinkers in bottles consumed per year are:
1 Spain: 145,000,000
2 France: 137,000,000
3 The U.S.: 117,000,000

The top 3 beer drinkers in quarts consumed per person per year are:
1 The Czech Republic: 169
2 Ireland: 149.3
3 Germany: 145.5

The top 3 coffee drinkers in cups consumed per person per year are:
1 Norway: 1,356
2 Denmark: 1,305
3 Finland: 1,293

The top 3 Coca-Cola drinkers in glasses consumed per person per year are:
1 The U.S.: 343
2 Mexico: 322
3 Germany: 201

11 Smile

46

(See page 64.)

47

(See page 65.)

48

(See page 65.)

49

(See page 65.)

50

a) I'd love to meet your friends—let's make a date now. We could try that new restaurant on 48th Street.
b) No, no, don't do it like that. Do it like this. Go on, do it again, and, oh, then get me some coffee.
c) No problem—I'm sure I can win. I know I'm faster than the others.
d) I'm working here to get some experience, but I'm going to start up my own company soon.

e) Yeah, whatever—I really don't mind. I'll be happy if we go out. I'll be happy if we stay in. Let's do whatever you want to do.
f) Look, are you sure you're O.K., because I can stay longer if you want. Anyway, you know where I am if you need me. Take care.

51

(See page 67.)

52

Laughter Clubs
Scientific research has proved that laughter reduces the effects of stress and helps the body to fight against illness and infection. In India, the health benefits of laughter are taken very seriously. There is a network of 600 "laughter clubs" where people meet every day just to laugh. They participate in "social laughter" (quiet tittering), suppressed laughter (snickering), and the loud, explosive laugh (roaring with laughter) that exercises the lungs.

12 Rebel

53

(I = Interviewer; J = Jake; D = Debbie; R = Ronny; C = Caroline)

I: It's May 1, and we are in the middle of a huge May Day demonstration. People are handing out leaflets with information. There are all kinds of people here, but what exactly are they protesting about?

Jake
I: Excuse me! Yes, you. What are you doing here?
J: I'm protesting against globalization. Multinational companies cause a lot of pollution. They are polluting the world's rivers and oceans, and they don't care—they just want to make as much money as possible. I'm also giving out peaceful protest leaflets and T-shirts. There are some people here who want violence, but most people are here to protest in a peaceful way. Me, I'm a supporter of peaceful action.
I: Thank you.

Debbie
I: Excuse me. Can you tell me what you're doing here?
D: Well, I'm in favor of many of the causes here, but I'm here today with a group of women from Texas. We're demonstrating for equal pay for women. Women still earn less than men in most jobs, and it's time for that to change. I'm not anti-men—I just want a fairer system. Would you like to sign our petition?
I: Uh, yes, sure, thank you.

Ronny
I: Hi there! Can you tell me what you're doing here?
R: I'm selling veggieburgers. I'm against cosmetic companies that use animals in their experiments. At home I have three dogs, two cats, and a pet mouse named Jerry. They are my friends. I support animal rights, and I'm protesting against cruelty to animals. All right?
I: Good luck.

Caroline
I: Excuse me. What are you doing here?
C: I'm having fun with my friends. I don't feel strongly about politics, and I don't know much about it. This is my first demonstration. I'm really against the destruction of the rain forest. You know, the logging companies are destroying the forests. This is really serious. Each of us has to be responsible for protecting the natural environment. I really care about a clean, safe environment for our children. We owe it to them.

54

(See page 71.)

55

explain, explanation
organize, organization
produce, production
legalize, legalization
educate, education
reduce, reduction
modernize, modernization
legislate, legislation

56

(See page 74.)

13 Dance

57

(I = Interviewer; J = Josh; S = Simone; A = Antonio)

Josh
I: Josh, how are you?
J: Uh, to be honest, I'm really beat! I've been dancing all night.
I: Hey, how come you don't have a tan? Don't you like sunbathing?
J: Uh, well, I haven't been to the beach yet.
I: How come? How long have you been here?
J: Dunno. Nine, ten days.
I: Well, what have you been doing since you arrived?
J: I've been clubbing every night and sleeping all day. I've met loads of people, especially girls.
I: So, have you had a good time?
J: Oh yeah, definitely. I reckon this is the best vacation I've ever had. The only problem is I'm broke. I've spent all my money, and I still have a few days to go.
I: Yeah, well, good luck and have a good trip home.
J: Thanks. Say…you couldn't lend me some money, could you?

Simone
I: Simone, how long have you been here?
S: Since 1997.
I: Where are you from originally?
S: Brazil, but I haven't been home in a couple of years now.
I: What have you been doing here since 1997?
S: Having a great time—I've been working in clubs. I've been a resident DJ at Amnesia for two years. Oh, and I've been building my own house.
I: Really? Do you make a lot of money working in clubs?
S: You can, but I've also married a guy from Ibiza. His father gave us the land to build a house.
I: I see. Do you think you'll ever go back to Brazil?
S: Well, I love the lifestyle here; it's so laid back. And anyway, all my friends and family come and visit me here.

Antonio
I: Good morning, Antonio. How are you today?
A: Not bad, not bad. But I've been working all night in my restaurant, so I'm going to go to bed soon.
I: Well, thanks for talking to us. How long have you been here in Ibiza?
A: All my life. I was born in the north, but I've been living in Ibiza since 1995. That was when I opened my own restaurant.
I: What's it like living here in Ibiza?
A: Ah, it used to be a wonderful place, but now the tourists have ruined it.
I: But tourists have been coming to Ibiza since the sixties.
A: That's true, but they've changed. Tourists used to behave much better than they do today. They used to be polite and quiet. Now it's all noise and wild parties.
I: What types of people come to your restaurant?
A: Well…uh…tourists.

58

(See page 81.)

14 Call

59

(M = Mom; L = Lorna)
M: Hello.
L: Hi, Mom. It's me.
M: Oh, hello, darling. How are you?
L: I can't hear you, Mom. It's a really bad connection.
M: Sorry, dear. I said how are you?

L: Terrible, Mom. My back's killing me, and the house is a mess.
M: Don't worry, darling, I'll come and help you clean the house.
L: But that's not all—the kids are driving me crazy. ELLA, PUT HIM DOWN!
M: Don't worry, darling. After we've cleaned the house, I'll take the children to the park.
L: Oh thanks, Mom. There is something else though. ELLA, I SAID PUT HIM DOWN! Sorry—the thing is, I'm expecting six people for dinner, and there's nothing to eat. Do you think you could do some shopping on your way over here?
M: No problem, darling. I'll stop at the supermarket, and then I'll make a dinner your friends will never forget.
L: Thanks, Mom. I don't know what I'd do without you. Could you do one more thing for me?
M: Of course, darling, what is it?
L: Well, I've run out of money. Could you possibly pay for the shopping, and I'll pay you back at the end of the month?
M: That's fine. You don't have to pay me back.

60

(L = Lorna; M = Mom)
L: Mom—you're an angel. How's Dad?
M: Dad? Darling, you know your father and I divorced when you were thirteen.
L: Divorced? Thirteen? Oh no—what number is this?
M: 555-4450.
L: Oh, no! I don't believe it. I dialed the wrong number.
M: Juliet?
L: I'm not Juliet—but please, wait—does this mean you're not coming over?

61

Conversation 1
(D = Dad; L = Lorna)
D: Hello.
L: Dad?
D: Hello, dear. How are you?
L: Oh, not too good actually.
D: Oh, dear, what's the matter?
L: PUT THAT DOWN!
D: What?!
L: No, not, not you, Dad—the children are driving me crazy. NO! FREDDIE, WHY DID YOU DO THAT?
D: Look, dear, I'm just going out to play golf. Can I call you back later? Or should I leave a message for your mother to call you when she comes in?
L: Yes. Please. Could you tell her it's urgent?
D: Yes, O.K., dear—I think she'll be home...
L: FREDDIE—DON'T TOUCH THAT! Dad, I have to go.
D: Oh—goodbye, dear.

Conversation 2
(J = Jackie; L = Lorna)
J: Hello.
L: Hello. Is this Jackie?
J: Yes. Hold on a minute...(Turn the music down!)
L: Jackie, it's Lorna. Lorna Carr.
J: Oh, hello, Mrs. Carr.
L: I was wondering if you could come over and baby-sit for a couple of hours this afternoon.
J: This afternoon? Uh...Would you mind hanging on a minute, please?...(I have to go and baby-sit.)... Is it O.K. if I bring my boyfriend?
L: Yes, that's fine. Would you like me to drive over and pick you up?
J: It's O.K. We'll take the bus.
L: NO! Uh, no, I need you right now. I'll be right over.

62

(See page 85.)

63

...and here are some useful phone numbers for tourists in the New York area. Remember — if you call on a cell phone, you do not have to dial the first one. And here are the numbers.

For trains to anywhere in the United States, call Amtrak for train schedules and fare information at one eight hundred... eight seven two...seven two four five.

For car rentals, call Budget Rent-A-Car. The number is one seven one eight...six five six...six oh one oh.

If you have problems with your car, call the Triple A emergency road service number at one eight hundred...two two two...four three five seven.

If you want to go by bus from New York City to anywhere, call the Port Authority Bus Terminal at one two one two...five oh two...two three four one.

For information about trains from New York to New Jersey, call PATH train information at one eight hundred...two three four...seven six two four.

And remember, if you need a phone number anywhere in the United States, call four one one for Directory Assistance.

64

A
A: Dad...Do you think I could have a Zoomatron for my birthday?... Please?
B: What's a Zoomatron?
A: It's a kind of space gun. It's really cool.
B: Oh, no. Not another one...
A: Please.

B
A: Could you tell me where the restroom is?
B: What?
A: Do you know where the restrooms are?
B: Sorry—I can't hear you.
A: WHERE'S THE RESTROOM?
B: Over there.

C
A: Can you remember where we left it?
B: Uhm, I think it was on the second level.
A: Well, this is the second level, and I can't see it.
B: I think we parked next to a white van....There it is.

D
A: Do you have any idea what the time is?
B: Dunno.
A: Well, it's twelve thirty. Where on earth have you been? I've been worried sick. Wait till your father hears about this!

E
A: Do you know if the last bus has left?
B: I'm afraid it left a couple of minutes ago.
A: Oh, no! Do you know where I can get a taxi?
B: Try the train station—there are usually a few taxis there.
A: Thanks.

F
A: Excuse me—do you know where the lions are?
B: They're over there next to the giraffes.
A: O.K. Thank you.

15 Review 3

65

(R = Reporter; H = Hyacinth; D = Derek; M = Maria; O = Oona; S = Sara)

Interview 1
R: Excuse me, ma'am, would you mind answering a few questions for 1010 Radio Sports News?
H: Certainly.
R: Well, could you tell me where you come from? Have you come far?
H: We don't live far from here. We live in Richmond, actually, so we usually get here very early in the morning. We like to be at the front of the queue, but Derek was slow getting up this morning, and there was a bit of a problem on the Underground, so we arrived a little later than usual.
R: Could you tell me how long you've been waiting?
H: Since about half past eight, something like that, I suppose. So, yes, it's been a long wait. What is it—about three o'clock now? Derek! What's the time now? Derek!
D: Yes, dear?
R: Do you think you'll get in?
H: Oh yes, I think we'll probably get in soon. Won't we, Derek? Derek, stop looking at that girl! You've been looking at her for hours. Haven't you seen enough? She's certainly not interested in you!
R: Well, it's a long queue. Do you know how many people there are in front of you?

H: I imagine there are about, what, twenty or thirty people. It won't be long now, will it, Derek?
D: Huh?

Interview 2
R: Excuse me, would you mind answering a few questions for 1010 Radio Sports News?
M: Excuse me? Can you speak a little more slowly, please?
R: Sure. Can I ask you a few questions for the radio?
M: Yes, of course.
R: How long have you been waiting here?
M: I have been waiting here since eight fifteen this morning. I did not know there was a long line.
R: You must be a real tennis fan!
M: Ah, so-so. I am a student of English. I have been in London for four weeks, and tomorrow I have to go back to Bogotá in Colombia, and I thought it was a good idea to come to Wimbledon before I go back to Colombia.
R: Do you think you'll get in?
M: Excuse me?
R: Do you think you will get in?
M: No, I do not think so. It has been raining since one thirty. I am wet and cold, and I am hungry, and there are many, many people in front of me in line. I think I will give up soon.

Interview 3
R: Excuse me, ma'am, would you mind answering a few questions for 1010 Radio Sports News?
O: Oh, come under the umbrella, dear. Would you like a strawberry?
R: Mm, thanks. Have you been here long?
O: Ooh, I'm not sure. What time did we arrive, Sara?
S: Mm, about eight?
O: Yes, we've been here since about eight this morning. We come every year on the Friday, you know.
R: What are your chances of getting in?
O: Not very good, I would say. It rained on the Friday last year, too, and we never got in. But you never know. There are probably about fifty people in front of us, but lots of them will give up and go home soon. Maybe we'll get the last match of the day. We live in Scotland, you know, so this is a big day out for us. We're not giving up now, not after coming all this way.
R: Isn't it a long time to wait for one match?
O: Ooh, no. We love the tennis, of course, but we really come for the atmosphere. We've met so many interesting people since we arrived. Have you spoken to that charming young girl from Colombia? We've been chatting for ages—she speaks English really well. And Sara always brings her radio, so we've been listening to that. We've been having a great day, haven't we, Sara?
S: Mm, another strawberry?
R: Mm, thanks. Well, good luck with the wait!

66

(See page 90.)

67

(S = Secretary; MK = Mrs. Knightly)
S: Mr. Rogers' office. Can I help you?
MK: Oh, hello. Can I speak to Mr. Rogers, please?
S: Certainly. Could you hold for a minute, please? I'm sorry, but Mr. Rogers is not in yet, ma'am.
MK: Uh, would you mind taking a message?
S: Certainly.
MK: Uhm, well, it's Joanna Knightly. I have an appointment with Mr. Rogers at 9:15, and I'm sorry, but I missed the bus…
S: Would you like to give me your telephone number, and I'll ask Mr. Rogers to call you when he gets in?
MK: That's all right, thanks. I'll call back later.
S: You're welcome. Goodbye.
MK: Thanks. Goodbye.

68

(See page 93.)

16 Lifestyle

69

(R = Receptionist; W = Woman)
R: New Life Center. Can I help you?
W: Yes. Could you give me some information about your center?
R: Certainly. Are you interested in losing weight or just improving your fitness?
W: Uhm, it's not for me. It's for my husband. He needs to lose weight and improve his fitness. I want to give him a week at your center as a surprise for his birthday.
R: Ah, lucky man!
W: Could you tell me something about the program?
R: Sure. As soon as he arrives here, he'll take a fitness test to see what kind of diet he needs to go on.
W: I see.
R: We start every day at 7:30 with a half-hour walk before breakfast.
W: Ha ha. He usually starts the day with a cigarette before breakfast!
R: I don't think so. If he has a cigarette here, he'll be in big trouble. It's a strictly no-smoking area.
W: Well, it's a good idea for him to give up smoking. He says he'll give it up as soon as he feels more relaxed.
R: Well, this is the ideal place to relax. We do at least two hours of yoga and meditation every day, and after the morning hike, he can have a sauna and jacuzzi.
W: Oh, he'll enjoy that. But what's this hike?
R: They go for a hike in the morning from 8:30 to 12:30. One of our instructors will take your husband and other people at the same level of fitness for a four-hour hike into the mountains.
W: Four hours! His idea of a walk is going from the front door to his car.
R: Oh, don't worry. When they get to the top of the mountain, they'll have a twenty-minute break before they come down again. The scenery is very relaxing.
W: They'll be starving!
R: Oh, don't worry. When they're hungry, they'll stop for a healthy snack. The instructor always carries a supply of fruit.
W: So no chocolate? Hmm. And what about the afternoon? Can he relax then?
R: No, not really. But he'll have time to relax after the afternoon hike.
W: Oh my goodness. I don't think he'll thank me for this.
R: Believe me, when he finishes the week, he'll feel like a new man.
W: If he finishes the week!

70

(See page 98.)

71

/ɪ/ lettuce spinach
/ʌ/ onion nut
/ə/ banana lemon
/i/ sardines beans
/ɑ/ orange olive
/ou/ potato tomato

72

(See page 98.)

17 Animals

73

1 Word A: tail – T A I L tail.
Word B: tale – T A L E tale.
2 Word A: deer – D E E R deer.
Word B: dear – D E A R dear.
3 Word A: bear – B E A R bear.
Word B: bare – B A R E bare.
4 Word A: right – R I G H T right.
Word B: write – W R I T E write.
5 Word A: wait – W A I T wait.
Word B: weight – W E I G H T weight.

74

(See page 103.)

75

a) Tim
(I = Interviewer; T = Tim)
I: Can you describe your pet?
T: She's very fat and not very pretty. But she has a beautiful curly tail.
I: What does she eat?
T: Anything and everything. She's very fond of banana skins.
I: Is she a good companion?

T: Yes, I always go and talk to her when I'm in a bad mood. She listens to my problems when no one else will.
I: When you go away, who takes care of her?
T: If I go away for work, my girlfriend looks after her. But if my girlfriend goes on the trip with me, we have to take her over to my parents. She doesn't like that very much because they have a dog that annoys her.
I: Do you and your pet look alike?
T: I hope not.
I: If you were an animal, what animal would you like to be?
T: I used to say a dolphin when I was younger, but I don't like the ocean very much now. I don't know—a giraffe maybe, though I'd hate to be stuck in a zoo.

b) Gus
(I = Interviewer; G = Gus)
I: Can you describe your pet?
G: He's black and has eight hairy legs.
I: What does he eat?
G: Insects.
I: What, he catches them?
G: No, I buy them frozen.
I: Is he a good companion?
G: Yeah. He's like a friend. We have a special bond.
I: When you go away, who takes care of him?
G: Well, I haven't been away since I got him, and I don't think anybody wants to take care of him. Certainly not my mom. He scares people away.
I: Do you and your pet look alike?
G: I'm not that hairy—but I think he looks cool, like me.
I: If you were an animal, what animal would you like to be?
G: A lion, because they're big and tough, and they rule.

c) Maxine
(I = Interviewer; M = Maxine)
I: Can you describe your pet?
M: She's very fluffy and very lovable. My boyfriend doesn't like her because she bit him—she's definitely a girl's girl.
I: What does she eat?
M: Her favorite foods are fresh vegetables, nuts, and cereal.
I: Is she a good companion?
M: Oh, yes, I love Page because she's good company for me when my boyfriend is away traveling. Besides, we have the same interests—she loves to sleep all day, eat, and then she parties all night long.
I: When you go away, who takes care of her?
M: I take her everywhere in her little cage.
I: Do you and your pet look alike?
M: I think that she's better looking than me—who could resist those brown button eyes?
I: If you were an animal, what animal would you like to be?
M: I am an animal.

76

I know somebody who has an iguana as a pet. It's a man I work with named Harry. The iguana is named Iggy, and it's probably about five years old—that's how long I've known Harry, and he got it soon after we met. It was a birthday present from his wife. It's just over three feet long from the tip of its nose to the end of its tail, and it's a lovely green color. Like all reptiles, iguanas never stop growing, so Iggy will get bigger and bigger. It's kind of shy and nervous, which is exactly the opposite of Harry, who's very outgoing and confident. It's definitely better looking than Harry though. Iggy doesn't sleep in a cage. For now, it lives at the top of the curtains in Harry's living room. When it was young, it ate crickets, but now that it's an adult, it doesn't need so much protein—in fact, it's completely vegetarian. Harry takes it for walks in the park on a leash. It's funny—when it's frightened, it runs up Harry's body and sits on his head.

18 Weird

77

(A = Anchorperson; I = Ida Gomez; K = Ken Crystal)
A: Let's hear now from our correspondent, Ida Gomez, in our studios in England with a strange and mysterious story. Ida?
I: This morning the residents of a small village in Wiltshire woke up to an amazing sight. It is the biggest crop circle ever seen in Britain. The press is calling it the mother of all circles, and the question everyone is asking: How did it get there? In the studio with me today is Ken Crystal, a crop circle expert. Ken, how long have you been interested in crop circles?
K: For about eleven years now.
I: Can you tell us something about this circle?
K: Well, we're very excited about this crop circle. The design is absolutely amazing, and it's enormous.
I: How big is it exactly?
K: It's about a half a mile! We've never seen anything like this before!
I: It's a very complex design. How many circles are there all together?
K: There are more than 400 circles—it really is incredible.
I: And do you know who made it?
K: No, I don't, but I believe that this is the work of strange forces.
I: What do you mean?
K: It's impossible for people to make something like this.
I: But I've heard that most circles are made by people. Is that true?
K: Yes, there are several groups of people who make crop circles. But they didn't make this one.
I: How do you know?
K: This circle appeared yesterday morning. The day before that, it wasn't there. There were only four hours of darkness that night—there wasn't enough time to make it.
I: How long does it take to make a crop circle?
K: Well, a simple circle takes a few hours. But a circle like this one would take several days.
I: How long have crop circles existed?
K: The first crop circles were reported in 1980. In the last eleven years, I've visited over a thousand. But I've never seen one like this.
I: Ken, a final question. Do you think that this crop circle is the work of aliens?
K: I think it could be a message…

78

(See page 108.)

79

(See page 109.)

80

(See page 110.)

81

1 Don's Story
I had a strange experience while I was working in Massachusetts.

One Friday, I left Boston and went to Cape Cod for the weekend. I remember I was walking down a road—I was alone, and I was wearing a coat with a hood over my head because it was snowing.

Suddenly I heard somebody call my name. When I looked around, I saw that it was a young woman I'd met the previous summer in San Francisco. I live in San Francisco, and she had been on vacation there. After the vacation, she'd returned to Boston, her hometown, and I hadn't been in touch with her since then.

She had no idea that I was in Massachusetts, and she didn't even live in Cape Cod—she was just visiting a friend. But somehow she recognized me, even though it was snowing and I was wearing a big hood.

After that we stayed in touch, and in fact, she came to my wedding ten years later.

2 Lidia's Story
My sister and my aunt had a strange experience the day after my mother died.

At the time of her death, my mother was living with my sister. My aunt came to stay with my sister to help her make arrangements for the funeral.

In the afternoon, the two women were sitting in the living room when my sister's little dog started barking.

They went out of the room to see why the dog was barking, and they both saw my mother's shadow on the wall. The shadow came down the stairs and disappeared.

They said they weren't frightened, but of course, they felt very emotional.

Actually, my mother's ghost often appears to different members of the family, in different forms.

I think this is because she was such a strong character, and her memory lives on in our minds.

19 Wheels

82

(K = Karen; R = Ron; J = Jill)

K: You're late!
R: Yes, I'm really sorry—I had to wait forever for a bus.
J: Why didn't you drive?
R: Ah, well. I sold my car.
K: Oh, are you getting a new one?
R: No, I'm not getting another car. I've decided to live without one.
J: Wow—what made you do that?
R: I think there are too many cars, and this city is far too polluted.
J: Well, that's true, but a car is useful.
R: I don't think so. Not in the city, anyway. I can never find anywhere to park, and you spend most of the time sitting in traffic jams.
K: But how are you going to get to work?
R: By bicycle.
K: Don't you think bicycles are dangerous?
R: Not really. I don't think they're as dangerous as cars.
J: Well, I couldn't do without my car. I have to take the kids to school every day.
R: I don't think children get enough exercise these days—they should walk to school.
K: Well, I don't have children, but I agree with Jill—I couldn't live without my car. I sometimes have to come home late from the office.
R: Why don't you take the bus? Public transportation is very good.
K: That's not true. The buses are not very regular where I work, and anyway, as a woman, I don't feel safe waiting for a bus late at night.
R: O.K., I see what you mean, but aren't you worried about pollution?
J: Of course, but you don't understand—it's easy for you to worry about the environment. I have to worry about carrying the groceries and kids and…
R: O.K., O.K., you're right! Come on. Let's change the subject. Hey, what do you think of my new haircut?

83

(See page 114.)

84

(P = Dave Pearl, talk show host;
C1 = Caller 1; C2 = Caller 2)

P: Welcome to the show. My name's Dave Pearl, and you're listening to *Road Rage*. O.K., let's see who's on the line. Hello—what's your name, and how can we help?
C1: Hello, Dave. Uh, my name's Mark, and my problem is traffic jams. I waste too much time sitting in my car in traffic jams in the morning on my way to work and on my way home after work, and I'm sick of it.
P: Ah, yes. I'm sure lots of people share your feelings, Mark. Why don't you work at home some of the time?
C1: I can't do that, Dave—I work in a store.
P: Oh, O.K. You could use public transportation. Then you could read a newspaper on your way to work, and your time wouldn't be wasted.
C1: I can't do that, Dave—I have to use my car at work for deliveries.
P: O.K. Well, Mark, if I were you, I'd learn a new language! Where do you want go on your next vacation?
C1: Uh, Mexico, Dave.
P: Great! You can buy a Spanish language course on CDs and play them on your car stereo. They're fantastic, and the time will pass quickly.
C1: Uh, Dave…
P: Thank you, Mark. Do we have another caller on the line—yes, hello—what's your name, and how can we help?
C2: Uh, hello, Dave. My name's… I'm, I'm Sharon, and I can't pass my driver's test.
P: Really? Why not?
C2: Well, I'm too nervous.
P: I see. How many times have you taken your test?
C2: Seven times, Dave. I'm fine when I'm practicing my driving, but then on the day of the test, I fall apart. I start shaking, and I can't see the road.
P: Well, Sharon,…

85

(See page 116.)

86

(See page 117.)

20 Review 4

87

(H = Host; A = Amy; J = Jack; V = Vera)

H: Hi, and welcome to *Speak Up!*, the radio talk show where *you* get the chance to say what *you* think about the stories in the news today.… In the news today is lottery winner Eva Alvarado. Yes, listeners, Eva Alvarado won $198 million, but she says she doesn't want to change her life. She loves her job in a children's home, and she wants to stay the way she is. Call us now at 212 555-8989 and tell us what *you* think.… We have our first caller—Amy Wilder. Go ahead, Amy.
A: Well, Mrs. Alvarado is obviously very fond of the children, but I'm sure she'll quit her job soon. When everybody knows how rich she is, life will be very difficult. Everyone will ask her for money, and she will soon get tired of all the letters. So she needs to think about the future now.
H: Good point there. We have Jack Nichols on the line. Go ahead, Jack.
J: Well, she doesn't sound very excited about winning the lottery. In fact, she's more interested in the children than in the money, so she'll probably give most of the money away—to the children's home, to her friends, you know? And I think she's right. If you have that much money, how are you going to spend it all?
H: Well, Jack, I'm sure I could help her! O.K., let's go to our next caller—Vera Baker.
V: It's a lot of money, and she'll need a financial advisor. She doesn't have to worry about the future anymore, but as soon as she has had time to think about it, I'm pretty sure she'll change her mind about just giving money to the children's home.

88

(See page 121.)

Macmillan Education
Between Towns Road, Oxford OX4 3PP
A division of Macmillan Publishers Limited
Companies and representatives throughout the world

ISBN 978 1 4050 2452 5

First published 2002
American Edition 2004

Project management by Desmond O'Sullivan, ELT Publishing Services.
Designed by Jackie Hill, 320 Design.
Illustrated by Martin Chatterton pp. 127, 128; Rebecca Halls pp. 62, 63, 77, 122, 123; Ed McLachlan pp. 17, 32, 42, 57, 88, 92, 116; Julian Mosedale pp. 24, 39, 54, 91, 121; David Shephard pp. 23, 59; Mark Thomas p. 117; Kim Williams pp. 124, 126.
Cover design by Andrew Oliver.
Cover painting *After Visiting David Hockney* © Howard Hodgkin.

Authors' acknowledgments
We would like to thank all our colleagues at the Lake School, Oxford, for their help and continued support; in particular, Pete Maggs, whose thoughtful comments on work in progress were much appreciated. Thanks also go to our pre-intermediate students who have kept us focused at all times on what works in the classroom (and made sure that we disregarded everything else).
We are especially grateful to Helena Gomm and John Hird for the *Inside Out* Teacher's Book, to Pete Maggs for the weekly *Inside Out* e-lessons, to Guy Jackson for running the *Inside Out* Web site at www.insideout.net, which has finally come of age, and to everybody involved in the *Inside Out* Resource Pack: a great team!
At Macmillan Education we would like to thank Sue Bale (publishing director), David Riley (publisher), and Pippa McNee (picture researcher). We would also like to thank Alyson Maskell and Celia Bingham (freelance editors), Jackie Hill (freelance designer), Helen Reilly (freelance picture researcher), Paulette McKean (freelance permissions editor), as well as James Richardson and Vince Cross (freelance audio producers). Thanks also go to the production and marketing teams who have worked so hard to make *Inside Out* what it is.
Once again, we reserve the biggest thank you of all for Desmond O'Sullivan (freelance project manager). We are indeed privileged to be working with such a talented and committed professional—long may it continue! Thanks for everything, Des.
In addition, we must thank our families, without whose support and understanding none of this would have been possible.
We would also like to thank Thalia Carr (The Swan School, Oxford), Jenny Johnson (International House, Barcelona), Beth Neher (International House, London), and Katarzyna Kowalczyk (Macmillan Polska) for their very helpful comments.

The authors and publishers would like to thank the following for permission to reproduce their material:
Excerpt from "E-How to remember names" by Valerie Singer from www.ehow.com, reprinted by permission of Blue Frogg Enterprises. *Stand By Me* composed by Jerry Leiber / Mike Stoller / Ben E. King, reproduced by kind permission of Hornall Brothers Music on behalf of Jerry Leiber Music / Mike Stoller Music/Mike & Jerry Music LLC. Excerpt from "They were the happiest couple in showbiz...but then it all went wrong" by Polly Graham from the *Mirror* 06.02.01, reprinted by permission of Mirror Syndication International. *Suspicious Minds* written by Francis Zambon, published by Sony/ATV Music Publishing, reprinted by permission of the publishers. *Money (That's What I Want).* Words and music by Berry Gordy and Janie Bradford © Jobete Music Co. Inc./Stone Agate Music, USA 1960, reprinted by permission of Jobete Music Co. Inc./EMI Music Publishing Ltd., London, WC2H 0QY and International Music Publications Ltd. All Rights Reserved. Excerpt from "Best of Times, Worst of Times: Bill Wyman" by Danny Danziger from *The Times* Magazine 04.30.00, copyright © Danny Danziger 2000, reprinted by permission of the author. *Don't Worry, Be Happy.* Words and music by Bobby McFerrin © Prob Noblem Music/BMG Music Publishing Ltd., Bedford House, 69–79 Fulham High Street, London, SW6 1994, reprinted by permission of Music Sales Limited. All rights reserved. International Copyright Secured. Excerpt from *Billy Elliot* by Melvin Burgess. Screenplay by Lee Hall (The Chicken House, 2001), text copyright © Melvin Burgess 2001. Original screenplay by Lee Hall © Universal Studios Publishing Rights, a division of Universal Studios Licensing Inc., 2001, reprinted by permission of the publisher. All rights reserved. Excerpt from "Why I Bought My Child A Gun" by Phil Hogan, copyright © the *Guardian* 2001, from the *Guardian* 07.04.01, reprinted by permission of the author. Excerpt from "104 Things to Do with a Banana" by Wayne M. Hilburn from www.dmgi.com/bananas.html, reprinted by permission of the author. Excerpt from "Balloon Buddies," the *Daily Mail* 06.28.01, reprinted by permission of Atlantic Syndication Partners. Excerpt from "Slip Sliding Away" by Sophie Radice, copyright © Sophie Radice 2001, from the *Guardian Weekend* 11.03.01, reprinted by permission of the author. Excerpt from *The Lost Continent* by Bill Bryson (Blackswan, a division of Transworld Publishers, 1999), copyright © Bill Bryson 1989, reprinted by permission of the publisher. *24 Hours from Tulsa.* Words by Hal David. Music by Burt Bacharach. © Hidden Valley Music Company/Casa David, USA. Universal/MCA Music Limited, Elsinore House, 77 Fulham Palace Road, London W6 8JA (50%), Windswept Pacific Music (London) Limited, Hope House, 40 St. Peter's Road, London W6 9BD (50%), reprinted by permission of Windswept Music (London) Ltd. and Music Sales Ltd. All rights reserved. International Copyright Secured.

Although every effort has been made to contact copyright holders before publication, this has not always been possible. If notified, the publisher undertakes to rectify any errors or omissions at the earliest opportunity.

The authors and publishers wish to thank the following for permission to reproduce their photographs:
Ardea pp. 102, 105 (t); Art Explosion p.112 (t); David Bebber p. 108 (tr); Big Pictures p. 31; Bridgeman Art Library p. 20 (b); Jenny Cockell p. 109; Corbis pp. 10 (tm, b), 13 (tm), 40 (tm), 43, 55 (t), 56 (all), 73 (bl), 112 (m); Paul Cousans p. 108 (tl); Empics pp. 22 (all), 26 (r); Fortean pp. 100, 107; FPG pp. 6 (br, tm), 14, 40 (a), 47 (all), 60; Getty Images pp. 4, 6 (bl, bm), 10 (tl, tr), 12, 13 (bm, t, b), 18 (both), 28 (t, b), 34, 40 (c), 41 (all), 44, 45, 58, 60 (br), 64 (a–c), 65 (all), 69, 71 (all), 78 (all), 82 (both), 83, 85, 95, 99, 100, 101, 102 (a, b, c, d, f), 103 (all), 108 (mr, bl), 110 (both), 114, 119, 125, 127 (m, r); Greg Evans Picture Library p. 112 (b); Hulton Getty p. 21; Image State pp. 6 (tl), 9 (b), 124 (a); Vaughan Jones p. 5 (t); Alberto Korda *Guerillero Heroico* (*Che Guevara*) © ADAGP Paris and DACS London 2002 courtesy of Couturier Gallery LA p. 74; Magnum p. 94; Desmond O'Sullivan p. 104; PA News pp. 5 (b), 37 (r); Photodisc pp. 26, 50, 99; Pictor International pp. 6 (tr), 38 (both); Popperfoto p. 70; Powerstock pp. 64 (t), 75; Retna pp. 9 (tr), 46, 67, 73 (br); Rex Features Ltd. pp.16 (all), 20 (a, c, d, e), 37 (ml), 73 (l), 77, 86, 117, 118, 127 (l); Ronald Grant Archive p. 30; Science Photo Library p. 111; Louis Stettner *Promenade Brooklyn 1954* © ADAGP Paris and DACS London 2002 courtesy of Gallery 292 / Howard Greenberg Gallery p. 68; Topham Picturepoint p. 37 (mr); Universal Pictorial Press p. 37 (l).

Commissioned photographs by Haddon Davies pp. 26 (Pauline Perkins), 48 (Ozone), 49 (Matt McKay), 97 (food images).
The publishers wish to thank Lou Wright.

Cartoons on p. 85 reproduced with permission from Tony Husband; pp. 7, 25, 84 with permission from *Private Eye*; pp. 8, 61 with permission from *The Spectator;* pp. 27, 79, 113 with permission from Cartoonstock; p. 86 with permission from *Business Life*; p. 72 with permission from *Punch*.

Printed and bound in Thailand

2012 2011 2010 2009 2008
14 13 12 11 10 9 8 7 6